Dr. Francis Tumblety
& The Railway Ripper

Michael L. Hawley

Mechanicsburg, PA USA

Published by Sunbury Press, Inc.
Mechanicsburg, PA USA

www.sunburypress.com

Copyright © 2023 Michael L. Hawley.
Cover Copyright © 2023 by Sunbury Press, Inc.

Sunbury Press supports copyright. Copyright fuels creativity, encourages diverse voices, promotes free speech, and creates a vibrant culture. Thank you for buying an authorized edition of this book and for complying with copyright laws. Except for the quotation of short passages for the purpose of criticism and review, no part of this publication may be reproduced, scanned, or distributed in any form without permission. You are supporting writers and allowing Sunbury Press to continue to publish books for every reader. For information contact Sunbury Press, Inc., Subsidiary Rights Dept., PO Box 548, Boiling Springs, PA 17007 USA or legal@sunburypress.com.

For information about special discounts for bulk purchases, please contact Sunbury Press Orders Dept. at (855) 338-8359 or orders@sunburypress.com.

To request one of our authors for speaking engagements or book signings, please contact Sunbury Press Publicity Dept. at publicity@sunburypress.com.

FIRST SUNBURY PRESS EDITION: August 2023

Set in Adobe Garamond Pro | Interior design by Crystal Devine | Cover by Lawrence Knorr | Edited by Jennifer Cappello.

Publisher's Cataloging-in-Publication Data
Names: Hawley, Michael L., author.
Title: Dr. Francis Tumblety & The Railway Ripper / Michael L. Hawley.
Description: First trade paperback edition. | Mechanicsburg, PA : Sunbury Press, 2023.
Summary: Nearly lost to history were seventy-six similar unsolved murders and brutal assaults of women in the United States during the late nineteenth century; heinous crimes that were committed along the railways. Shockingly, one of Scotland Yard's prime Jack the Ripper suspects cannot be eliminated as having committed each of these crimes. That suspect was the tall, transient hater of women, Dr. Francis Tumblety.
Identifiers: ISBN: 979-8-88819-084-5 (paperback) | ISBN: 979-8-88819-085-2 (ePub).
Subjects: TRUE CRIME / Historical | TRUE CRIME / Murder / Serial Killers | HISTORY / Europe / Great Britain / Victorian Era | HISTORY / United States / 19th Century.

Product of the United States of America
0 1 1 2 3 5 8 13 21 34 55

For the Love of Books!

CONTENTS

Foreword *v*
Preface *ix*
Author's Note *xi*
Acknowledgments *xiii*

CHAPTERS

1.	Dr. Francis Tumblety and the Whitechapel Murders	*1*
2.	I Quite Expect a Similar Experience in New York	*14*
3.	On the Strength of Important Information	*28*
4.	Ripper-like Murder in the Big Apple in May 1888	*49*
5.	Bookends to the Whitechapel Murders in the United States	*62*
6.	A Narcissist's Secret	*80*
7.	A Taste for Releasing Rage Upon Women – 1880 to 1882	*100*
8.	Unsolved Murders & Assaults Between 1883 and 1886	*122*
9.	Jack the Tripper and Post-1888 US Murders & Assaults	*144*
10.	Tall Man in a Gray Coat and a Derby Hat	*178*
11.	Ruthless to the Bitter Century's End	*194*
12.	A Late-Nineteenth Century Serial Killer – The Railway Ripper	*211*

Chronology of the Unsolved Murders & Assaults From 1880 to 1901 *231*
Bibliography *233*
Index *237*
About the Author *240*

FOREWORD

The murders ascribed to the killer dubbed Jack the Ripper in the East End of London during the autumn of 1888 are, without doubt, the most infamous unsolved murders in criminal history. The longer the killer remained uncaught the greater the mystery became, and with each murder becoming increasingly horrific, the media sensation intensified. Consequently, Jack the Ripper went viral, to use modern parlance, and metamorphosed into something of an omnipotent demon or bogeyman across Britain. Almost any attack, serious assault, or murder committed by an unknown assailant would rapidly escalate through each word-of-mouth retelling to something far more horrible, and lo! And behold! Jack the Ripper was up to his old tricks again and the press were not above repeating these concerns in print—all in the public interest, of course.

The sending of letters—claiming knowledge of the killer or even purporting to come from the killer himself and threatening to carry out attacks—that were sent to the police or public officials was not limited to London either. Many of the letters containing threats were also reproduced in the provincial newspapers where the letters were received, and local scares erupted too. Britain was gripped by an 'Autumn of Terror,' during which many wondered and feared where the killer would strike next, and many folks thought twice about stepping out onto the street after dark. Such were the caution and dark fascination with Jack. Although the climate of fear did fade over the years after 1888, it never completely disappeared. It would suddenly manifest again—even into the early years of the twentieth century, just like Jack was imagined to leap out of the shadows—when another horrible murder was committed and there was no immediately apparent no suspect, almost as some ghastly reminder of the past. Not to mention all these years since, long after anyone who could have committed the Ripper murders is dead and gone, Jack lingers in the popular psyche of the British people to such an extent that any killer stalking the streets of Britain and believed to have committed more than one murder of a woman, regardless of the weapon used or type of wounds inflicted, is soon dubbed a 'Ripper' in the press. Cases of serial killers in the late twentieth century, such as the 'Yorkshire Ripper' and 'The Ipswich Ripper,' left the British public under no illusions of just how dangerous and vile the killer was.

My maternal great-great-grandmother saw Jack the Ripper. She was training as a midwife in London in 1888, when newspapers, especially the illustrated broadsheets, carried lurid images and gruesome stories of the murders committed in the East End and attributed to the murderer dubbed 'Jack the Ripper.' When she returned to her home county of Norfolk, her siblings and younger family members all clamoured to know if she had seen Jack the Ripper. Of course she had, and she told them earnestly that he crept around and lurked in the dark shadows of the East End, he turned and looked at her once, she saw his eyes 'burned like the coals of hell!' and she ran for her life to escape him. It was a story she regaled, on occasion, to successive generations of my family when tall tales were told, and it was related to me by my dear old Gran and her brothers with all the eeriness that Great-Great Granny would employ when she told it to them all those years ago. So entranced would I be at the telling of the story that it took just one tap on the shoulder as it reached its denouement, and I would jump out of my skin. Jack the Bogeyman strikes again! Consequently, I have known and shuddered at the name Jack the Ripper for as long as I can remember.

As a teenager in the 1980s, I remember well, and with quite some affection, books such as Gordon Honeycombe's *Murders of the Black Museum* (1982), *The Murderer's Who's Who* (1979) by J. H. H. Gaute and Robin Odell, *The Complete Jack the Ripper* (1976) by Donald Rumbelow, and *Jack the Ripper: The Final Solution* (1976) by Stephen Knight that fostered my ever-growing interest in true crime. However, it was the unsolved murders of Jack the Ripper that really captured my imagination and, having read and absorbed books on the subject for years, my fascination was piqued by the much-anticipated two-part TV drama *Jack the Ripper* starring Michael Caine, which appeared on our screens for the first time on the centenary year of the murders in 1988. These were the years of Royal conspiracies and many books, magazines, and newspapers articles (we did not have the internet in those days), even the TV drama pointed the finger of accusation at Sir William Withey Gull, one of the Physicians-in-Ordinary to Her Majesty Queen Victoria.

Any suspect drawing such a spotlight will have the theories around them subjected to close scrutiny, and with diligent research the case against the great physician has been greatly diminished over the years since. Other suspects have been suggested, and cases arguing for each of them can sound extremely compelling but, for me at least, the evidence presented fails to convince in all of them . . . with one exception—Francis Tumblety.

No books on Jack the Ripper had mentioned Tumblety as a Ripper suspect until a chance discovery of a single document was made by crime historian Stewart P. Evans. The revelation came in the text of one of four letters Stewart purchased from antiquarian book dealer Eric Barton in 1993. The pertinent letter was addressed to the noted author, playwright, and journalist George R. Sims in reply to an enquiry from Sims relating to the Jack the Ripper murders. It was written by Chief Inspector John Littlechild of Special Branch, the only senior police officer to be in post before, during and after the Whitechapel murders. Written on 23 September 1913 Littlechild not only named Tumblety as a likely suspect for Jack the Ripper, he added that there was 'a large dossier concerning him at Scotland Yard.'

Recognising the significance of what has become known as the 'Littlechild Letter,' Stewart embarked on researching Tumblety with co-author Paul Gainey and they published their groundbreaking findings in *The Lodger: The Arrest and Escape of Jack the Ripper* (1995). A Channel 4 (UK) television documentary, presented by respected investigative reporter David Jessel, followed a year later. In the documentary, a short interview with Vivien Allen, the biographer of Sir Thomas Henry Hall Caine, one of the most popular authors of the late nineteenth century but almost forgotten today, revealed a connection between him and Francis Tumblety. On hearing this, a starling connection occurred to me. I recalled that Bram Stoker's enigmatic dedication in Dracula was, 'To my dear friend Hommy-Beg.' Hommy-Beg was Manx for 'Little Tommy'—the affectionate name given to Hall Caine by his Manx grandmother. I began to research these links but was only able to briefly mention them in *A Grim Almanac of Jack the Ripper's London* (2004), my first book about those crimes and times published almost twenty years ago.

While researching Jack the Ripper's London, it was my good fortune to be introduced by my editor to crime historian Stewart P. Evans, and we have enjoyed an enduring friendship ever since. Stewart and I have discussed and debated the Ripper case as well as many others at length, but it was the connection between Hall Caine, Tumblety, and Stoker that really captured my imagination. As time went on, more and more resources became available on the internet, notably online newspapers in America and Canada, which allowed me to trace far more about Tumblety than had been previously possible in the United Kingdom.

The problem of further research into Hall Caine was that his papers were not easily accessible. They were hundreds of miles and a ferry journey away from me on the Isle of Man. Furthermore, the cataloguing of the papers had only begun after their closure period expired on 1 January 2000, and was still, to some extent, ongoing. In 2011, my work as a historian brought me to the Isle of Man for a short project, and I took the opportunity of enquiring about the availability of the Hall Caine papers at Manx National Heritage. I arranged to meet with their archivist, Wendy Thirkettle; the welcome was warm, and the reply was that the papers were now available. My wait was over, and I soon made a return journey to the archive where I found not the handful of letters I was expecting but instead a cache of fifty letters and telegrams from Tumblety to Hall Caine. Despite their impeccable provenance, I also had the letters independently authenticated and a sample examined by an expert witness, forensic graphologist Ruth Myers. I published this groundbreaking discovery along with the only fully authenticated real photographic portrait of Francis Tumblety, which I discovered in a private collection, in my book *The Dracula Secrets* (2012). I am very proud to say that the Tumblety letters I published are acknowledged as and remain the greatest collection of letters from a contemporary Jack the Ripper suspect ever to be published. The research and comparison with some of the key letters purporting to have been sent by Jack the Ripper is ongoing.

For nearly thirty years Francis Tumblety has been the subject of scrutiny and continuous research by crime historians all over the world, but I knew it would take dedicated researchers in America to take the story to the next level. I got to know Michael Hawley in the latter stages of the research for *Dracula Secrets* when I reached out to a number of Americans as I was completing my research. We soon found we were kindred spirits and have struck up an enduring friendship, and we have often discussed the case over the years. No truer words were ever spoken than 'the more you dig the more you find.' Tumblety had fled bail in Britain and had returned to the United States in 1888. Despite it being known for serial killers to stop killing, almost as if a switch turns off, there was always a strong suspicion Tumblety did continue to kill in the States. After years of painstaking research, Michael has pieced together compelling evidence that Tumblety did indeed leave a trail of horrible murders behind him ... wherever he went, before, during and after the Whitechapel murders of 1888. *Quod erat demonstrandum.*

Neil R. Storey
Norfolk, England

PREFACE

It is certainly true that recent research into Dr. Francis Tumblety has produced an unbelievable amount of discoveries—discoveries that continue to build upon the groundbreaking research from the 1990s made by retired Suffolk Constabulary police officer and crime historian Stewart P. Evans. Stewart had predicted that much on Tumblety was to be discovered in the United States and Canada, and he was right. I have been asked on numerous occasions how I have discovered so much new information on Tumblety, and my answer is that Tumblety research in America is actually a team sport. I am the freshman on the team, following in the footsteps of two seasoned active researchers, Joe Chetcuti and Roger Palmer. Borrowing from researcher Robert Anderson, who has affectionately referred to his group of researchers on syphilis as "Team Syphilis," I call us "Team Tumblety." Whenever I believe I have found something new and pertinent, I contact Joe and Roger. I can guarantee that if I have made a factual error, Joe will find it. Joe forgets nothing. It is the huge volume of discoveries in this book where Roger comes into play. As I began to find evidence of damning information about Tumblety in America, I was shocked that no one had ever discovered it. When I presented the evidence and my conclusions to Team Tumblety, I was surprised to learn that Roger, of course, had made many of these discoveries and conclusions fifteen-plus years ago! The exciting aspect of this is, since our research was entirely separate, we come from completely different angles, which makes for two powerful and complementary works. I want to thank Roger for allowing me to use some discoveries that he first came across. I will, however, allow Roger to present his own findings, which we will see in the near future.

When cold-case detectives solve a decades-old murder case and family members are interviewed, the overwhelming response is that they experience a certain level of closure, even if the murderer may have died years earlier and justice was never served. The rediscovery of murdered and brutalized women discussed in this book died well over a century ago, so their families and friends have long since passed. Thus, I cannot offer them closure or justice. But, by presenting the victims' stories here, at least they now have a voice, and they are no longer forgotten.

Acknowledgments

I am honored to have been assisted by such great people, and my sincere gratitude goes out to each and every one. Thank you to Joe Chetcuti and Roger Palmer for being on Team Tumblety and keeping me on track. Thank you, Stewart Evans, for not only your much-needed expert advice but also for starting it all. Much appreciation also goes out to Neil Storey, Robert Anderson, Brian Young, Al Warren, Andy Struthers, Mark Ritchie, A.j. Griffiths-Jones, Steve Blomer, Jason Figgis, and John West. I would like to thank Monica Mooney, Kevin Gallivan, and the Clarence Public Library's Sherlock Holmes group for allowing me to use them as test subjects with my recent discoveries.

I am so grateful to my editor, Jennifer Cappello, for keeping my research and arguments readable and cogent, and to Lawrence Knorr for creating such an amazing book cover. Thank you, Gary Smith and Scott Benson, for your valuable advice, and Karen Grundy for allowing me access to Canadian sources. Lastly, thank you to Sunbury Press for all of your support.

AUTHOR'S NOTE

Because this book relies heavily on original source material, every effort has been made to preserve the integrity of the original language—including spelling and grammar. While the author and publisher are aware that some of these dated and unusual conventions may appear to be errors on the part of the author, they have been checked against original source material and have been left untouched and unmarked to retain the historical accuracy and flavor of the primary source. Since marking every single "error" would have been tedious and distracting to the reader, this note serves as the disclaimer that those "mistakes" knowingly exist in the manuscript. In addition to this note, there are still several prominent instances of mistakes in quoted source material, which have been marked (using "[sic]") throughout the following pages, as determined by editorial discretion.

To clarify, the use of brackets in quoted material throughout this book refers to interjections by the author; the use of parentheses in quoted material refers to either notes and asides found in the original source or this author's citation of said material.

Additionally, since much of the scholarship and primary and secondary source material in this genre comes from British authors, the UK spellings (and some punctuation) have been left unedited. While these conventions may seem unusual to an American reading audience, they are indicative of traditional British spelling and grammar practices and are not errors.

All efforts in these areas have been made to ensure quality scholarship practices and to help clarify the origins of source material for readers and other researchers in the field.

CHAPTER 1

DR. FRANCIS TUMBLETY AND THE WHITECHAPEL MURDERS

Almost lost to history was one of Scotland Yard's most notorious Jack the Ripper suspects, Dr. Francis Tumblety. And Tumblety would have faded into obscurity if not for the tenacity of an enterprising young London correspondent at one of the largest New York newspapers in 1888, the *New York World*. His name was E. (Edwin) Tracy Greaves. At the time, the highly respected T. C. Crawford was the chief London correspondent for the *New York World*, having been in the position for three years. Greaves was newly assigned as his subordinate in January 1888. Before this, Greaves was the editor of their evening paper, the *Evening World*. In the summer of 1888, Crawford was reassigned to the United States, specifically to work the famous Hatfield–McCoy feud story and, thus, never returned to London. By early August, E. Tracy Greaves was the sole London correspondent. Because of the tutelage of the experienced T. C. Crawford, not to mention inheriting his London connections, and Greaves's own hard work, he had acquired a Scotland Yard informant. His office was just feet away from Scotland Yard, which was then the common name for the headquarters of the Metropolitan Police Department. Greaves stated twice that fall—as reported in the *Chicago Tribune*, October 7, 1888, and the *Evening World*, October 9, 1888—that he had a Scotland Yard man who updated him weekly on the Whitechapel murders investigation.

It was this source, on November 17, 1888, who helped Greaves break the story in a *New York World* news cable communication of Dr. Francis Tumblety being arrested on suspicion for the Whitechapel murders, although it was a subordinate story to the arrest on suspicion of a member of the Royal family.

Multiple US newspapers ran the news cable, including the *Chicago Daily Tribune*, November 18, 1888:

> LONDON, Nov. 17. — Just think of it. One of the Prince of Wales' own exclusive set, a member of the Household Cavalry . . . getting into custody on suspicion of being the Whitechapel murderer! . . . That was the case of Sir George Arthur of the Prince of Wales' set. He put on an old shooting coat and a slouch hat and went to Whitechapel for a little fun. He got it. It occurred to two policemen that Sir George answered much the popular description of "Jack the Ripper." . . . and he was released with profuse apologies for the mistake. The affair was kept out of the newspapers . . .
>
> Another arrest was a man who gave the name "Dr. Kumblety of New York." The police could not hold him on suspicion of the Whitechapel crimes, but he has been committed for trial in the Central Criminal Court under a special law passed soon after the modern Babylonian exposures. The police say this is the man's right name, as proved by the letters in his possession from New York, and that he has been in the habit of crossing the ocean twice a year for several years.

After a search through contemporary newspapers in the United Kingdom, Greaves's Scotland Yard source was correct that the Sir George Arthur incident was indeed kept out of the British press. What was also kept out of the British press was the arrest on suspicion of "Dr. Kumblety from New York"; it seems the source misread the report and told Greaves the slightly misspelled name. It was actually New York City Chief Inspector Thomas Byrnes who informed the press who Dr. Kumblety really was—Dr. Francis Tumblety. For Byrnes to so quickly and confidently profess that this Jack the Ripper suspect was Tumblety, it is clear that the chief inspector had inside information from Scotland Yard. There would have been no other way for Byrnes to have connected Kumblety, a name given to no one, to Francis Tumblety, and to believe it with such confidence that he allowed the press to announce it to the world. Indeed, it was at this exact time we have record of Scotland Yard, specifically, Assistant Commissioner Robert Anderson, in cable communications with two other major US police officials about Tumblety and the Whitechapel murders, San Francisco's Chief of Police Patrick Crowley and Brooklyn's Police Superintendent Patrick Campbell.

The "Scotland Yard man" relayed to Greaves that the American doctor "was in the habit of crossing the ocean twice a year for several years." Evidence suggests his trip to England began around June 1888, and he stayed until late November 1888. If Greaves's source is correct that he made two trips to England, Tumblety may very well have traveled to England soon after he visited Toronto in January of that year.

According to an article in the *New York World*, dated November 19, 1888, Tumblety was seen in New York City "five months earlier," meaning around June 1888. The earliest record we have of Tumblety in London is July 27, 1888, because this was the date he was charged with committing the misdemeanor offense of gross indecency on the first young man, Albert Fisher. On the luxurious and famous steamship *City of Rome*, Tumblety left for London on May 25, 1887, and returned on the same ship on October 7, 1887. If he took this ship in 1888, it left New York harbor on June 13 and on July 11; either trip would allow him to be in London on July 27. Something very curious about the July 11 *City of Rome* trip to London is that Richard Mansfield and his *Strange Case of Dr. Jekyll & Mr. Hyde* company were onboard. They performed at the Lyceum Theatre from August 4 (three days before the Martha Tabram murder) until the end of September. The London papers quickly connected Mr. Hyde with Jack the Ripper, stating that the performance may very well have incited the killer into action against sex workers.

Greaves reported in his November 17, 1888, news cable article that "Dr. Kumblety of New York," was initially arrested on suspicion of the Whitechapel murders, but because they had little evidence to directly link him to the murders, they "committed him for trial under a special law passed after the Babylon exposures." This was the Criminal Law Amendment Act of 1885, known as the Maiden Tribute Act, which was primarily designed to protect young maidens from criminal vice. Part of the special law, though, was called "gross indecency," which made it easier to convict men committing homosexual acts. Even though the public and the press did not know Tumblety was specifically arrested for gross indecency, the November and December 1888 criminal court calendars for Central Criminal Court stated this fact.

In view of this and other corroborating evidence, sometime before November 7, 1888, Tumblety was arrested on suspicion. According to the November and December Central Criminal Court calendars, he was then received into custody at Holloway Prison on November 7. Under nineteenth-century British law, the *Writ of Habeas Corpus* mandated that within twenty-four hours of incarceration and identification, the prisoner must either be charged with the crime and presented to the judicial branch of government, (i.e., the police court magistrate) or be released. This is the reason Tumblety was released after being arrested on suspicion of the Whitechapel crimes: No one saw the murders, so convicting any suspect without a confession would have been a losing battle.

Once someone was arrested on suspicion by a police constable or divisional detective, the prisoner was taken to the local police station to be identified, meaning the authorities would determine their name and residence. They would then cable the Metropolitan Police headquarters, aka, Scotland Yard, to see if there was already a file on the prisoner. During the mass arrests of October 1888, the police would quickly collect this information and then release the suspects. In the case of Tumblety, we have inside information on what happened when Scotland Yard was cabled by the local police and discovered his file, which was likely when Tumblety became a target of interest. In a private return letter to famed British journalist George R. Sims, dated 1913 and written by retired Chief Inspector of Special Branch John G. Littlechild—a man who was in the inner circle of Scotland Yard at the time of the murders—Littlechild mentioned Tumblety:

> I never heard of a Dr D. in connection with the Whitechapel murders but amongst the suspects, and to my mind a very likely one, was a Dr. T. (which sounds much like D.) He was an American quack named Tumblety ... I knew Major Griffiths for many years. He probably got his information from Anderson who only "thought he knew."

Major Griffiths was the Inspector of Prisons from 1878 to 1896 and was a close acquaintance to all the senior-ranking Scotland Yard officials at the time of the murders. Littlechild mentions Tumblety's large "dossier" and comments upon pertinent information. He states that Tumblety was an American quack doctor, and, at the time, it was believed that Jack the Ripper might be an American with anatomical knowledge. According to Littlechild, what was more concerning was that Tumblety had an unusual and bitter hatred of women, "a fact on record." Because Littlechild also wrote that Tumblety was "a very likely suspect," this suggests that these top Scotland Yard officials had a serious discussion about him. Corroborating this was the fact that, at this very time, Assistant Commissioner Anderson—the official ultimately in charge of the Whitechapel murders investigation—corresponded with US chiefs of police requesting background information on Tumblety.

Even though Littlechild's comments in his private letter had given details only known to Scotland Yard, he did make one error. Littlechild stated, "... He [Tumblety] shortly left Boulogne and was never heard of afterwards. It was believed he committed suicide . . ." Tumblety never did step foot in England again, but he did not commit suicide and actually lived until May 1903. How could Littlechild have relayed such accurate information unknown to the press and public, such as Tumblety being charged and remanded at Marlborough Street Police Court, but end in a blatant error? The answer is, Littlechild did indeed believe he heard that a Whitechapel murders suspect had gone to America and then committed suicide because Scotland Yard received reports of a murderer having been tracked to New York who then committed suicide. Beginning on June 1, 1889, Melville Macnaghten was assigned as the Assistant Chief Constable of CID (Criminal Investigation Department) and immediately became the number-two man in charge of the Whitechapel murders case under Assistant Commissioner Anderson. Macnaghten had detailed knowledge of the entire Whitechapel murders investigation up until the case closed in 1892. Even though the case was no longer actively investigated, any subsequent leads would have crossed Macnaghten's desk and been pursued. Ex-Chief Inspector Tom Divall stated in his 1929 autobiography, "Assistant Commissioner of CID, Sir Melville Macnaghten, received some information that the murderer had gone to America and died in a lunatic asylum there." Not only does this match a Whitechapel murder suspect going to America, but it also matches the suspect soon dying. Further, Commissioner Monro generated a report for the Metropolitan Police Force for 1889 and discussed a prisoner who was tracked to New York and committed suicide while incarcerated. Monro reported, "The criminal returns for the year. . . . That 17 murders are recorded without a single conviction having been obtained may seem to need explanation. . . . In 4 of 9 remaining cases the persons against whom coroners' juries found verdicts of willful murder had committed suicide before their crimes were discovered. In one, the murderer was tracked to New York, and arrested there, but committed suicide in prison." Littlechild retired from Scotland Yard just after this, in 1893, so he was in the position to listen to Macnaghten and company discuss the case at least until 1892. So, while Littlechild was not mistaken in his knowledge of persons of interest in murder cases traveling to America and, thereafter, committing suicide, his error was in thinking that Tumblety was among that demographic.

Incidentally, the case closing in 1892 and Littlechild's 1893 retirement also explains why he did not know of a Dr. D., as in Montague Druitt, and that he assumed Major Griffiths got the information from Anderson, as opposed to Macnaghten. Montague Druitt did not enter as a suspect in the official records until Macnaghten submitted it in his 1894 memorandum, and the memorandum was unknown to the public. Even if Druitt came under the radar of Macnaghten before Littlechild's retirement, Macnaghten admitted that he kept this information private. It was later discovered that Arthur Griffiths, a friend of Macnaghten's, read the 1894 memorandum and knew Macnaghten was convinced of Druitt's guilt. Griffiths then told Sims about a Dr. D as a top suspect.

Littlechild also knew Griffiths was a friend of Anderson's, and by the writing of this 1913 letter, Anderson was already speaking to the press about the Whitechapel murders case and stating that the identity of the killer is an "ascertained fact." While Anderson published that the killer was a Polish Jew, he purposely avoided naming him. It makes sense that Littlechild believed the information came from Anderson, especially if Sims failed to mention in his letter that Dr. D died in the Thames. Littlechild could easily have assumed that Sims was stating that Dr. D was the suspect Anderson had claimed was an ascertained fact. Corroborating this is Littlechild's rebuttal, stating that "Anderson only thought he knew."

The fact that Littlechild recalled quite accurately in 1913 unpublicized details of Tumblety's 1888 file means that he was aware that high-ranking police officials took Tumblety seriously at the time of the murders. It also explains why Littlechild even mentioned Tumblety to Sims, clearly—in his mind—a suspect more significant than Major Griffith's Dr. D. Littlechild also made it a point to end the paragraph on Tumblety by writing that, after he left England, ". . . certain it is that from this time the 'Ripper' murders came to an end."

On important cases in the late nineteenth century, Scotland Yard had the Director of Public Prosecutors (DPP) under the Treasury Solicitor prosecute, but with Tumblety, it was a private organization called the National Vigilance Association (NVA) that took charge of prosecution. This was perfectly legal and appropriate at the time. This association was formed in 1885, specifically to prosecute cases involving the Maiden Tribute Act relating to criminal vice and public immorality. Some have suggested that if Scotland Yard took Tumblety seriously as a Ripper suspect, it would have had the DPP prosecute the case. But the DPP always had the authority to take over a case if it was dissatisfied with the NVA prosecutors, thus, it would have kept a close eye on the case. Why alert a prisoner that he's a serious suspect in a high-profile murder case that may cause him to go to prison for the rest of his life? Rarely would a law enforcement agency inform a suspect that they are being investigated until they are charged. Using the NVA, the normal method to prosecute crimes under the Maiden Tribute Act, would likely not have raised a red flag to Tumblety and his highly paid legal counsel. If the DPP was used, Tumblety's legal counsel would have known immediately that his case was being treated differently, and since Tumblety was just arrested on suspicion of the Whitechapel crimes, this would have been the first thing that came to mind. Keeping Tumblety completely ignorant of their investigation may have worked for a short time. There is evidence that Tumblety had no idea he was being investigated for the Whitechapel murders after his initial arrest on suspicion. Note what he stated to a *New York World* reporter in late January 1889, as published in multiple US newspapers, such as the *Buffalo Times*, January 30, 1889:

> "My arrest came about in this way," said he. "I happened to be in England when these Whitechapel murders attracted the attention of the whole world, and in company with thousands of other people I went down to the Whitechapel district. I was not dressed in a way to attract attention, I thought, though it *afterward* turned out that I was. I was interested by the excitement, and the crowds and the queer scenes and sights, and *did not know that all the time I was being followed by English detectives*."
>
> "Why did they follow you?"
>
> "My guilt was very plain to the English mind. Someone had said that Jack the Ripper, must wear a slouch hat. Now I happened to have on a slouch hat, and this, together with the fact that I was an American, was enough for the police. It established my guilt beyond any question."
>
> "How long were you in prison?"
>
> "Two or three days; but I don't care to talk about it. When I think of the way I was treated in London it makes me lose all control of myself. It was shameful—horrible."
>
> "What do you think of the London police?"
>
> "I think their conduct in this Whitechapel affair is enough to show what they are. There was absolutely not one single scintilla of evidence against me. I had simply been guilty of wearing a slouched hat, and for that I was held and charged with a series of the most horrible crimes ever recorded." [Author emphasis added.]

Notice that Tumblety stated he was unaware he was being followed by the London police, and that he was a Jack the Ripper suspect. Tumblety's last statement, however, is a lie: He was never charged for the Whitechapel murders—what this narcissist called 'the most horrible crimes ever recorded'—though he was indeed initially arrested on suspicion. It may also be true that the only reason he was first arrested on suspicion was because he was merely walking alone on the Whitechapel streets at night and wearing a slouch hat. At this exact time, Sir George Arthur was walking the streets in Whitechapel at night, wearing a slouch hat, and he was arrested on suspicion. What Tumblety did not say correctly, however, something he may never have known, was why they suspected him enough to have detectives secretly follow him. Chief Inspector Littlechild stated that in Tumblety's file—a file Tumblety himself was not privy to—it was clear that his hatred of women was "remarkable and bitter in the extreme."

There is an eyewitness account of someone who knew Tumblety and interacted with him in London in October 1888 and saw his gross misogyny firsthand. The *Buffalo Courier*, December 7, 1888, interviewed a Buffalo man, C. A. Bloom, who knew Tumblety for fifteen years and reported on his peculiar change of behavior when forced to be near women. Bloom's encounter with Tumblety occurred just after the September 30, 1888, murders of Elizabeth Stride and Catherine Eddowes:

> During the past summer and early fall I [C. A. Bloom] was in London, England, for three months. One pleasant day in October [1888], in company with my wife and another lady, I was going down Regent street. At Oxford street I was greatly surprised to see this same Dr. Tumblety enter the omnibus. . . . But what surprised me was his actions when he found that I was in company with the ladies. When I introduced my wife to him his actions were so strange that she has spoken about it several times since . . . He seemed to be very ill at ease and never raised his eyes from the floor after he had learned that the ladies were with me.

Tumblety's response was more than just ignoring the gender he despised; he could not even have a cordial conversation with Bloom when these women were so close to him. The significance of this event is that it shows Tumblety's attitude while he was in London during the Whitechapel murders.

Because the *Writ of Habeas Corpus* in nineteenth-century British law mandated that a prisoner be presented to a magistrate within twenty-four hours of their arrest, we know that Tumblety had his remand hearing in front of Marlborough Police Court Magistrate James Hannay on or about November 7, 1888. According to the Central Criminal Court calendars, he was charged with gross indecency and indecent assault upon four young men. They were Albert Fisher, occurring on July 27; Arthur Brice on August 31; James Crowley on October

14; and John Doughty on November 2, 1888. The purpose of a remand hearing is to give the police court magistrate the ability to either remand (incarcerate) the prisoner until the scheduled committal hearing one week later or offer them bail. The subsequent committal hearing allowed the magistrate to hear both sides of the case and then determine if it should be committed up to the next judicial level for trial in front of a judge at Central Criminal Court for City of London cases or Middlesex Sessions for Middlesex cases or be dropped. When a case was committed, a grand jury was automatically assigned for jurors to review the case. If a "true bill" was returned by the jurors at the grand jury, then the case was committed up. If the jurors returned a "no bill," then the case was dropped.

Tumblety's case was treated differently than other cases of gross indecency at the time, begging the question as to why. It was normal for remand hearings to be in open session, meaning British reporters were allowed in the police court examining room to report on each case. London reporters were specifically assigned by their respective papers to attend police court, which guaranteed the case getting published in the London newspapers. Tumblety's case never made the papers, and the obvious reason for this would have been that his case was in closed session. Hannay had the authority to have a closed session, which meant that reporters were excluded from the examination room. Records in the British papers and Central Criminal Court show Hannay commonly had gross indecency cases in open session, so Tumblety requesting a closed session due to embarrassment would likely have been futile. If, though, the prosecutors and Scotland Yard agreed to a closed session, Hannay would likely have allowed it. If Scotland Yard merely wanted a boy molester in prison for gross indecency, it stands to reason that they would have wanted it in open session for all to see. If, however, their real concern was that Tumblety might be Jack the Ripper, having a closed session and keeping this part of the investigation private as long as they could would clearly have been appropriate.

Tumblety's committal hearing was scheduled for November 14, 1888. Mary Kelly was murdered on November 9, 1888. Some have claimed that Tumblety was remanded in Holloway Prison from November 7 to November 14, so he could not have been the killer. Strangely, there are no official Central Criminal Court records on Tumblety's case, but we know Hannay allowed bail at the November 14 committal hearing because Tumblety posted bail on November 16. It makes no sense that a magistrate would have offered bail at the committal hearing and not have offered bail at the earlier remand hearing. Tumblety always had a large sum of money on his person and would have been able to immediately post bail.

We have record of Magistrate Hannay's past practice when dealing with gross indecency cases during his tenure. One particular case even involved a retired medical officer, Hamilton De Tatham, committing gross indecency against four young men, just like Tumblety. Luckily, this case was in open session, so the reporters were in the examining room, providing us with a record of Hannay offering bail at both the remand hearing *and* the committal hearing. According to a *Reynolds Newspaper* article from May 3, 1891, titled, "Serious Charge Against a Member of the Junior United Service Club," and Old Bailey records, Detective Sergeant Nearn, C Division, received a warrant on April 21, 1891, to arrest forty-seven-year-old Hamilton De Tatham, a retired medical officer of the Indian army. De Tatham was residing at Due Street, St. James, and thus, was charged at the Marlborough Street Police Court. Against De Tatham were sworn testimonies from four young men at Junior United Service Club. Detective Sergeant Nearn said he received a communication from the Junior United Service Club, and he and Sergeant Bowden "went and saw the secretary, and took down the boy's statements." Even though it was considered a serious case, Magistrate Hannay allowed £400 bail, which De Tatham posted, and, thus, was released from Holloway Prison until the committal hearing seven days later. Tumblety's case in front of Magistrate Hannay was nearly identical, but we have no record of the amount of bail he set at the remand hearing. Hannay was clearly allowed to set bail at a remand hearing, since he did so in the De Tatham case, and if he was consistent with his duties as a magistrate, then he likewise offered Tumblety bail. Since it was Tumblety's habit to have a roll of cash totaling at least £1000 on his person, then he had the funds available. Tumblety posting bail is a certainty.

At De Tatham's committal hearing on April 29, 1891, Hannay judged that there was enough evidence for the case to be sent up to Central Criminal Court and set bail at £500, "accepted in two sureties of £250 each," which De Tatham posted. In Tumblety's case, bail was set at the committal hearing for £300, and there are court records showing that Tumblety posted bail.

Although there is no evidence of a grand jury having been convened in the De Tatham case, since the case made it to Central Criminal Court on May 4, 1891, a grand jury had to have convened and returned a true bill. De Tatham was found not guilty. On November 18, 1888, the grand jury for Tumblety's case was held, and, as stated earlier, the jurors returned a true bill. Tumblety's case was held in front of the judge in Central Criminal Court during the November 19/20, 1888, session. Tumblety was not in court and had his attorney request an extension. The case was postponed until December 10, 1888. We have evidence of Tumblety cabling his New York bank on November 20, 1888, for enough money to purchase a transatlantic ticket back to New York. Tumblety requested £260 1s. 6d. from his New York bank and reprinted his bank's response letter in his 1889/1893 autobiographical pamphlets:

> No later than November of last year Dr. Tumblety received a letter from Drexel, Morgan & Co., which contained the subjoined passage, quoted here to show the pleasant business relations existing between them.
>
> "In accordance with your order of the 20th inst., we have forwarded you by this mail our sterling letter of credit for £260 1s. 6d., upon Messrs. Drexel, Morgan & Co., of New York.
>
> We are, etc.,
J. S. Morgan & CO."

If Tumblety was the killer, it makes sense that the last Jack the Ripper victim was murdered just a day or so after he was arrested, sent to Holloway Prison, charged, and finally released on a misdemeanor charge. His indignation—even rage—would have been at its most intense. Recall what he stated about the incident a full two months later, ". . . I don't care to talk about it. When I think of the way I was treated in London it makes me lose all control of myself. It was shameful—horrible." There is actually an eyewitness account of a suspicious person leaving the direction of the final murder, seemingly in an emotional state of having lost control, who fits the description of Francis Tumblety:

> On Saturday afternoon a gentleman engaged in business in the vicinity of the murder gave what is the only approach to a possible clue that has yet been brought to light. He states that he was walking through Mitre square at about ten minutes past ten on Friday morning, when a tall, well-dressed man, carrying a parcel under his arm, and rushing along in a very excited manner, ran plump into him. The man's face was covered with blood splashes, and his collar and shirt were also bloodstained. The gentleman did not at the time know anything of the murder (*Daily News* (UK), 12 November 1888).

By November 22, 1888, Tumblety was making his way to France. Chief Inspector Littlechild stated that he was first seen in Boulogne. Since he eventually boarded the steamship *La Bretagne* in Havre, France, before its noon departure time on November 24, 1888, he likely traveled east out of London to Folkestone Harbour, crossed the channel, and arrived in Boulogne on or before November 23, 1888, ultimately taking a train from Boulogne to Havre. Tumblety's normal method of departure across the ocean began west in Liverpool, thus, he was clearly sneaking out.

On December 1, 1888, E. Tracy Greaves finally broke the story of Tumblety jumping bail and being last seen in Havre, France, which had to have come from his Scotland Yard source. The information is not only true, but it also reveals inside information, as Tumblety's last-known whereabouts being Havre was a detail not publicized or published anywhere. Curiously, a warrant for his arrest was not issued until December 10, 1888, when he was a no-show for his trial at Central Criminal Court. The fact that Littlechild knew Tumblety was *first* seen in Boulogne, France, around November 23, and that E. Tracy Greaves's source was a Scotland Yard informant, supports the notion that Scotland Yard was attempting to track Tumblety ever since he posted bail on November 16. If their concern for Tumblety was only for the gross indecency case, then their interest in finding him would only have started after his December 10, 1888, warrant.

Between the arrest on suspicion sometime before November 7, 1888, and jumping bail sometime around November 22, 1888, there is evidence that Tumblety left London and visited his niece, Catherine Way, of Bath, England. Catherine was the daughter of Tumblety's older sister, Julia Moore, so Catherine was only a few years his junior. Researchers Roger Palmer and Robert Linford independently uncovered a record of oral family history at Ancestry.com, pertaining to Catherine Way being visited by Tumblety. A member of Ancestry.uk stated:

> Oral family history included a relative from America questioned in the Whitechapel murders in 1888 named Maurice Fitzsimmons. He was a man who dressed dramatically (with a cape) and was the somewhat-wild son of a doctor and uncle to Catherine, whose mother's maiden name was Powderly. The hosts of that visit were the Joseph & Catherine Way family of Bath, Somerset. Interviews with the oldest relatives showed a familiarity with the name Maurice Fitzsimmons but not with Powderly. It turned out, after records research, that both surnames were connected to Catherine's family—they were the married names of two of her maternal aunts. There was also only one person in all of the connected families who was ever called doctor for any reason—Francis Tumblety, Catherine's youngest maternal uncle, also somewhat wild. That Catherine and her uncle were only a few years apart in age could account for the impression that he was her cousin. Another source of confusion could have been the waning memories of the oral historians.

Tumblety's fourth-oldest sister was Elizabeth, who married a Thomas Powderly and had five children, though none of them were named Catherine, so the "mother's maiden name was Powderly" recollection is one of those "waning memories." Catherine's maiden name was Moore. Tumblety's sister Julia Moore married a Joseph Moore and settled in Bath, Somerset. Tumblety's oldest sister was Alice, who was twenty-two years his senior. She married a Michael Fitzsimmons, having three children together: Michael, Charles, and Mary. Michael Fitzsimmons was only five years younger than Tumblety. Not only was there no one named Maurice Fitzsimmons, but none in the Fitzsimmons family were doctors. It is beyond doubt that Francis Tumblety and Maurice Fitzsimmons were one and the same.

On December 2, 1888, Tumblety arrived in New York Harbor. New York City Chief Detective Inspector Thomas Byrnes had received notice that Tumblety was on his way one week earlier. In 1884, Byrnes explained that he was in constant communication with Scotland Yard about prisoners transiting the Atlantic. The cable communication was significant enough for Byrnes to order two detectives who knew Tumblety by sight to identify him disembarking *La Bretagne* and then to follow him.

CHAPTER 2

I QUITE EXPECT A SIMILAR EXPERIENCE IN NEW YORK

The following December 21, 1888, article in the evening edition of the *New York World* reports upon Scotland Yard Detective Inspector First-Class Walter Andrews being directed by his Scotland Yard superiors around December 9 or 10, 1888, to add to his original assignment of escorting Canadian prisoner Roland Barnett from London, England, to Toronto, Canada, and assist two other Scotland Yard men in finding Jack the Ripper in America before returning to England:

ALL THE WAY FROM SCOTLAND YARD.
An English Detective Coming Here in Search of Jack the Ripper.
[SPECIAL TO THE WORLD].

MONTREAL, Dec. 20 – Inspector Andrews, of Scotland Yard, arrived here to-day from Toronto *and left to-night for New York*. He tried to evade newspaper men, but incautiously revealed his identity at the Central Office, where he had an interview with Chief of Police Hughes. He refused to answer any questions regarding his mission, but said there were twenty-three detectives, two clerks and one Inspector employed on the Whitechapel murder cases. And that the police were without a jot of evidence upon which to arrest anybody.

"How many men have you working in America?"

"Half a dozen," he replied; then hesitating, continued: "American detective agencies have offered to find the murderer on salaries any payment of expenses. But we can do that ourselves, you know."

"Are you one of the half dozen?"

"No, my boy; don't say anything about that. I meant detective agencies."

"But what are you here for?"

"I had rather not say, just at present, anyhow."

Ten days ago Andrews brought Roland Gideon Israel Barnet [*sic*], charged with helping wreck the Central Bank of Toronto, to this country from England, *and since his arrival he has received orders from England* which will keep him in America for some time. It was announced at Police Headquarters today that *Andrews has a commission, in connection with two other Scotland Yard men, to find the murderer in America.* His [Jack the Ripper's] inaction for so long a time, and the fact that a man suspected of knowing considerable about the murders left England for this side three weeks ago, makes the London police believe Jack has left that country for this.

It is said among Irish Nationalists here that they have information that Andrews is remaining in America for the purpose of hunting up certain men and evidence to be used by the London Times in the Parnell case. [Author emphasis added.]

The only Jack the Ripper suspect who left England for America "three weeks ago" from the date of the article was Francis Tumblety, who left England on or about November 24, 1888. Further, Andrews was intending on traveling to New York, and Tumblety arrived in New York Harbor on December 2, 1888, then vanished three days later. Montreal, Canada, is due north of New York and situated on the shortest railway connection to New York City. This would have been the logical location for Andrews to take a train to New York, while any other Canadian location he stopped at would not.

A claim has been put forth that Andrews never "left to-night for New York," because he never received new orders from Scotland Yard to help two other Scotland Yard men find "Jack the Ripper in America." The authors of the claim state that the *New York World* correspondent made it up, deceptively adding the New York story to the article in order to sell papers. The conclusion is that Andrews had only one mission: escort the Canadian prisoner, Barnett, to Toronto, then return to England. Other than questionable comments made by newspaper reporters, they claim that there is no evidence that Andrews ever traveled to New York, a trip adding no value to Andrews's Toronto extradition orders. In support of their claim is the fact that a reporter from the *Montreal Herald*, who was also in Montreal Police Headquarters, or Central Office, listening to Andrews, never mentioned in his article published on the same day (December 21, 1888) anything about Andrews's next stop being New York:

Inspector Andrews, of the Scotland Yard detective force, London, who brought over the celebrated Gideon Barnett, was in the city yesterday on his return to England. At the Central Station, which he visited yesterday morning, he met several members of the press, and to their inquiries about the Whitechapel murders, said that so far the force was at sea, having no clue to work upon. They have arrested scores of suspected persons, but were forced to release them for want of sufficient evidence. The search is still kept up and will be until the culprit is captured. Twenty-three detectives, two clerks and an inspector are specially detailed for the Whitechapel affair, and they have received as many as 6,000 letters from police officers and others trying to give clues to the fiend."

Further, they explain that if it is true Andrews boarded the SS *Sarnia* in Halifax on his way back to England, which left only two days later, on December 22, 1888, this gives little time to accomplish the new set of orders. The *New York World* reporter stated in the December 21, 1888, article, "and since his [Andrews's] arrival he has received orders from England which will keep him in America for some time." If Andrews did depart on the SS *Sarnia* on December 22, then this statement made by the *New York World* reporter demonstrates that his comments are suspect.

There actually is evidence conflicting with the entire claim, the first of it discovered by researcher Roger Palmer. A local Halifax reporter with the *Morning Herald*, along with many reporters, spotted Inspector Andrews embarking on a steamship for the transit back to England. The steamship was the SS *Oregon*, not the SS *Sarnia*. An article in the *Morning Herald* (Halifax), on March 22, 1889, reported this event:

> The inspector [Andrews] returned home by way of Halifax, and as he stepped from the train at the deep water terminus and on board the steamer Oregon he was accosted by the reporter and questioned upon this delicate point. The inspector did not appear any too well pleased at the question, but allowed himself to be drawn into conversation when he admitted, as far as professional etiquette would allow, that such was his mission. But he would go no further...

The SS *Oregon*, as well as the SS *Sarnia*, was considered a mail steamer with the Dominion Lines slated for "Liverpool services," but it also carried passengers. According to the *Montreal Gazette*, December 20, 1888, rates of passage from Portland, Maine, to Halifax to Liverpool were $50, $65, and $75, with a return of $100, $125, and $150, "according to position of stateroom, with equal saloon privilege, Second cabin, $30. Steerage, $20. These steamers have Saloon, Staterooms amidships, where but little motion felt, and they carry neither cattle nor sheep . . ."

The SS *Oregon* changed its sailing schedule two times a year, its "summer arrangements" and "winter arrangements." According to the *Gazette*, October 30, 1888, for the summer arrangements, the SS *Oregon* serviced both Montreal and Quebec, then transited directly to Liverpool. It did not stop in Halifax. Its winter arrangements for Liverpool services, on the other hand, did stop in Halifax two days after it received mail and passengers in Portland, Maine. While Montreal and Quebec were located on the St. Lawrence River, which froze over in the winter, Halifax, Nova Scotia, and Portland, Maine, were coastal harbor towns that did not freeze over.

The Dominion Line began its winter arrangement for its steamships in early December, placing announcements of the change in newspapers in late November. For example, the following announcements in the *Gazette*, November 29, 1888, have the sailing dates of both the SS *Sarnia* and the SS *Oregon*. Specific to the SS *Sarnia*:

> Liverpool Service Sailing Dates
> —From Portland, *Sarnia* . . . Thurs. Dec. 20, From Halifax, Saturday Dec. 22.

This corroborates the SS *Sarnia* leaving Halifax for Liverpool on December 22, 1888. Note, though, the sailing dates of the SS *Oregon* in the very same list:

> Liverpool Service Sailing Dates
> —From Portland, *Oregon* . . . Thurs. Jan. 3, From Halifax, Saturday, Jan. 5.

This particular announcement from Dominion Lines began in late November 1888 and continued throughout December 1888 and never varied, thus, the SS *Oregon* did not receive passengers throughout the entire month of December. Corroborating this is the SS *Oregon* departure date from Liverpool on December 13, 1888, as reported in the *Portland Daily Express* (in all issues from the end of November to the middle of December), along with the *Portland Daily Press*, December 27, 1888, reporting that the SS *Oregon* arrived in Portland from Liverpool on December 25, 1888, to start its winter schedule. Andrews could not have embarked on the SS *Oregon* in Halifax until January

5, 1889. It was docked in Portland, Maine, until it left on January 3, transiting to Halifax.

This debunks the argument that Andrews could not have been in New York because he quickly left the shores of North America two days after he was in Montreal. This, in fact, supports the *New York World* reporter's comment that Andrews's new orders, "will keep him in America for some time." Researcher Roger Palmer made another revealing point. The Halifax reporter's comments about Andrews embarking on the SS *Oregon* were published on March 22, 1889, and he never gave a date to his transit across the Atlantic back to England. The SS *Oregon* had returned from Liverpool and arrived in Halifax on February 16, 1889. The next time it arrived in Halifax was March 2, 1889, followed by March 30, 1889. This means that the Halifax reporter may have even spotted Andrews on February 16 or March 2.

The Achilles' heel of the *New-York-World*-reporter-lied claim is, if Andrews, indeed, intended to travel to New York, this would verify the new orders. Further, if true, this would mean Scotland Yard took seriously the possibility that Tumblety was the Whitechapel fiend since they were investing time, money, and energy into three Scotland Yard detectives searching for him. Note what a reporter for the *Montreal Gazette*, who was also at Central Office, reported on the very same day:

> Inspector Andrews of Scotland Yard, London, who brought Barnett to Toronto, called at the Central police station yesterday and was shown round the city by Detective Robinson. Inspector Andrews will leave for England via New York to-morrow [December 21].

Although the reporter made no mention of why Andrews was traveling to New York, he did indeed independently verify his planned visit to America. This demonstrates that the New York trip was not a product of the imagination of the *New York World* reporter but was a statement made at Central Office heard by multiple independent reporters. It makes sense that the *Montreal Gazette* reporter—and the *Montreal Herald* reporter, for that matter—did not publish the details of Andrews's New York trip. Note that this information did not come from the interview Andrews gave to the group of reporters but from an announcement at Central Office that day. The Canadian reporters heard the announcement, but New York affairs did not involve their respective country or cities. Andrews making his way to New York to find Jack the Ripper would have been huge news for a New York reporter.

Might Andrews's planned trip to New York have been just a rumor in the halls of Central Office and not really true? The following record seems to refute Andrews's trip to America. An official letter written by Assistant Commissioner Robert Anderson stated on March 17, 1890, that Andrews was never in the United States:

> Perhaps I should add for Mr. Matthews information in the event any supplementary Q begin asked, that at the date specified there was another of my Inspectors across the Atlantic (since pensioned) had taken an extradition prisoner to Canada (as papers in H.O. will [explain]) but he was not in the United States at all. This whole story is a stupid fabrication. —HO 144/478/X27302

In order for Anderson's claim to be true, his boss, Home Secretary Henry Matthews, must then have lied. On that very day, March 17, 1890, the home secretary commented to members of the House of Commons about the *Times* attempting to procure witnesses in the United States against Charles Stewart Parnell by using Metropolitan Police Inspectors Jarvis and Shaw. Anderson's anger must have been festering for a full year, because on March 21, 1889, the home secretary admitted Andrews went to America. Home Secretary Matthews was asked a question in the House of Commons on March 21, 1889. According to the *Evening Star*, March 21, 1889,

> *Home Secretary Matthews, in reply to a question, admitted that Police Inspector Andrews had visited America* since the passage of the Parnell commission bill, but he did not know whether Andrews had seen Le Caron, the informer, there. [Author emphasis added.]

Recently discovered evidence, though, has put the issue to rest. Inspector Andrews was quoted discussing his upcoming trip to New York, and by extension, he did indeed receive orders to find the murderer in America, regardless of whether Anderson stated the truth.

On the very same day the *New York World* article was published, the *Ottawa Daily Citizen* published its own account of the Andrews interview at Montreal Police Headquarters, yet it is clearly not a reproduction of the *New York World* article. The article certainly does repeat Andrews's comment on the detectives, clerks, and inspector dedicated to the Whitechapel murders case and even uses the phrase "jot of evidence," but this correspondent reported upon entirely different aspects of the interview:

Ottawa Daily Citizen, December 21, 1888.
THE WHITECHAPEL SLAYER.
Twenty-three Detectives Anxious to Capture Him.

Montreal, 20th. — Inspector Andrews, the Scotland Yard detective who brought R. G. Barnett from England to Toronto, is in the city. Talking to several members of the press about the Whitechapel murders, he said: "We are utterly powerless, as we have not a jot of evidence or clue of any kind moral or legal, against any man. I am of the opinion that the man has some surgical knowledge. This was shown in at least five of the six murders. They may continue for years, and I quite expect that he will go on with his work. He and his victim always avoid the police. No one has ever seen him approach or leave his victim. At Toronto the other day a man was at my hotel before I was up to give me the name and full description of the murderer. I said, 'My dear sir, why don't you go over to London and secure the $75,000 now offered as a reward and, also, in all probability, something for life?' I quite expect a similar experience in New York. We have a special staff of 23 detectives, two clerks and an inspector doing nothing else but working on this case. They have received at least 6,000 letters, each having a distinct idea on the murders." Inspector Andrews is a handsome man of about 40, with full brown beard and moustache.

This report also commented upon Inspector Andrews being interviewed by more than one newspaperman and even gives a firsthand account of what Andrews looked like. Of supreme importance in the *Ottawa Daily Citizen* article is what Andrews stated after explaining to the reporters that when he was at his Toronto hotel an armchair detective gave him advice on how to catch Jack the Ripper. Andrews clearly took the advice personally, then stated,

"*I quite expect a similar experience in New York.*"

The *Ottawa Daily Citizen* reporter quoting Andrews's comments about what he expects in New York verified the inspector's intentions to go to New York. This can mean only one thing: Andrews did, indeed, receive new orders to find Jack the Ripper in America. This also explains why the *New York World*'s Montreal correspondent thought Andrews was on his way to New York—because he said so.

The *New York World* reporter was clear that the announcement at Central Office about Andrews being commissioned to work with two Scotland Yard detectives was the reason he was going to New York City. There certainly was a Scotland Yard detective reported to have been in New York City at that very time watching Tumblety specifically because of the Whitechapel murders investigation. Note how a *New York World* correspondent stationed in New York City reported the incident:

> It was just as this story was being furnished to the press that a new character appeared on the scene, and it was not long before he completely absorbed the attention of every one. He was a little man with enormous red side whiskers and a smoothly shaven chin. He was dressed in an English tweed suit and wore an enormous pair of boots with soles an inch thick. He could not be mistaken in his mission. There was an elaborate attempt at concealment and mystery which could not be possibly misunderstood. Everything about him told of his business. From his little billycock hat, alternately set jauntily [*sic*] on the side of his head and pulled lowering over his eyes, down to the very bottom of his thick boots, he was a typical English detective. If he had been put on a stage just as he paraded up and down Fourth avenue and Tenth street yesterday he would have been called a caricature.
>
> First he would assume his heavy villain appearance. Then his hat would be pulled down over his eyes and he would walk up and down in front of No. 79 staring intently into the windows as he passed, to the intense dismay of Mrs. McNamara, who was peering out behind the blinds at him with ever-increasing alarm. Then his mood changed. His hat was pushed back in a devil-may-care way and he marched by No. 79 with a swagger, whistling gayly, convinced that his disguise was complete and that no one could possibly recognize him.
>
> His headquarters was a saloon on the corner, where he held long and mysterious conversations with the barkeeper always ending in both of them drinking together. The barkeeper epitomized the conversations by saying: "*He wanted to know about a feller named Tumblety, and I sez I didn't know nothink at all about him; and he says he wuz an English detective and he told me all about them Whitechapel murders, and how he came over to get the chap that did it.*" [Author emphasis added.]
>
> When night came the English detective became more and more enterprising. At one time he stood for fifteen minutes with his coat collar turned up and his hat pulled down, behind the lamp-post on the corner, staring fixedly at No. 79. Then he changed his base of operations to the stoop of No. 81 and

looked sharply into the faces of every one who passed. He almost went into a spasm of excitement when a man went into the basement of No. 79 and when a lame servant girl limped out of No. 81 he followed her a block, regarding her most suspiciously. At a late hour he was standing in front of the house directly opposite No. 79 looking steadily and ernestly [sic].

The *New York Herald* reporter's eyewitness account was less detailed yet clearly identified the same Englishman:

I found that the Doctor was pretty well known in the neighborhood. The bartenders in McKenna's saloon, at the corner of Tenth street and Fourth avenue, knew him well. And it was here that I discovered an English detective on the track of the suspect. This man wore a dark mustache and side whiskers, a tweed suit, a billycock hat and very thick walking boots. He was of medium height and had very sharp eyes and a rather florid complexion. He had been hanging around the place all day and had posted himself at a window which commanded No. 79. He made some inquiries about Dr. Tumblety of the bartenders, but gave no information about himself, although it appeared he did not know much about New York. It is uncertain whether he came over in the same ship with the suspect.

Both the *New York World* and *New York Herald* had competing stories on December 4, 1888, of an English detective in New York City staking out Tumblety's room with a reported mission to come over and get the chap who had committed the Whitechapel murders. Two independent reports actually clarify where the English detective came from—Scotland Yard. In the December 14, 1888, issue of the *Cincinnati Enquirer*, an Associated Press article discussed an investigation on Tumblety going on in Cincinnati, which states,

... Dr. Francis Tumblety, one of the suspects under surveillance by the English authorities, and who was recently followed across the ocean by Scotland Yard's men. From information which leaked out yesterday around police headquarters ...

In the December 16, 1888, issue of the *San Francisco Examiner*, the article referred to the English detective in New York City as the "detective from Scotland Yard." This man was certainly one of the detectives Inspector Andrews would have gone to New York to collaborate with.

Just days earlier, in Toronto, on December 11, 1888, Inspector Andrews told a *Toronto World* reporter the reason he wanted to meet Tumblety. He wanted to interview him. "Do I know Dr. Tumblety, of course I do. But he is not the Whitechapel murderer. All the same we would like to interview him, for the last time we had him he jumped his bail. He is a bad lot." When Andrews stated "we," he meant Scotland Yard as a whole; thus, his superiors wanted Tumblety interviewed, regardless of whether Andrews believed Tumblety was the murderer or not. This conforms with Andrews's new commission received around December 9 or 10, 1888. In these days, in order to interview someone, the interviewer had to be present with the suspect—which means Inspector Andrews was in New York City, where Tumblety was.

There has been a claim that Andrews wanted to interview him for the gross indecency case he jumped bail from, though an interview for that would have been of absolutely no value. The case was done; the grand jury returned a true bill on November 19, 1888, meaning the prosecution's case against Tumblety was so solid that it convinced the jurors to send the case up to Central Criminal Court. Also, New York Chief Detective Thomas Byrnes stated publicly that Tumblety had jumped bail on a non-extraditable misdemeanor case, thus, Tumblety was untouchable by British authorities. Byrnes, though, would have allowed Scotland Yard officials to interview him. Now, an interview about the Whitechapel murders investigation, an ongoing case, may very well have been fruitful, especially when Byrnes also stated that if Scotland Yard issued an extraditable warrant, then he would allow extradition.

When Inspector Andrews was at the Montreal police station on December 20, 1888, the Scotland Yard detective, or detectives, in New York City would have told him by cable that Tumblety was not in New York City, and they did not know where he was. Tumblety had vanished from New York City on December 5, 1888; less than one day after two New York City dailies reported on the English detective casing his room at 79 E. Tenth Street with the reported intent to "get the chap that did it." Unbeknownst to the Scotland Yard officials and the New York City officials, on December 20, 1888, Tumblety was hiding out with his sister's family in Waterloo, New York. In a small-town New York newspaper, the *Waterloo Observer*, in its December 12, 1888, issue, a Waterloo correspondent reported on Tumblety being in their town. (Waterloo is about forty miles east of his family residence in Rochester, New York.) The report states:

> Wild rumors are afloat about villains in many villages and cities assaulting, insulting and molesting women and young girls on public streets after dark.

All these places have a modified prototype of the White Chapel murderer, "Dick the Slasher." The announcement that *Dr. Tumblety* had come to New York and departed for a rural retreat, in the fancy of many timid females *has been located in Waterloo*. And this is the more certain; since the veritable doctor spent a summer here some ten years ago. [Author emphasis added.]

A Waterloo reporter had his article published in the local newspaper, so no one other than locals would have read the paper. Even though the *Waterloo Observer* may have received Associated Press news cables, stories they initiated would not have been wired. Tumblety hid for the next month and a half, yet Scotland Yard and the New York City Police Department had no idea when, or even if, he would return.

The *Daily Telegraph* correspondent who reported that Andrews did arrive in New York in what seemed to be a firsthand account does have corroboration. Andrews certainly did state that his next destination after Montreal was New York City. Once Andrews arrived, he would have been greeted by the New York City-based Scotland Yard detective and would have been informed that Tumblety was not available for an interview with him, a first-class inspector. This would also allow Andrews to receive any documents acquired by the detective stationed in New York City.

The whereabouts of Francis Tumblety also explain the second skeptical claim about "finding the murderer in America." The *New York World* article states that on or about December 10, 1888, Andrews had a commission, or an amendment to his assignment, involving the Whitechapel murders. This was about five days after Tumblety vanished from New York City. Scotland Yard and the New York City Police Department knew this, so Andrews's orders would have been to first find Tumblety before he could interview him. Andrews himself was quoted by the *New York World* correspondent discussing finding the murderer in America when he stated that half a dozen *American* detective agencies, "have offered to find the murderer on salaries any payment of expenses. But we can do that ourselves, you know." "American detective agencies," such as the Pinkerton Detective Agency, would have been referring to a search in America, especially since the question to Andrews was about the Whitechapel murders investigation in America. Andrews commenting upon Scotland Yard officials "do[ing] that ourselves," means Scotland Yard detectives were searching in America.

This now explains the comments made by Guy Logan in his book *Masters of Crime* (1928):

The murders ceased, I think, with the Miller Court one, and I am the more disposed to this view because, though the fact was kept a close secret at the time, I know that one of Scotland Yard's best men, Inspector Andrews, was sent specially to America in December 1888, in search of the Whitechapel fiend on the strength of important information, the nature of which was never disclosed. Nothing, however, came of it, and the Inspector's mission was a failure.

Andrews being unable to meet up with Tumblety in New York to interview him would have been considered a failure. An argument against the credibility of Logan's comments is that Andrews was not sent to America, but to Canada. While Andrews certainly was sent to North America in December 1888, this comment is still accurate; even if Logan meant the "United States" when he wrote "America," it still makes sense. Recall that Andrews was sent to Canada in order to escort Barnett to Toronto and then received new orders specific to the Whitechapel murders. Logan was clearly referring to the second set of orders, which pertained to the Whitechapel murders and involved Andrews traveling from (Montreal,) Canada to (New York City,) America. If Logan's Scotland Yard source was privy to inside information as he claimed, then the British reporter may have been correct, and Andrews did, indeed, make it to New York City.

In *Ripperologist 134*, October 2013, Logan authority, author, and rheumatologist at Cardiff University, Jan Bondeson, wrote the first of a two-part article on the history of Guy Logan and his literary connections to the Whitechapel murders. In 2013, Bondeson also edited and republished Logan's first true crime novel on the Whitechapel murders, which Logan wrote in 1905, titled *The True History of Jack the Ripper*. Logan wrote *Masters of Crime* in 1928, and his first chapter was on the Whitechapel murders. Bondeson characterizes Logan as having strong Scotland Yard connections, stating, "Guy Logan and George R. Sims moved in the same circles: both were playwrights and journalists, and they shared an interest in criminal history . . ." Sims knew Assistant Chief Constable (CID) Melville Macnaghten and Major Arthur Griffiths, all three promoting the same the Dr. D theory mentioned by Littlechild in his letter. Logan's 1905 *The True History of Jack the Ripper* follows closely with this theory, suggesting Logan shared Sims's sources. Further, Bondeson explains that former Assistant Commissioner at Scotland Yard Sir Basil Thomson wrote the preface to Logan's 1935 book *Verdict and Sentence*. This suggests that Logan certainly did get this information in his 1928 *Masters of Crime* from a credible Scotland Yard source.

What is now difficult to dispute is that Tumblety was, in the eyes of Scotland Yard at the peak of the murders, a Jack the Ripper suspect significant enough to have detectives spend time and resources in America. It makes sense why Chief Inspector Littlechild thought it important enough to inform Sims of Tumblety in the 1913 letter. He clearly remembered CID taking Tumblety seriously in the last few months of 1888. Why, then, is Tumblety's name missing from British records involving the Whitechapel murders, from newspapers to government archives, causing modern-day researchers for years to miss him?

Note the coincidences of omission:

1) While the US papers were reporting extensively on Tumblety in November and December 1888, the British papers were totally silent, not commenting upon Tumblety until February 1889. We know that Scotland Yard did have some influence over what the British press was publishing, as evidenced by a news cable from the *New York World's* London correspondent E. Tracy Greaves dated November 17, 1888. Greaves reported on Sir George Arthur's arrest on suspicion of the Whitechapel crimes and how they successfully kept the story out of the British press. The story was not front-page news in the British papers.

2) While all other *remand* hearings in front of a police magistrate involving gross indecency cases were reported in the British press, Tumblety's case never was. The prosecutors had to have convinced the magistrate for a closed session since he would have rejected the request from Tumblety.

3) While all other *committal* hearings in front of a police magistrate involving gross indecency cases were reported in the British press, Tumblety's case was not. We know it occurred because the November and December Central Criminal Court calendars stated that he posted bail two days later and then was released.

4) Tumblety's case made it to Central Criminal Court. It should have been recorded in official Central Criminal Court records, as all other gross indecency cases committed up by the magistrate were. Yet, it is missing. We know the records had to have been there because the November and December 1888 Central Criminal Court calendars recorded his case.

5) The archived records of Scotland Yard make no mention of Tumblety in the Whitechapel murder case or any other case, even though Chief Inspector Littlechild stated that Scotland Yard had a large dossier on him. The file is missing.

A pattern of omitting and/or deleting any knowledge of Tumblety in the British papers, court records, and Scotland Yard archives might be merely a series of similar coincidences, but it screams of a nineteenth-century concerted effort to erase him from having ever been connected to the Whitechapel murders case. It certainly worked perfectly for over a century until Stewart Evans acquired the Littlechild letter. Recall that Guy Logan, a man with Scotland Yard sources at the highest levels, stated Andrews's mission in America and the information he held was kept a close secret. If there was a CID effort to eliminate Tumblety, this also explains why Littlechild was willing to discuss Tumblety with Sims. Littlechild was not in CID, so he would not have been privy to any private directive to CID to keep Tumblety a secret.

It is also clear why the British government, including Scotland Yard, wanted the Tumblety investigation kept a close secret and then buried. Tumblety successfully escaped their grasp by jumping bail and returning to the United States, which would have been a huge embarrassment if it was revealed that he was a Jack the Ripper suspect. Once Inspector Andrews returned to England unsuccessful, it was clear that Tumblety was beyond their reach.

CHAPTER 3

ON THE STRENGTH OF IMPORTANT INFORMATION

There can now be little doubt that the investigation on Tumblety continued in North America. Researcher Roger Palmer identified a possible answer as to why Scotland Yard performed a North American investigation on the Whitechapel murders case involving Tumblety by examining Scotland Yard's past practices on similar cases. They completed a thorough background check in hopes of uncovering damaging information. For example, in the investigation of the 1891 Francis Coles murder, Chief Inspector Donald Swanson conducted an extensive background check on suspect Thomas Sadler, seeking a chronology of his movements during the 1870s and 1880s. He discovered an incident in the mid-1880s involving a knife. Palmer also points out another case with Dr. Thomas Neill, who was suspected of poisoning sex workers. Scotland Yard sent a man to America for the sole purpose of investigating his past activities. It seems to be the same reason why Tumblety always brought with him fake letters from prominent people attesting to his high standing in society. He knew police officials relied heavily upon a suspect's past behavior and character. Regardless of whether this was a successful practice, this is what they did in the late nineteenth century, and it should not be a surprise that they attempted to discover Tumblety's antecedents in America.

Recall the last statement from Guy Logan in *Masters of Crime* (1928):

> ... Inspector Andrews was sent specially to America in December 1888, in search of the Whitechapel fiend *on the strength of important information*, the nature of which was never disclosed. Nothing, however, came of it, and the Inspector's mission was a failure. [Author emphasis added.]

Scotland Yard's interest in Tumblety's history in America was based upon the strength of certain information they possessed. Notice the similarity of this comment and the following report out of Cincinnati (*Daily Picayune*, December 17, 1888) just days before Andrews arrived in Montreal:

> It has been known for some days past that the detectives have been quietly tracing the career in this city [Cincinnati] of Dr. Francis Tumblety, one of the suspects under surveillance by the English authorities, and who was recently followed across the ocean by Scotland Yard's men.... The investigation in this city is understood to be under the direction of English officials now in New York, *and based upon certain information they have forwarded by mail.* [Author emphasis added.]

The similarities are too close to be mere coincidence, especially when both quotes deal with Scotland Yard's investigation of Tumblety. Logan was told by his Scotland Yard source about this important information on Tumblety, which was sent out to various cities seeking something about Tumblety's past. What "important information" in North America would have helped bring Francis Tumblety to justice in a court of law for the crime of murdering unfortunates on the east side of London in late 1888? It is true that Assistant Commissioner Anderson was in cable communication with numerous US chiefs of police in November 1888 for all information on Tumblety, including examples of his handwriting. This, though, seems incomplete since Scotland Yard would have received this information by mail.

Three possible discoveries about Tumblety's antecedents would certainly have counted as important information. First, an extreme hatred of women, especially sex workers; second, any connection to anatomical organs since Jack the Ripper collected anatomical organs; and third, any possession of a knife or use of a knife against another human being, especially a woman. Any history of these would be damning in a Jack the Ripper murder case.

Recall, Chief Inspector Littlechild stated in his letter to Sims that Scotland Yard mentioned Tumblety's hatred of women, having this "fact on record." There is a large volume of events in the United States and Canada attesting to Tumblety's unusual hatred of women. Note for example the sworn statements of Richard Norris, the young man Tumblety met up with each New Orleans Mardi Gras season from 1881 to 1901. Norris testified to Judge Gabriel Hernandez in 1905 that one year for a joke he took Tumblety to a sporting house (a brothel):

... I did not tell him it was a sporting house until I got right in front of the place. Then I told him there was a lady friend of mine bothering me about money matters, and threatening to send to the office, and being in the neighborhood I was going in, and wouldn't he go in with me. I told him that as a joke, and I told the girls what a peculiar man he was, and when I got him in, he began to treat to some champagne, and I told the girls I know we would both have to leave, because he hated your kind of people—your class of people.

Norris likely knew Tumblety better than any other nonfamily member, and his comments make it clear that Tumblety had an aversion to female sex workers. Still, additional facts about Tumbley's misogyny in the United States may not have been needed in a court case in London. Littlechild stated that his misogyny was recorded in the Scotland Yard file.

There is even evidence that Scotland Yard knew of Tumblety's connections to anatomical organs, and it may have come out of London. While it was E. Tracy Greaves who broke the story through his Scotland Yard informant about Tumblety being arrested on suspicion, it was the London correspondent for the *New York Sun*, the highly respected Arthur Brisbane, who first reported *why* Scotland Yard suspected him. Brisbane would certainly take advantage of the telegraph to send time-sensitive stories, but he also wrote a multicolumn article in the Sunday paper. To reduce expenses, he sent it on a steamer, making it to New York in a week. He sent his Sunday, November 25, 1888, article around the same time as E. Tracy Greaves broke the story of Tumblety being arrested on suspicion. In it, Brisbane stated that Tumblety was being held on suspicion partly because of Coroner Wynne Baxter's theory that some American medical institution wanted uterus specimens.

In a November 10, 1888, article in the *New York Sun*, Brisbane recounted his trip into the Whitechapel District just after Mary Kelly was murdered. He then stated how he got the police to give him information on the case when they were ordered not to speak. He handed them a half crown: "The police do nothing but observe secrecy—a secrecy easily melted with a half crown, by the way..." Neither Scotland Yard nor even Brisbane would likely have known Tumblety did have a uterus collection during the Civil War. Yet, another London correspondent of a New York paper made a similar accusation. The *New York Tribune's* London correspondent was George W. Smalley, and he also had the opportunity to report firsthand. Note what an article in the December 4, 1888, issue of the *Tribune* stated about Tumblety:

DR. TUMBLETY ARRIVES IN NEW-YORK.
DETECTIVES KEEPING THEIR EYE ON HIM
—HIS ARREST IN LONDON HAS EXCITED PEOPLE HERE SOMEWHAT.
Doctor Francis Tumblety or, as he is known in England, Twomblety, is in New-York. He was arrested on suspicion of being implicated in the Whitechapel butcheries. When the French steamer La Bretagne arrived at her pier on Sunday . . . *He has been charged with a fondness for collecting anatomical specimens, and this has made his connection with the Whitechapel atrocities appear probable.* It is a fact that after he was discharged for lack of evidence from the accusation of being implicated in the Whitechapel horrors he was re-arrested in London for a violation of the "Maiden Tribute" act and released under 500 pounds bail. He "jumped" his bail and came to America. [Author emphasis added.]

When the paper reported "It is a fact," this suggests firsthand knowledge, and for the *Tribune*, it would have been from Smalley himself. Additionally, the knowledge of collecting anatomical specimens had to have been known by Scotland Yard, since their charge was connected to his collection, and this caused their strong suspicions.

It was published that the American medical student Baxter spoke about was an esteemed gynecologist out of Philadelphia. Once this became known, modern theorists immediately ignored it, but interestingly, many in Scotland Yard at the time did not. Years later in 1907, famed journalist George Sims, an acquaintance of Guy Logan—one with Scotland Yard connections—stated in the *Sunday Referee* that some Scotland Yard officials continued to take seriously the Baxter uterus theory, which was based upon "startling evidence," even adding that the organ had to be removed from "the almost living body."

Logan and Sims knew each other. How curious that they discussed an internal organ that was removed *and* startling information/evidence.

With regards to Tumblety's unusual interest in anatomical organs, the investigation must have started in Canada, from Toronto to St. John. At the beginning of Tumblety's career as a quack doctor operating in "Canada West," or Ontario, from 1856 to 1860, Tumblety was successfully prosecuted for practicing medicine as a physician, as opposed to distributing medicine as a druggist. In Canada West, physicians coming from the United States possessing a valid diploma were not allowed to practice medicine until they were approved by the governor's local medical board, which would then issue a license. Physicians had to go through an oral examination in front of the medical board. Tumblety initially planned on permanently running his operation out of Toronto for good reason. In only three years, Tumblety earned over one million dollars in today's value. Tumblety actually owned three thousand acres of land just west of Toronto in a town called Guelph.

Questions from the oral board came from each aspect all physicians were trained in: medicine, anatomy, surgery, and midwifery. Since Tumblety never went to medical school, even though he presented a fake Philadelphia medical diploma in the Toronto court case, he clearly had to study and practice on his own. Tumblety had knowledge of medicine covered because the board grudgingly accepted herbal medicine from eclectic medical schools, such as the Philadelphia Eclectic Medical School. Evidence that Tumblety had excellent medical knowledge, including surgery, came from Dr. J. H. Zeigler, the physician who cared for Tumblety each night for the three weeks he was in the St. John Catholic Hospital just before his death. When asked under oath if Tumblety had medical knowledge, Zeigler explained that the questions Tumblety asked him each night required medical knowledge. He then stated that they discussed surgery often, recalling a discussion on amputations, tying up arteries, and sewing up flesh.

It was less than a year after Tumblety lost the Toronto case that we see his interest in anatomical organs. After losing the case of practicing medicine without a license in Canada West, he continued to keep his Toronto office open but also opened an office in Buffalo, New York, in January 1858. It was here and at this time that a Buffalo resident recalled seeing Tumblety giving medical lectures with thespian emphasis. Medical lectures by surgeons in the late nineteenth century were generally illustrated medical lectures—illustrated with anatomical organs of their own creation. By 1861, Tumblety established himself in New York City. A *Vanity Fair* reporter complained of Tumblety's pictures of anatomical organs displayed in his office window.

At the onset of the Civil War, also in 1861, Tumblety followed the troops to Washington DC, claiming to offer his surgical services to Commander of the Army of the Potomac General George Brinton McClellan. Colonel C. A. Dunham, a New York lawyer by trade, recalled he and other officers were invited by Tumblety to his illustrated medical lecture, similar to what Tumblety had done in Buffalo, New York, one year earlier. Tumblety illustrated the lecture with anatomical organs, with Dunham claiming that Tumblety's favorites were his jars of uterus specimens. Possessing and successfully preserving human organs was Tumblety's way of proving his surgical prowess. General McClellan quickly became aware of Tumblety's deception, so he was rejected. A few months later, in early 1862, Tumblety shifted gears and began to promote his quack business in DC as an Indian herb doctor for the next two years, which by all accounts was very successful.

But the Civil War illustrated lecture was not the first time Tumblety was connected to the extraction of organs from a dead body. A *San Francisco Call* reporter contacted a reporter from St. John, New Brunswick, who responded with information about Tumblety operating his quack business in their city in 1860. As published in the *St. Louis Globe-Democrat*, January 5, 1889, the *Call* reporter stated:

> During the inquest [for the death of James Portmore], and before the Doctor fled, those present at the hearing were horrified at the nearly *successful attempt to abstract the heart and liver of the dead man* from the receptacle in which they lay. [Author emphasis added.]

The *only* suspect that can be connected specifically to the organs taken by Jack the Ripper—the kidney, the uterus (twice), and the heart—is Tumblety. In January 1888, the year of the Whitechapel murders, Tumblety told a *Toronto Mail* reporter that he was suffering from kidney and heart disease and was constantly in dread of sudden death.

The nineteenth-century *Anatomical Venus* was a wax display of a naked, beautiful woman with removable organs, reclined on a bed and dressed in a sexy negligee. The woman represented the famous reclining goddess, Venus. Venus was the Roman goddess of heterosexual love. The *Rokeby Venus Velazquez* painting of Venus with her son, Cupid, was displayed at the National Gallery in London. Tumblety would have hated the idea Venus represented since he believed beautiful women decoyed young men away from their intended lovers—other men. Tumblety would have loved the *Anatomical Venus*, however, since it was the *Reclining Venus* in a state of mutilation. Both Catherine Eddowes and Mary Kelly were displayed exactly like an *Anatomical Venus*.

Curiously, in January 1888, in New York City, in the Bowery District near where Tumblety lived, "several" wax museums were raided by the police, and their *Anatomical Venuses* were destroyed. This would have angered Tumblety. How coincidental that this occurred in the same year as the Ripper murders.

A possible motive for Jack the Ripper collecting anatomical organs, especially the uterus, was to cure himself of disease or even aging. Scotland Yard actually investigated the possibility that Jack the Ripper was a medical maniac searching for the elixir of life. While the idea of an elixir of life today is relegated to fantasy, in the late nineteenth century, the possibility of extending life was a valid scientific question. And the connection between an elixir and the murders didn't escape the notice of the press. E. Tracy Greaves, the London correspondent for the *New York World*, had his office within walking distance of Scotland Yard and claimed on three separate occasions in October 1888 that his Scotland Yard source was "engaged in working on the case." From an October 7, 1888, *New York World* news cable dispatch, the *St. Louis Post-Dispatch* published an article with the title, "Jack, The Ripper. The London Police Think He Is The Whitechapel Murderer. An Herb Doctor Under Suspicion . . ." In it, Greaves stated:

> An American who used to live in New York now keeps an herb shop in the Whitechapel district. A detective called at his place this week and asked him if he had sold any unusual compound of herbs to a customer since August. Similar inquiries were made at other shops in the neighborhood. The basis of this investigation has a startling Shakespearian flavor as an eminent engineer of London suggested to the police the theory that the murderer was a medical maniac trying to find the elixir of life, and was looking for an essential ingredient in parts taken from murdered bodies.

Coincidentally, the Associated Press reported in December that Tumblety kept an herb shop near Whitechapel Road: "His oddity of manner, dress and speech soon made him notorious as the 'American doctor.'" The source for this story had to have come from London since few in America knew he was accurately referred to as the American doctor in England. Since Tumblety never advertised in London, we do not have advertisements to corroborate this earlier in his career.

Mansfield's *Jekyll and Hyde* began to play at the Lyceum Theatre in London's wealthy West End just days before the first Jack the Ripper murder in August 1888. An elixir was an integral part of the story. Mansfield's performance had been playing in New York City in early 1888, as well, when Tumblety was in town.

Tumblety had a passion for the theater and claimed to have frequented London's Lyceum Theatre at its exclusive Beefsteak Club. Bram Stoker, the author of *Dracula*, was the business manager at the Lyceum Theatre, and his best friend was Sir Henry Hall Caine. Hall Caine was Tumblety's friend and companion in the mid-1870s. The employees at the Lyceum Theatre began a masonic group called the Order of the Golden Dawn. One of their goals was to find the elixir of life.

Amazingly, Tumblety discusses an elixir of health in his autobiographies, stating, "In the vegetable kingdom there may be found the elixir of health—there may be found the healing balm." Tumblety was very concerned about his youthful appearance, waxing his mustache black even in his thirties. It is not beyond reason to suggest that when Tumblety aged and contracted a progressive disease, he extended his search for an elixir into the animal kingdom, and perhaps, even, how that search led him to the literal womb of the human species.

Tumblety even commented in 1880 upon how his youthfulness was as if he'd discovered the elixir of life, demonstrating his preoccupation with the idea of such an elixir. He stated, referring to himself in the third person, in the *Montreal Gazette*, September 16, 1880, "The Doctor (himself) is little changed since his last visit to Montreal, and appears to have discovered an elixir which grants perennial youth."

The medical community attempting to determine why humans die and how to extend human life was a natural scientific question in the late nineteenth century.

Coincidentally—or not—a contemporary theory of the Whitechapel murders was a Dr. Jekyll and Mr. Hyde killer, wherein the Ripper lived two lives. During the day he was an upstanding citizen, and at night his evil side came out and he became a ruthless murderer. The *Birmingham Daily Post*, October 3, 1888, published a number of theories of who the killer, or killers, might be. The following is a partial list:

> THE GANG THEORY – Some think that such a series of murders could only have been successfully executed by a gang of two or more.
>
> THE WORK OF A RELIGIOUS MANIAC – The murders point to one individual, and that individual was insane . . . He may be an earnest religionist with a delusion that he has a mission from above to extirpate vice by assassination . . .
>
> THE BURKE AND HARE THEORY – Suggested by Mr. Wynne Baxter that the murderer is employed to get anatomical specimens for some experimentalist.
>
> THE JEKYLL AND HYDE THEORY – That the murderer lives two lives, and inhabits two houses or two sets of rooms.

Curiously, in the 1880s, Tumblety was known to rent out more than one room when he visited a city, conforming to the Jekyll and Hyde theory. It was on Friday, February 25, 1881, that Tumblety arrived in New Orleans and quickly met young Richard Norris at the Saturday evening performance at the Charles Theater. Richard Norris stated under oath that Tumblety brought him up to his room in the St. Charles Hotel and continued to visit his room for the next month. Norris then stated that by late March 1881, Tumblety switched rooms to 109 Canal Street. He thought it was strange that Tumblety had done this. The reality is, Tumblety never switched rooms but actually rented out both rooms at the same time, just not telling Norris about the other room. According to the *Daily Picayune*, March 25, 1881, the landlady of 109 Canal Street stated to the police and press that Tumblety arrived in New Orleans on Friday, February 25, 1881, and rented out one of her rooms. Incredibly, Tumblety rented out three rooms, at the St. Charles Hotel, 109 Canal Street, and the posh City Hotel. According to the *Times-Democrat*, March 25, 1881: "His [Tumblety's] board bill at the City Hotel, he boarded, was always promptly paid and as was his room rent at his establishment on Canal street."

If Tumblety was searching for an elixir of life, he seems to have stopped by the mid-to-late 1890s. Around this time, he began dressing more like a vagrant and did so for the rest of his life; he no longer cared about his appearance, youthful or otherwise. Notice what he wrote in his 1893 autobiography, a statement not included in his 1889 version: "Since, however, there is no panacea that can give us everlasting youth, let us bow before this inexorable law, but endeavor to prepare for ourselves a green old age by avoiding every other source of organic deterioration."

Interestingly, in 1907, George R. Sims referred in the *Sunday Referee* to a particular theory he received from Scotland Yard officials:

> The other theory in support of which I have some curious information, puts the crime down to a young American medical student who was in London during the whole time of the murders, and who, according to statements of certain highly-respectable people who knew him, made on two occasions an endeavour to obtain a certain internal organ, which for his purpose had to be removed from, as he put it, *"the almost living body."* [Author emphasis added.]

Dr. Wynne Baxter, the coroner, in his summary to the jury in the case of Annie Chapman, pointed out the significance of the fact that this internal organ—the uterus—had been removed. This certainly conforms to the elixir of life theory.

There is an argument that Jack the Ripper was not collecting specific organs but was merely mutilating. That the type of organ was random. This stems from the question as to whether Jack the Ripper had anatomical knowledge or not. The contemporary police surgeons had mixed conclusions, but for a reason. After Mary Ann "Polly" Nichols's murder, Dr. Rees Llewelyn concluded that the killer had rough anatomical knowledge. Dr. George Bagster Phillips believed the killer had to have a working knowledge of anatomy: "Some anatomical knowledge." After the Catherine Eddowes murder, Dr. Frederick Gordon Brown stated, "The killer would have had a good knowledge of the positions of the organs . . ." He concluded that the killer was a medical man or a butcher. Coroner Wynne Baxter stated that the killer had considerable anatomical skill and knowledge and stated that he was accustomed to the postmortem room. First-Class Inspector Walter Andrews stated to an *Ottawa Daily Citizen* reporter on December 21, 1888, "I am of the opinion that the man has some surgical knowledge . . ."

One well-respected police surgeon disagreed. After the Kelly murder, Assistant Commissioner Anderson asked Dr. Thomas Bond, the A Division police surgeon, to do a postmortem examination, review the reports of the previous murders, and give an evaluation. His report included what kind of man the killer would be. It seems to have been the first attempt at criminal profiling. He concluded that at least five victims were killed by the same person. The killer was solitary and eccentric. Bond was convinced that the killer was not an expert in anatomy and had no anatomical knowledge, stating in his report:

> The mutilations in each case excepting the Berner's Street one were all of the same character and shewed clearly that in all the murders, *the object was mutilation*. In each case the mutilation was inflicted by a person who had no scientific nor anatomical knowledge. [Author emphasis added.]

The Berner Street murder victim was Mary Kelly. The *only* reason Bond gave as to why he believed the killer had no anatomical knowledge was because of his conclusion that the offender's motive was mutilation and not harvesting of organs. This means that, in his opinion, collecting the kidney, uterus, and heart was merely random. Point: If Jack the Ripper's motive was truly harvesting specifically the kidney, uterus, and heart, then Bond would likely have agreed Jack the Ripper had anatomical knowledge (not necessarily anatomical skill).

Conflicting with the "mere mutilation" conclusion is that the offender *moved Chapman's intestines* in order to extract the uterus. Mere mutilation would suggest that any organ, like the intestines, would have been collected first, since he could have collected them more easily and quickly. Still, if Jack the Ripper was collecting organs at random, the increased level of mutilation still fits with Francis Tumblety being further enraged by his understanding that his mind was going.

Even toward the end of his life, Tumblety carried around a flask of a brown "elixir" that he would pull out and drink. Tumblety's Baltimore attorney, Robert H. Simpson, was questioned under oath in 1905:

> Simpson: "I was his counsel and he seemed to be all right mentally and physically until about the year 1902, along about the fall; in appearance he was large and robust."
> Attorney: "Up to this time?"
> Simpson: "Yes, sir; in appearance he was always large and robust; he was bloated; he was a man who drank a great deal of brown stuff; almost invariably he would have a bottle of the stuff in his pocket . . ."

In another facet of the investigation, the reports of Scotland Yard being interested in Tumblety's handwriting in November 1888, are arguably connected to anatomical organs. Assistant Commissioner Anderson of Scotland Yard sent private cable communications to US chiefs of police requesting some inquiries on Ripper suspect Francis Tumblety, as reported in the *Brooklyn Citizen*, November 23, 1888:

> "Is He The Ripper?"
> A Brooklynite Charged With the Whitechapel Murders.
> Superintendent Campbell Asked by the London Police to Hunt Up the Record of Francis Tumblety—Captain Eason Supplies the Information and It Is Interesting.
> Police Superintendent Campbell received a cable dispatch yesterday from Mr. Anderson, the deputy chief of the London Police, asking him to make some inquiries about Francis Tumblety . . .

In the cable exchanges with San Francisco Chief of Police Patrick Crowley, the inquiries requested included handwriting samples. The *San Francisco Examiner*, November 23, 1888, states:

> Dr. Tumblety.
> The London Detectives Ask Chief Crowley about Him.
> Dr. Francis Tumblety, the suspect arrested at London in connection with the Whitechapel murders . . . and a good deal of importance seems to be attached

to his apprehension. All facts in relation to the suspected "doctor" are being carefully collected, and, as Tumblety was once in the city, there has been considerable telegraphing between the Police Departments of San Francisco and London ... When the Chief of Police learned these facts, and that the bank still had several letters written by Tumblety, he telegraphed to the Superintendent of Police of London that he could, if desired, furnish specimens of Tumblety's handwriting. The dispatch was sent on the 19th instant, and yesterday this answer was received:

HIS HANDWRITING.

"P. Crowley, Chief of Police, San Francisco, Cal.: Thanks. Send handwriting and all details you can of Tumblety. ANDERSON 'Scotland Yard.'"

While it is clear by the report that Scotland Yard initiated contact with the Brooklyn chief of police, it is not clear what type of information they were requesting. After numerous correspondences between Scotland Yard and San Francisco Chief of Police Crowley about *all* facts relating to Tumblety, Crowley singled out letters with Tumblety's handwriting. Notice how Anderson capitalized "HIS HANDWRITING" as the title of his cable to Crowley, which suggests a high level of interest in and importance of that piece of information.

The only reason he would have been interested in Tumblety's handwriting was to compare it to the Jack the Ripper letters they'd received, and one of the very few they took seriously was a letter that also accompanied a kidney. On October 16, 1888, the president of the Whitechapel Vigilance Committee, George Lusk, received what is now known as the "From hell" letter. Lusk received a small cardboard box in his mail, which had a letter and half a human kidney preserved in wine. The last Ripper victim, Catherine Eddowes, had her left kidney taken by the killer. Lusk quickly handed it off to the police. Note the following article transmitted by multiple newspapers throughout the United Kingdom:

> A statement which apparently gives a clue to the sender of the strange package received by Mister Lusk was made last night by Miss Emily Marsh, whose father carries on business in the leather trade at 218 Jubilee Street, Mile End Road. In Mr Marsh's absence, Miss Marsh was in the front shop, shortly after one o'clock on Monday last, when a stranger, dressed in clerical costume, entered, and, referring to the reward bill in the window, asked for the address of Mr Lusk. . . . The stranger is described as a man of some forty-five years of age, fully six feet in height, and slimly built. He wore a soft felt black

> hat, drawn over his forehead, a stand-up collar, and a very long black single-breasted overcoat, with a Prussian or clerical collar partly turned up. His face was of a sallow type, and he had a dark beard and moustache. The man spoke with what was taken to be an Irish accent. No importance was attached to the incident until Miss Marsh read of the receipt by Mr Lusk of a strange parcel, and then it occurred to her that the stranger might be the person who dispatched it. His enquiry was made at one o'clock on Monday afternoon, and Mr Lusk received the package at eight pm the next day. —*North-Eastern Daily Gazette*, October 20, 1888

It is difficult not to accept that this tall man with a Prussian-style collar was Tumblety. Even though all of the extant pictures and photos of Tumblety never showed him with a beard, he did wear a beard at times. Under sworn testimony, Tumblety's New Orleans attorney, George F. Bartley, commented on his beard. The attorney asked Bartley what habits Tumblety had that were peculiar in nature. Bartley responded:

> Well, he took my appetite away from me by running his fork through his beard. He cleaned his beard with his fork. It was the first time I had seen that done, and it gave me a further insight into the man than before.

Regardless, if Scotland Yard did interview Emily Marsh, then any tall suspect with a mustache, meaning Tumblety, would have been on the top of the investigation list. Curiously, on this date *and* in Mile End, City of London detectives were interested in another suspicious tall man in a long overcoat and a mustache that made the papers. In the *Evening News*, October 19, 1888, an article titled, "A Remarkable Story" was published:

> The City Police have under observation a man whose movements in Whitechapel, Mile End, and Bermondsey are attended with suspicion. A man, who is said to be an American, was arrested in Bermondsey at one o'clock yesterday morning, and taken to the police station. His conduct, demeanor, and appearance gave rise to great suspicion, and his apprehension and general particulars were wired to the City police. Following this a conference took place yesterday afternoon, between a young man named John Lardy, of Redman's-row, Mile End, and the head of the detective department at the Old Jewry, at which he stated as follows: "At 10.30 last night I was with a friend and a young woman outside the Grave Maurice Tavern, opposite the London Hospital, when I

noticed a man whom I had never seen before come across the road, look into each compartment of the tavern, and enter the house. He came out again directly, and carefully looked up and down the road, and then walked over the road to the front of the hospital, where two women were standing talking. They were, I believe, loose women. The man said something to them, but I did not hear his words. The women shook their heads and said 'No.'"

IS HE THE MURDERER?

"I said to my friend, 'What a funny-looking man! I wonder if he is the murderer.' My friend replied, 'Let us follow him.' We said good-night to our friend and followed the man. When opposite the Pavilion Theatre he drew himself up in an instant, and looked carefully round. We believe that he saw us following him, and he disappeared into a doorway. We stopped for a moment or two, and he came out of his hiding-place and went into a newspaper shop next door. During the whole time we saw him his right hand was in his overcoat pocket, apparently clutching something. He bought a paper at the shop, and folded it up on his chest with his left hand, and then left the shop, looking up and down the road as he did so, and carefully reading the placards outside the shop window. He afterwards started off towards Aldgate, and we followed him."

HE NOTICES THAT HE IS PURSUED.

"When he got to the corner of Duke-street (the street leading to Mitre-square) he turned, and, seeing that we were following him, recrossed the road and walked back to Leman-street and went down it. When he reached Royal Mint-street he went into King-street, which is very narrow, and my friend and I ran round to the other end of the street, hoping to see him come out there. Just as we got to the other end of King-street we heard a door close, and we waited to see if the man reopened it, for we felt sure that he was the man, although we had not seen him go into the house. We both waited for 25 minutes, when we saw the same man come out of the house. He came up the street, and we stepped back and allowed him to pass, and he went in the direction of the Whitechapel-road. He went away so quickly that we lost sight of him in the fog, which was then very thick. The time then was just after 12."

REAPPEARS DIFFERENTLY DRESSED.

"When he reappeared from the house we noticed that he was very differently dressed to what he was when we first saw him, the most noticeable being his overcoat. At first he was wearing a sort of short frock-coat, reaching his knees only, but when he came out of the house in King-street he had on a large overcoat which reached to within three inches of the ground. From what I could see he appeared to be between forty and forty-five years of age, and from 5ft. 11in. to 6ft. high." (A man 5ft. 11in. was placed before Lardy, who said, "My man was a little taller than you.")

LOOKED LIKE AN AMERICAN.

"He wore a low hat with a square crown, but I cannot describe either his trousers or boots. He had the appearance of an American. His cheek-bones were high and prominent, his face thin, cheeks sunken, and he had a moustache only, his cheeks and chin being clean shaven. The moustache was, I believe, a false one, for it was all awry, one end pointing upward, and the other towards the ground. His hair was dark, apparently black, and somewhat long."

It is clear that both the London City Police and the Metropolitan Police were interested in a particular tall, well-dressed man before Tumblety was received into custody for gross indecency on November 7, 1888. E. Tracy Greaves's Scotland Informant revealed to him that Tumblety was arrested on suspicion of the Whitechapel crimes before November 7. Recall, per the *Writ of Habeas Corpus*, his remand hearing was held at Marlborough Street Police Court on or about November 7, then based upon overwhelming evidence he was released on bail by November 8. The following eyewitness account of a tall, well-dressed man occurred in the late morning of November 9, 1888, the very day Mary Kelly's body was discovered. This was at a time when Tumblety was already on the suspect list. Per the *Daily News (UK)*:

> On Saturday afternoon a gentleman engaged in business in the vicinity of the murder gave what is the only approach to a possible clue that has yet been brought to light. He states that he was walking through Mitre square at about ten minutes past ten on Friday morning, when a *tall, well-dressed man*, carrying a parcel under his arm, and rushing along in a very excited manner, ran plump into him. The man's face was covered with blood splashes, and his collar and shirt were also bloodstained. The gentleman did not at the time know anything of the murder. —November 12, 1888 [Author emphasis added.]

It might not be a coincidence that a tall, well-dressed suspect was seen in the vicinity of Mitre Square. It is difficult to fathom that Scotland Yard did not take seriously a suspect who fit this description.

The third possible fact of "important information" may have been Tumblety in possession of the type of knife that Jack the Ripper may have used, and New Orleans would have been a boon to the investigation with respect to evidence of Tumblety traveling with surgical knives. Young Richard Norris, a resident of New Orleans, stated under oath in 1905 that in the early 1880s, in his later teens, he used to "take extra tricks" and earn cash by acting as a male sex worker. He met up with Tumblety each year during Mardi Gras and the carnival season in late February and early March from 1881 to 1900. In 1881, Norris stated that he and a friend watched a performance at the St. Charles Theatre, and Tumblety introduced himself during intermission. Tumblety told him he'd just arrived in New Orleans for the Mardi Gras holidays. He told Norris that he had a room at the St. Charles Hotel. After buying Norris and his friend dinner, Tumblety asked Norris to come to his room to write a letter. Norris was initially apprehensive, but then he "took a chance." Norris stated what he saw when he was in Tumblety's room:

> He then opened a large trunk (but in the meantime ordered some more ale) and he pulled out a velvet chest which had, I judge—three or four medals on each side—they looked to me like gold medals. He told me they were awarded to him by the English Government. *Then there was a sort of tray in the trunk, and there were all sorts of large knives in there, surgical instruments*—that is, I did not know what they were at the time. [Author emphasis added.]

Tumblety was actually arrested around the same time he met Norris, and the details of the arrest corroborate Norris's story about surgical knives. On Thursday evening, March 24, 1881, Francis Tumblety was arrested in New Orleans by private detective Dominick C. O'Malley of O'Malley Detective Agency and Police Protection and jailed in the Third Police Precinct Station. He was charged with petit larceny for allegedly pickpocketing the pocketbook of young Henry Govan, a clerk in the US district attorney's office in the Customhouse. Govan claimed his pocketbook had between $50 and $100. According to two daily New Orleans newspaper reports in the March 25, 1881, issues of the *Times-Democrat* and *Daily Picayune*, O'Malley's arrest report stated that Tumblety and Govan first met on Canal Street on Tuesday, March 22, 1881, then had a social drink for about an hour at Wenger's Saloon. Tumblety asked Govan to meet up again the following morning on Wednesday. After waking, Govan changed his mind and decided to go straight to work instead. Just outside the Customhouse awaited Tumblety, who engaged Govan and pressured him to walk with him and smoke cigars. After their smoke, Govan insisted he had to go to work and left, but once he reached his office, he realized that his pocketbook was missing from his breast pocket. He returned home and searched but could not find it.

He then recalled that Tumblety's hand was near his breast pocket and became convinced that Tumblety stole his money. Govan rushed to the police station to report the theft to Captain Malone. Govan had no idea where Tumblety was rooming, so Malone explained that he would first need to assist a police officer in finding him. Govan, though, felt frustrated that the captain was not placing a priority on his complaint, so under the recommendation of workmates, Govan hired a local private detective, Commissioned Special Officer D. C. O'Malley. O'Malley immediately escorted Govan on the streets and quickly determined that Tumblety was rooming at a boarding house on Canal Street. No address was given in the papers. The *Times-Democrat*, March 25, 1881, details the encounter, which included O'Malley seeing medical instruments:

> The doctor was at home and seemed glad to see his visitors until O'Malley accused him of the theft when he signified his willingness to go to jail, but, according to O'Malley's statement, attempted to compromise by offering to make the amount good. O'Malley was, however, firm and called on Officer Landrigan to watch the room while he conveyed the prisoner to jail. Landrigan, however, refused to have anything to do with the case, and O'Malley was therefore forced to escort the prisoner to jail, leaving the room which, as he states, contained lots of burglars' tools and *a box of medical instruments* to take care of itself. [Author emphasis added.]

Further support for Norris's recollections came from the *Times-Democrat* reporter who visited Tumblety's Canal Street room the night he was arrested. He reported on the medals he witnessed in the March 25, 1881, issue:

> Dr. Tumblety is in possession of a number of medals and decorations which should be a guarantee to his respectability. He has an elegant gold medal, presented by the citizens of Montreal, Canada, on March 4, 1858, for his skill as a physician; a Maltese cross presented on September 24, 1860 (?), by His Royal Highness, Prince of Wales; a cross of the legion of honor presented by Napoleon; an iron cross from the emperor of Prussia; a decoration from the emperor of Austria, another from the czar of Russia, and a number of other medals and decorations from other notables.

Incidentally, the pickpocket case against Tumblety was quickly thrown out by the presiding judge due to a lack of evidence. Supporting Tumblety's innocence in this case is the fact that Tumblety had no history of pickpocketing, burglary, or theft of anyone's money for that matter. What O'Malley thought were burglar's tools were likely the surgical implements underneath the tray of knives.

In Chief Inspector Littlechild's 1913 private letter to George Sims, he made it clear that the fact on record in Tumblety's Scotland Yard file was his unusual and bitter hatred of women. This suggests that the classified important information used to initiate the US investigation into Tumblety was related to this and was possibly evidence of misogynistic behavior. If Tumblety acted upon his hatred of women in America, then this would definitely help in a case where a killer acted upon his hatred of Whitechapel sex workers. Tumblety certainly had a history of personifying his hatred by threatening and even giving poor treatment to women for decades. An article in the *Boston Herald*, November 25, 1888, discusses an eyewitness account of Tumblety opening an office in Saint John, New Brunswick:

> About the time that the war broke out, in 1860 or 1861, Dr. Tumblety made his appearance at St. John, N.B., where he immediately proceeded to cut a great dash. . . . After a while the more intelligent people got their eyes open to the fact that he was a charlatan, and pretty soon afterward stories began to go round about his *indecorus* [sic] *treatment of some of his lady patients*. [Author emphasis added.]

Tumblety actually published this treatment of women in St. John:

> My friends of the press were lavish in their encomiums, and frequently indulged their poetic fancy in complimentary effusions, among which, the following, from the St. Johns (N.B.) Albion, is a humorous sample:
>
> DR. TUMBLETY.
> Dr. Tumblety rode a white steed
> Into St. Johns in its time of need,
> Determined to cure with herbal pills
> All the ailing of all their ills.
> Dr. Tumblety had a greyhound—A beautiful animal I'll be bound—
> The dog looked up in the Doctor's face
> As he rode along at a slapping pace.
> *Tumblety had a killing air,*
> Though curing was his professional trade,

Rosy of cheek, and glossy of hair,
Dangerous man to widow or maid . . . [Author emphasis added.]

The so-called newspaper reporter's statement of him having a "killing air" and being "dangerous . . . to widow or maid" is quite damning. Not only did Tumblety personally write the poem, but he also added it to his 1865 autobiography. Some have suggested that in this poem Tumblety was merely stating his prowess as a womanizer. Scouring over forty sworn testimonies and multiple private letters makes one point clear: Tumblety hated single women and anything to do with them. He would have abhorred the thought of being a seducer of the very gender he believed was a curse to the land. Nowhere in any of his advertisements from the late 1850s to the late 1870s had he ever commented upon womanizing. As stated in the *Boston Herald*, Tumblety's treatment of "some of the women" was indecorous, meaning rude and inappropriate. The following shows that this treatment not only continued in his office, but it also implied danger. It was reported in the *Liverpool Leader*, January 9, 1875, over thirteen years before the Whitechapel murders:

> There comes to us a tale of a decent woman from the Isle of Man who sought his advice respecting a bad leg. He told her it was due to the immorality of her parents, but would cure it for 3 pounds. This she declined, whereon he [Tumblety] ordered her to get out legs and all or else he would kick her out! Other women young and unmarried, have fled in alarm from his premises, and say his language and *conduct suggested danger*. [Author emphasis added.]

Notice how the article clarified which type of women, the young and the unmarried, similar to the "widow or maid" statement in the poem. The aim of Tumblety's misogynist rage shows a direction. The evidence points only to Tumblety hating women who have the ability to lure young men toward a life of heterosexuality, and he was known to warn young men he had relationships with about these women. Thanks to the efforts of historian Neil Storey, we have actual private letters written by Tumblety to a young man of his interest explaining how these degrading women lure, or decoy, young men. In the mid-1870s, Tumblety struck up a relationship in Liverpool, England, with young Henry Hall Caine. In a private letter to Hall Caine, Tumblety stated:

> In morals and obscenity they [Chinese women] are far below those of our most degraded prostitutes. Their women are bought and sold, for the usual

purposes and they are used to decoy youths of the most tender age, into these dens, for the purpose of exhibiting their nude and disgusting person to the hitherto innocent youths of the cities.

There were even reports of Tumblety actually threatening sex workers—including East End London sex workers. The *Evening Post*, December 3, 1888, reported:

> In Boston, says the American correspondent of the Daily Telegraph . . . It is reported by cable from Europe that a certain person, whose name is known, has sailed from Havre for New York, who is famous for his hatred of women, and who has *repeatedly made threats against females of dissolute character*. [Author emphasis added.]

Tumblety was even known to threaten with a surgical knife, albeit his intended victim in this instance was a young man. During Norris's first interaction in Tumblety's St. Charles Hotel room in February 1881, he saw the "big knives" in a tray in Tumblety's travel chest. It was at a later time in his room on Canal Street in March 1881 that Tumblety took one of those knives and placed it on Norris's throat. The veracity of Norris's account is supported via the room number detail. Never did the newspapers report that the Canal Street room was old number 190. According to Norris:

> . . . he never attempted to do anything wrong with me until one night he took me to his room, and he locked the door on me. I don't know whether he was humbugging or not, but he did make a bluff at me with one of those big knives. He said, "You cannot get out of this room while I have this."
>
> . . . He was not at the Charles hotel then, he had changed his place—I don't know for what cause he had changed his place, but he had changed to Old No. 190 Canal street.

Norris then gave an account of how Tumblety sexually molested him while under the threat of a knife at his throat. After assaulting him, Tumblety peppered Norris with apologies and cash. This seemed to work on Norris since Norris continued to meet up with him for twenty years. Curiously, instead of offering money for sex at the outset—an act that would have worked since Norris admitted he used to take money in exchange for sex—Tumblety preferred to force himself upon Norris with the use of a knife. This is yet another implication of Tumblety's violent streak and further proof of knives as his weapon of choice.

Just as O'Malley reported the medical equipment in a box, Norris referred to a "sort of tray." This is exactly how Civil War-era surgical knives were housed. The knives were in an actual tray that fit into the thin box on top of the other instruments. The landlady of 190 Canal Street stated to the police that she saw Tumblety's closed travel chest, but she did not see surgical instruments in the room. Recall, though, that Norris stated, "There were large knives *in* the trunk," (emphasis mine) so the landlady not seeing the knives makes sense.

CHAPTER 4

RIPPER-LIKE MURDER IN THE BIG APPLE IN MAY 1888

The most substantial type of "important information" of Tumblety's antecedents in America that Scotland Yard may have been attempting to collect just after his arrest and, for that matter, Mary Kelly's murder in November 1888, would have been about him being linked to any assault and/or murder of a woman, especially with the use of a knife. Evidence corroborating Scotland Yard's interest in this was an article written by an investigative reporter from the *Oakland Tribune* published in their December 8, 1890, issue. The *Tribune* learned that Tumblety had operated his quack doctor business in the area years ago, and then discovered that his brother still lived in Oakland. Although they did not disclose his name, they interviewed the brother for the article. Tumblety's brother Lawrence did, in fact, live in Oakland in 1890, confirming the veracity of the report. In it, the reporter commented upon Scotland Yard's investigation into Tumblety's past in the United States:

> The London police could not learn much of Tumblety's antecedents, and to the present they are trying to identify him with other crimes.

This report also fits with Guy Logan's comments about Scotland Yard's Inspector Andrews's mission in America coming up empty-handed, stating, ". . . [Andrews] was sent specially to America in December 1888, in search of the Whitechapel fiend on the strength of important information, the nature of which was never disclosed. Nothing, however, came of it, and the Inspector's mission was a failure." The article, which was written after Andrews returned to England, confirms that Scotland Yard did not find enough evidence of other crimes committed by Tumblety in America that they could have used in the Whitechapel murders case, even by 1890. Scotland Yard's motivation to have continued the investigation into 1890, albeit without Inspector Andrews, does suggest that the "important information" was there, just not complete.

Information the local police possessed in any city Tumblety had a history in would not only have been information that likely did not make the papers, but it would also have been damning information about his character. Notice what Tumblety's Baltimore attorney, Robert Simpson, said under oath in court in 1905 about an incident in 1900 when Tumblety took a young boy to Druid Hill Park:

> Simpson: ". . . there was a lady, I never could find out who she was, he told me she lived on Pierce Street; he had taken a little boy out . . ."
>
> Attorney: "Do you mean Dr. Tumblety had taken a little boy out?"
>
> Simpson: "Yes, sir; he had met him on the street and talked to him and bought him some candy, some confectionary and such as that and took him to the park."
>
> Attorney: "What park?"
>
> Simpson: "Druid Hill Park; he put him on the car and took him out to the park and it seems as if the little boy went home and told his mother where Tumblety could be found; I do not know what occurred; but I drew my influence from what I hear from different policemen and what I heard about it . . . My candid opinion about it is that he had a habit of resorting to unnatural practices on little boys; he was watched very closely and frequented our parks a good deal."
>
> Attorney: "Watched by whom?"
>
> Simpson: "The policemen, and he would dodge around and sometimes he would be at Patterson Park and sometimes at Druid Hill Park."

Simpson learned about Tumblety's activities through the local police. Simpson also learned from the police an even greater kept secret specific to his sexual anatomy (which had absolutely nothing to do with his depraved desires to prey upon little boys). When Simpson discovered that Tumblety was what the local police called a "hermaphrodite," he asked Tumblety about it: ". . . the reason I asked him was I had heard it before; I had heard so much from various police about him I thought I would put the question to him just for curiosity." Tumblety replied, ". . . do not ever tell that to anybody; that is a misfortune which has followed me all through my life . . ." Note, "hermaphrodite" is an outdated and inaccurate term. Today, Tumblety would be considered an intersex person, where his sexual anatomy does not fit perfectly in the category of male or female. At this point in history, however, Tumblety's anatomical formation was not viewed as favorable or socially acceptable, thus causing him anguish and shame.

There is a London newspaper report referring to Tumblety's antecedents, which likely did not receive its facts from a US source but from a London source, such as Scotland Yard. The *Sheffield and Rotterdam Independent*, December 5, 1888, picked up the following cable dispatch from a foreign correspondent of a London paper, the *Daily Telegraph*. Even though Tumblety's name was not used, note the clear references to him:

> It is reported by cable from Europe that a certain person, whose name is known, has sailed from Havre for New York, who is famous for his hatred of women, and who has repeatedly made threats against females of dissolute character.

The antecedents referred to, specifically, "repeatedly made threats against females of dissolute character," seem to have come out of Tumblety's history in England. This would explain why Assistant Commissioner Anderson was so interested in Tumblety's history in America. On numerous occasions, Tumblety was known for being a suspicious character on the streets in America. In the *St. Louis Globe-Democrat*, January 5, 1889, an article taken out of the *San Francisco Call* stated:

> He was compelled to leave that city [Chicago], and went to England, where he was seen chiefly in London and Liverpool. Between 1875 and 1878 he was in New York, and was regarded as a suspicious character.

Tumblety was even arrested for being a suspicious character, although he was never convicted. In the *St. Louis Post-Dispatch*, November 18, 1890, Tumblety was reported to have been arrested in Washington DC, stating that he was, "arrested in this city last night on the charge of being a suspicious character." The police clearly thought Tumblety, whose pastime was to walk the slums at night, was up to no good.

The Scotland Yard North American investigation was headquartered in New York City. Tumblety had a checkered history in New York City that clearly showed both his hatred of women and his nefarious nightly activities. After initially scoffing at the idea of Tumblety being Jack the Ripper, San Francisco Chief of Police Patrick Crowley reconsidered after hearing about his activities in New York. In the *San Francisco Examiner*, November 23, 1888, he stated to a reporter:

> There may be more in the arrest than was at first supposed. This man Tumblety is evidently a crank. His course with the bank here does not indicate that he was a man of good instincts, and in New York his *behavior* was that of a man who had *no liking for women* . . . [Author emphasis added.]

If a case did not make the paper, we would have no idea if local officials ever suspected Tumblety of assaulting or murdering women. Chief Crowley's comment suggests that it was the New York City Police who informed him. The police response to him certainly did give Chief Crowley pause for concern. Crowley's comment on behavior referred not to what Tumblety said but to what he did. This poor behavior against women may very well have been in police records and, thus, could have been part of this important information, as in the *Daily Telegraph*'s report stating that Tumblety made repeated threats against women of dissolute character.

Time and time again we see Tumblety arrested for inappropriate behavior, such as sodomy, and then going to court but ultimately beating the charge. His nickname could have been "Teflon Tumblety," having so very few charges stick to him. If he was convinced he was going to lose the case he simply vanished, as he did with the manslaughter charge in St. John in 1860, and in London in 1888. Being able to afford the best attorneys who merely had to argue against opposing testimony was certainly an advantage as well. It is only because of the use of modern forensics and DNA evidence that officials have been able to scientifically connect many criminals to their crimes, especially elusive serial killers, *beyond* the oftentimes imperfect witness testimony. Take for example Joseph DeAngelo, the Golden State Killer. We would never have known that he was the Golden State Killer if it were not for familial DNA. Additionally, we would never have known he was also the Visalia Ransacker, the East Area Rapist, the East Side Rapist, the East Bay Rapist, the Creek Bed Killer, the Diamond Knot Killer, and the Night Stalker, murdering thirteen victims and raping fifty in a crime spree spanning over two decades. It would not be a surprise if he was guilty of more murders and rapes. His plan was to take his past with him to his grave, but his DNA finally caught up with him.

Even with the damning evidence that led Scotland Yard to take Tumblety seriously as being Jack the Ripper, plus the recently discovered evidence corroborating their suspicions, a perfectly appropriate question has been asked by researchers today:

> *Why would Tumblety, an American quack doctor, travel across the Atlantic Ocean to kill casual sex workers when cities across the United States have sex workers?*

On the surface, it makes no sense for an American killer to only kill when he was visiting London. The solution to this answer is that he murdered on both sides of the Atlantic. And, as we know, he had other reasons for traveling as much as he did—perhaps not so much motivated by a search for victims but to flee from his other crimes and reputations in many of the American and Canadian cities in which he resided. Then, while stateside or across the pond, he simply murdered wherever he hung his hat at that particular time; and we know Tumblety was living in London in 1888 when the Whitechapel murders occurred. A follow-up question naturally asks:

> *Were there any unsolved Ripper-like murders of women in America where Tumblety cannot be excluded as having committed the crime?*

This question asks us to assess the plausibility of Tumblety having been Jack the Ripper. If he was a serial killer, maybe he had murdered in other locations, as some have been known to do. Ripper-like behavior would include murders of women who had recently been walking the streets at night, the victim not having been raped or robbed, their throats cut from ear to ear, and the body showing no signs of sadistic behavior. Jack the Ripper mostly attacked out on the street and did not rape his victims, and with the exception of Annie Chapman's rings, he did not rob their bodies. In the case of Chapman's rings, taking them was not robbery for the sake of financial gain but for the serial offender act of collecting trophies. In view of this, if a murder victim in America shows that she was robbed and "collection of a trophy" is a plausible reason, then this will be taken into account. Also, the victims were mutilated *postmortem*, thus, the killer was not sadistic. Tumblety's motive to commit these crimes would have derived from his bitter hatred of unmarried women; it is clear the Ripper hated his victims. Tumblety was not attracted to women—in fact, he was repulsed by them. The Ripper did not sexually assault or sadistically inflict pain upon his victims but attacked their faces (in the cases of Eddowes and Kelly) and their gender (in the cases of Nichols, Chapman, and Eddowes). He was disgusted by them.

If Jack the Ripper did commit murders outside of London, it is logical to assume that they would have occurred in the slums and red-light districts of any major city where prostitution was commonplace. The fact that Tumblety considered New York City his home and that it was a large city not too dissimilar to London, it seems appropriate to start here. Not only was the Whitechapel District a place of terrible poverty, but it was also known for its vice.

In New York City in the late nineteenth century, a lower Manhattan neighborhood called Five Points was the poorest neighborhood of the city and, unsurprisingly, a place of prostitution as well. The southern edge of Five Points was located near the approach ramp of the Brooklyn Bridge, and Tumblety spent much of his time in Brooklyn. Five Points, located in present-day Chinatown, was the setting of the 2002 film *Gangs of New York*, based upon Herbert Asbury's historical novel of the gang wars between the 1840s and 1860s. The Five Points Gang was an Irish-American gang that warred with rival gangs. According to historian Dr. Sarah Handley-Cousins, PhD, Five Points was considered the most miserable slum in the Western Hemisphere. In an alleyway infamously known as "Murderers Row," a boarding house openly rented rooms to sex workers on the ground floor while running a saloon in the basement.

A nineteenth-century red-light district in Manhattan also known for its prostitution was the Tenderloin, which was well north of Five Points between 24th and 42nd Streets and 5th Avenue and 7th Avenue. The well-known Madison Square Garden was, and is, located in this neighborhood. An 1885 study estimated that half of the buildings in Tenderloin were connected with vice. The Tenderloin, though, was not considered a slum, just a red-light district. While more upscale than Five Points and other areas of prostitution, it was still populated by brothels, saloons, nightclubs, music halls, and theaters. The reputation of the Tenderloin was that of high crime and police corruption.

A third place of prostitution was the theater district along Broadway Avenue. Prostitution was prevalent along Broadway between Houston and Fulton Streets in the late nineteenth century. According to Handley-Cousins, Broadway was the center of city life, shopping by day, and attending theaters, shows, and other kinds of amusements by night. This included vice entertainment with concert saloons, gambling establishments, and brothels. Handley-Cousins also explained that there was a link between the theater and prostitution. The third-tier balconies were known as the "guilty third tier," which was generally reserved for prostitution.

The Manhattan neighborhood most similar to London's Whitechapel District in the late nineteenth century was definitely the Bowery. The Bowery was a large boulevard that began in the Five Points neighborhood and traversed northerly for about ten city blocks through the Lower East Side of Manhattan to Cooper Square on 4th Street. The Bowery was very impoverished, yet it was filled with nighttime entertainment and vice, peppered with brothels, saloons, low-rate concert halls, flophouses, pawnshops, and German biergartens, or beer gardens. The Bowery was not as destitute as the Five Points slums, having a thriving working-class community. The famous gang out of the Bowery was the Bowery Boys, an anti-Catholic, anti-Irish criminal gang, which fought with the Five Points gang on numerous occasions. The gang was made up of tradesmen, butchers, and mechanics.

The Bowery is the neighborhood that Tumblety roomed nearest to, always taking up residence in lodging houses at the Bowery's northern border just east of Washington Square. Because of Tumblety's taste for young men, it is not a surprise that he lived so close to the Bowery. Not only was it a center for prostitution, but the Bowery was also known for bars catering to gay men and lesbians, such as The Slide at 157 Bleecker Street opened up by Frank Stevenson in the late 1880s and forced to close in 1892, and in the 1890s, Columbia Hall at 5th Street, then called Paresis Hall. According to the *Sun*, August 27, 1882, south of the Bowery on the western border of Five Points at 18 Lafayette Street was just one of the Russian and Turkish baths establishments, a common meeting place for gay men in the 1880s. Tumblety always raved about baths. In an article in the *New York Times*, November 13, 1881, titled, "The Baths of New York," Tumblety discussed the health benefits of the city's Turkish, Russian, and Roman baths.

Other baths reported in the *New York Times* were at 9 East 46th Street (January 8, 1882), just north of the Tenderloin, and at 7 West 24th Street inside the Tenderloin (January 28, 1882). According to the *Sun*, May 3, 1888, one of the most famous New York City Russian and Turkish bath establishments known to be frequented by gay men was owned by James Everard, opening in the Tenderloin at 28 and 30 West 28th Street in May 1888.

Unknown until now was a Ripper-like murder that occurred in May 1888, on the southern boundary of the Bowery near Five Points in a neighborhood known as Little Italy. A Bowery sex worker was murdered with her throat cut from ear to ear and was neither raped nor robbed. It was front-page news, such as in the *Evening World*, May 19, 1888. The following is a firsthand account of when officials first saw the body, since the *Evening World* reporter was there to assist:

EXTRA
Last Edition.
WOMAN MURDERED.
Found in a Wood Box with a Frightful Gash in Her Throat.
Ragpicker Vincenzo Arrested for the Crime.
. . . An Evening World reporter accompanied Dr. William A. Conway, Coroner Messemer's assistant, to the house at noon. The policeman, carrying a piece of candle, went down the narrow, rickety stairway, the Evening World man next, with Dr. Conway in the rear of the procession. The policeman led the way along the hall of the cellar to the front wood-hole. On opening the door the form of a woman, apparently thirty-five years of age, was found on her right side lengthwise of the box, with her head held up by a carpet bag supported by a pile of waste paper. Her features were terribly emaciated. The body was dressed in a black dress and sack. She wore stockings and button shoes. The left hand hung over across the body. The right hand, which was doubled up under the body was found to contain a few pieces of silver and pennies . . . Dr. Conway, assisted by the policeman and The Evening World man, turned the body over. The cloak, which was doubled around the woman's neck, was pulled aside. A horrible sight presented itself. There was a long, clean cut clear across the neck, which appeared to have been caused by a slash with a stiletto [long, thin, dagger]. The jugular vein and carotid artery was severed.

According to the *Evening World*, May 19, 1888, resident Johan Fralato of a lodging house at 81 Mulberry Street, New York City, went to the cellar for a "scuttle of coal" at seven A.M. Each resident had their own wood box to keep their coal in. In the front end of the cellar was a small iron grating, which allowed sunlight to enter. The cellar also had a ragpicker's shop. When Fralato approached his wood box, he noticed that the wood box next to his was open. He tried to close the door, but something was blocking it. He then saw why; the body of a woman was lying crosswise on a heap of rags with her feet partially protruding. Over her head was a carpet bag. Fralato quickly ran upstairs and informed the landlord, Vincenzo Daneto. The landlord called Policeman Bernard McMahn, who stood guard until the arrival of a representative of the coroner's office. An *Evening World* reporter accompanied Dr. William A. Conway, "Coroner Messemer's assistant," to the house at noon.

Further details were given by the *Sun*, May 20, 1888: "The body was partially on its side, the right hand doubled under the back and closed over a few small coins, and the left hand pointing the index finger toward the throat."

Robbery was clearly not the motive. The wound to the throat was ragged and extended from the right jaw to the breast. Both the jugular vein and the carotid artery were severed. No weapon was found, although according to the *Sun*, Dr. Conway believed the cut was consistent with a long-bladed stiletto.

A resident named Antonio Divino informed the police that a woman in the house, Maria Calusio, said the dead person was Tillie Smith, a well-known Bowery sex worker. Being in Little Italy, 81 Mulberry Street was an area with a high concentration of Italian immigrants. In the *Evening World*, May 19, 1888, it was stated that Calusio recalled seeing Smith at eleven thirty in the evening with whom she believed to be the resident ragpicker, Vincenzo Di Cantio. She claimed she saw the two arguing in the backyard. Calusio spoke to the man, who replied, "Go away, or I'll do the same to you." Calusio threatened to call the landlord, and the man replied, "Oh, go away!" She claimed she then went to bed. A slightly different account was given in the *Sun*, May 20, 1888, which had a more detailed article. It stated that Calusio reported to the police that she saw the victim with the ragpicker at twelve thirty in the morning and heard the woman cry out. She then yelled, "What have you been doing with that woman?" She claimed he swore at her and bade her be gone, "Or I'll beat you as I did the other one." Detectives stated that Di Cantio left 81 Mulberry Street in the morning to collect more rags. He was then arrested in the afternoon.

It was discovered that Tillie Smith's real identity was Minnie Moscowitch from 157 South Street, Philadelphia, where her husband and parents still lived. She was around thirty years of age and had been married for less than five years. Her husband and parents "cast her off on account of her dissolute habits." According to the *Sun*, Moscowitch came to New York and frequented "stale beer saloons" as a sex worker.

Newspapers were already reporting that the Italian ragpicker was the killer. The *Brooklyn Daily Eagle*, May 20, 1888, titled the article, "Stabbed with a Stiletto. A Dissipated Woman Killed by an Italian Ragpicker." This was a rush to judgment. According to the *Evening World*, November 19, 1888, Di Cantio "proved his innocence. The murderer is still at large." According to the *New York Times*, May 22, 1888, another witness named Steen saw a Vincenzo Di Vito in the hallway with three other men acting suspiciously near Di Cantio's room. The other men were actually his brothers, Giuseppe, Finnecello, and Giovanni. All were arrested but were quickly released. The investigation quickly dried up, and the case remains unsolved to this day.

Calusio claimed a tall man with a black mustache was the ragpicker Di Cantio, not just because he fit the physical description but likely because the body was found in the cellar near the ragpicker's shop. This, though, would also have been where a Bowery sex worker would have taken a customer for quick service and privacy. In the *Lawrence Daily Journal*, June 1, 1888, per an article titled in all-caps, "LIFE IN THE SLUMS," ragpickers and landlords along Mulberry Street actually rented out their cellar rag-picking shops as bedding for the night or week:

> High Rents Paid by New York's Poor for Wretched Tenements. You will return from your first visit to the slums with two strong impressions: One, of the utter hopelessness of trying to do anything; the other, of the necessity for doing something immediately, lest the heavens fall . . . But, as you stand in "the Bend" in Mulberry street and gaze about you, it will be to say in despair . . . In a semi-circle of sheds occupied by rag-pickers one woman pays $1 a week for the end of one shed.

The Mulberry Bend was considered the "foul core of New York's slums." In Jacob Riis's *How the Other Half Lives*, Riis comments, "There is but one 'Bend' in the world, and it is enough . . . Around 'the Bend' cluster the bulk of the tenements that are stamped as altogether bad . . . Here, too, shunning the light, skulks the unclean beast of dishonest idleness. 'The Bend' is the home of the tramp as well as the rag-picker." The lodging house at 81 Mulberry Street where Smith/Moscowitch was murdered was on the northern edge of the Mulberry Bend—a bend in the road.

Notice some similarities between the Bowery sex worker murder and the Polly Nichols murder. Both showed evidence of first being choked to death before having their throats cut with a long blade. The cut from a stiletto in the case of the Moscowitch murder would have been identical to the cut from a long, thin-bladed amputation knife, as in the case of the Whitechapel murders. Also, neither showed signs of being raped nor robbed. While it is highly likely that Polly Nichols met up with Jack the Ripper on Whitechapel Road, then she brought him to the more secluded Buck's Row to "do the business," it is less obvious how the evening transpired with Minnie Moscowitch. Two possibilities are that she brought the killer to 81 Mulberry Street from the saloon as a customer, or she left the saloon and he followed her without her having knowledge of his presence.

There are a number of reasons why we cannot rule Tumblety out as being the offender of this unsolved murder. Maria Calusio claimed she saw Minnie Moscowitch with Di Cantio in the backyard thirty minutes after midnight, yet it was not Di Cantio. He had a solid alibi. It was very likely dark even if there was a lantern in the backyard. Maria Calusio may very well have seen the Bowery sex worker with the murderer. The papers gave the physical description of Di Cantio as six feet tall with a dark mustache with side whiskers. This physical description matches perfectly with that of Francis Tumblety, who was also six feet tall and wore a dark mustache and side whiskers. Also, Tumblety was reported as having been seen in New York City around June 1888 before departing for England, so he was most likely in New York City in May. According to the *New York World*, November 19, 1888:

> During the past few years Twomblety has opened a branch office in London, and has been making regular trips across the ocean at intervals of five or six months. *He was last seen here [New York City] about five months ago, when he appeared on Broadway*, just as he did 20 years ago, with his leather-peaked cap, white overgaiters and buttonhole bouquet. [Author emphasis added.]

The southern section of Broadway was just two blocks away from the western borders of Five Points, Little Italy, and all of the Bowery, then it traveled north directly into the Tenderloin. Broadway was the perfect street to quickly enter into any of the slums and red-light districts in Lower Manhattan, then quickly leave. Broadway was only four blocks away from the murder site of Minnie Moscowitch.

Lastly, numerous people who knew Tumblety stated that each night he would walk the streets in the slums of every city he visited, so Tumblety would have been walking the slums of New York City. He lived next to the Bowery, which suggests he would have been on the streets of the Bowery exactly where Minnie Moscowitch was prostituting each evening.

The question should be asked, why had, or has, no one ever heard of the Moscowitch murder when it had so many details in common with the Whitechapel murders and it occurred in 1888 just a few months before? Here was a brutal unsolved murder of a sex worker who was not raped or robbed and who had her throat cut from ear to ear. The answer is probably that American murders were not on the radar of those interested in the London murders. However, because of the similarities and when it occurred, it can be argued that the murder of this sex worker may have been connected to the Whitechapel murders—especially when considering that a potential Ripper suspect like Tumblety was in each of those places at the times the murders occurred.

The chief of detectives for New York City at the time of the Moscowitch murder was the charismatic Detective Inspector Thomas Byrnes, having held the position since March 12, 1880. After the double event murders in London on September 30, 1888, many were questioning Scotland Yard's ability to catch the killer. On October 1, in an article that was published in the *San Francisco Examiner*, October 2, 1888, a *New York World* reporter asked Inspector Byrnes if he and his detective division in New York City would be able to catch Jack the Ripper if the murders occurred in New York. Byrnes responded:

> I sincerely hope that such a series of offenses will never be inaugurated in this city, but if such a thing should come about, I cannot believe that the guilty person could escape detection. We caught a fellow who had a mania for throwing vitriol upon women's dresses red-handed. Immediately after it was reported, his crime was localized. He frequented Fourteenth street. I found victims for him and my men were thickly scattered through the district. We have no such autocratic powers as the London police, we would most assuredly arrest the perpetrators in short order.

Yet, Scotland Yard did localize the crimes and "thickly scatter" detectives throughout the district in early October 1888. E. Tracy Greaves, the London correspondent for the *New York World*, was there and in communication with Scotland Yard sources. Notice what Greaves stated in an October 7, 1888, *New York World* news cable dispatch as reported in the *St. Louis Post-Dispatch* after exclaiming what he "learned to-day from a Scotland Yard man engaged in working up the case":

> The Whitechapel district is swarming with detectives. Some, disguised as laborers, are talking with dissolute women and endeavoring to find out from them something to give the police a tangible basis to work upon. Some private detective agencies, tempted by the $8,000 reward, obtained from private sources, have posted decoy women upon the streets, but all of this avails nothing. Innumerable arrests have been made, but there is no one now in custody ... The police are beginning to think "Jack, the Ripper," who wrote the letter and postal card to the Central News, the real murderer ... Hundreds of amateur detectives have also been ordered on police duty.

Byrnes's criticism of Scotland Yard's handling of the Whitechapel murders case was relatively short-lived, possibly because he found out Scotland Yard was indeed flooding Whitechapel with detectives. By November, Byrnes resisted reprehending Scotland Yard in this matter. Just after the Mary Kelly murder, Byrnes was again asked the same question by a reporter, and this time he refrained from being critical. In the *Boston Globe*, November 13, 1888, Byrnes stated:

> In my position as inspector of police and in charge of the detective force of this city I would say that, if we ever had in New York the misfortune of meeting such outrages, or any similar to those which were perpetrated at Whitechapel, I would consider it an act of great imprudence for me to advertise what schemes I should resort to or what action I should undertake with the detective force of this city for the purpose of apprehending and prosecuting the person who committed the offenses . . . It is easier always to condemn others than it is to succeed in their special line of work, and appreciating the difficulties that surround the London police . . .

It strains credulity to believe that Byrnes and his detective department were not reminded of the unsolved Moscowitch murder in their own backyard when every newspaper in New York was publishing at great length the Whitechapel murders, especially since they occurred only a few months later. Regardless of if Byrnes was critical of Scotland Yard's investigation or not, the question about Jack the Ripper possibly being in New York City was forced to the forefront of his mind.

Byrnes certainly would have had the incentive to keep the Moscowitch murder quiet if he was now investigating the possibility that Scotland Yard's Jack the Ripper suspect cut the throat of a Bowery sex worker just before he left for England.

CHAPTER 5

BOOKENDS TO THE WHITECHAPEL MURDERS IN THE UNITED STATES

Many victims actually survive a serial killer encounter. Peter Sutcliffe, infamously known as the Yorkshire Ripper, murdered thirteen women—mostly sex workers—in England between 1975 and 1980, although he likely murdered more than twenty-two. Sutcliffe was known to follow a woman on the street, brutally bludgeon her over the head with a ball-peen hammer, then repeatedly stab them with a knife or sharpened flat-headed screwdriver. Surprisingly, no fewer than seven women survived the vicious attack. On a number of occasions, the attack was interrupted, and Sutcliffe fled. A silver lining to attempted murders and assaults is that many of these victims can give a physical description of the assailant. For example, fifteen-year-old Kara Robinson Chamberlain was kidnapped by serial killer Richard Evonitz. He assaulted her in his apartment for eighteen hours. His preferred assault was to molest a teenage girl for a period of time and then murder her. Kara was set to be his fourth victim, but when Evonitz was asleep, Kara escaped. She was able to free a hand from the handcuffs and unclip the leg restraint. Because she survived, Kara was able to help in Evonitz's arrest and conviction. Because we know some victims survive a serial killer encounter, the original question, "Were there any unsolved Ripper-like murders of women in America where Tumblety cannot be excluded as having committed the crime?" should more appropriately be amended to:

> Were there any unsolved Ripper-like murders *or assaults* of women in America *who were neither raped nor robbed*, and where Tumblety cannot be eliminated as having committed the crime?

When we say, "Ripper-like murders," the assumption is that the offender only killed in a certain way, which experts call modus operandi (MO) and offender signature. In short, MO is what the offender must do in order to commit a crime, such as leading the victim away from public places, the method of control, and the type of weapon used. The offender signature serves to satisfy the emotional and psychological needs of the offender through fantasy, such as torture, location of mutilation, or staging and posing the body. The MO between successive murders may be similar but may change and evolve with time, environment, or when the offender discovers a better method of accomplishing his agenda. The term used to refer to the murders attributed to Jack the Ripper is "canonical," as in the canonical five victims: Polly Nichols, Annie Chapman, Elizabeth Stride, Catherine Eddowes, and Mary Kelly. This term was used because the offender's MO was so similar as compared to the numerous other murders of unfortunates at the time, yet even with these murders the MO was not identical. Organs were taken from just three of the five victims, while none were taken from the bodies of Nichols and Stride. It may very well have been that the killer was interrupted, so he had no time to collect organs. The cut to Elizabeth Stride's throat was not deep to the spine as the others were, and her body was not found prone. This may also have been because the killer was interrupted. Mary Kelly's murder was different because she was murdered indoors.

Two of the victims universally accepted as having been killed by Jack the Ripper were Polly Nichols and Annie Chapman. The similarities and location of each murder convinced even Detective Inspector First-Class Frederick Abberline, a detective assigned to the case, who at first concluded that there was no single killer. In both cases, there were clear signs of the victim first being rendered unconscious or killed by strangulation, followed by their throats being cut "from ear to ear," and then lastly postmortem mutilation of the abdominal region. In one respect, the killer could have been nicknamed Jack the Strangler.

In some cases, though, the method of murder changes. Take for example the Sunday Morning Slasher, Carl Eugene Watts (1953 – 2007), who murdered between fourteen and one hundred victims from about 1974 to 1982. While he almost always killed young White women, his known victims ranged from ages fourteen to forty-four. Of the victims he was convicted of murdering, his methods of killing varied, using strangulation, stabbing, bludgeoning, and drowning. Rarely were the victims sexually assaulted, but on occasion he did so.

Richard Cottingham (born in 1946), aka, the New York Ripper, aka, the Times Square Killer, aka, the Torso Killer, was a sado-sexual serial killer of mostly sex workers who began his crime span in 1967 until he got caught in

1980. While he generally drugged his victims and then strangled them, his MO varied, which caused authorities to not connect the first few murders to one killer. Although Cottingham claimed to have started killing as an adolescent, his first known victim was seventeen-year-old Mary Ann Della Sala on January 24, 1967, in Hackensack, New Jersey, by strangulation, yet she was not a sex worker. His next victim was a twenty-nine-year-old mother of two he strangled in Ridgefield Park, New Jersey. In July 1973, Cottingham murdered thirty-three-year-old Sheila Heiman in North Woodmere, New York, by bludgeoning her and stabbing her. In August 1974, he beat and raped Lorraine Kelly, aged sixteen, and Mary Pryor, aged seventeen, in Montvale, New Jersey, then murdered them by drowning. In December 1979, Cottingham bound, tortured, and cut off the heads and hands of two sex workers at a Travel Lodge Motor Inn in New York City. In May 1980, Cottingham strangled Jean Reyner in New York City, cut her throat, then severed her breasts.

Recall that when Tumblety sneaked out of London and then arrived in New York City onboard the *La Bretagne* on December 2, 1888, he was wearing an Ulster overcoat without a cape. According to the *New York Herald*, December 4, 1888:

> He wore a long English cloth Ulster, without a cape, a derby hat, and carried an umbrella and two canes tied together. It was the now famous Dr. Tumblety . . .

The Ulster coat, or Ulster overcoat, derives its name from the Irish province of Ulster, whose residents used to wear a type of tweed overcoat. The Ulster coat can be defined by seven elements: it is a long coat and double breasted with two vertical, parallel rows of buttons. It also has notched lapels, as opposed to peaked lapels. It has patched pockets, cuffs, contrast stitching along the edges and cuffs, has a belt, and is generally made of tweed. The Ulster coat sometimes came with a cape and a hood, such as the fictional character Sherlock Holmes wore.

Tumblety may have purchased an Ulster coat in New Orleans in 1881. Under sworn testimony in 1905, being questioned by Judge Hernandez, Richard Norris spoke of the time Tumblety bought him a suit: "On my way back from the Post Office he asked me if I was going to his room and I told him no. He stopped over at H.B. Stevens to buy a coat for himself, and then he bought me a suit." H. B. Stevens advertised in the local newspapers, such as the *Times-Picayune*, March 30, 1880, stating that they sold gentlemen's clothing, "A large and choice assortment in all the late styles," and added, "Clothing made to order, from best English, French and Scotch materials and latest patterns." This would have included the English cloth Ulster that Tumblety was wearing when he disembarked the *La Bretagne*.

While the Bowery sex worker murder in May 1888 does indeed answer the question to the affirmative that Tumblety was in the area of a murder of a woman, a surprisingly Ripper-like murder, this is actually only the tip of the iceberg. For starters, there were at least eight unsolved outdoor attacks and murders of women in America just before and just after the Whitechapel murders, when Tumblety was known to have been, or reported to have been, in the area. Local officials saw neither rape nor robbery as a motive, just as in the case of the Whitechapel murders. Upon reviewing these crimes, it will be apparent that there were additional similarities to the Whitechapel murders, leaving the possibility that these assaults and murders of women on both sides of the Atlantic were connected.

THE WATERLOO ATTACK, NEW YORK – EARLY DECEMBER 1888

According to the *Waterloo Observer*, December 12, 1888, "During this past week," two separate accounts of women walking the streets at night were surprised by a threatening man. The correspondent reported that:

> Moreover, during this past week a young lady was met about seven o'clock in the evening on a public street in the first ward by a man who said, "You are the girl I want," and tried to *seize her by the neck* when she beat him in the face . . . and he fled. In the lower ward, a woman was followed for a long distance in a menacing manner, and sought safety . . . [Author emphasis added.]

The reporter also commented upon Francis Tumblety being in town, stating prior to the above comment, "The announcement that Dr. Tumblety had come to New York and departed for a rural retreat, in the fancy of many timid females he has been located in Waterloo . . ." Of significance is that the reporter implied that Tumblety was the man who assaulted the woman! Note the article in its entirety, in which attacks are introduced, then Tumblety's arrival is noted, followed by a description of an attack:

> Wild rumors are afloat about villains in many villages and cities assaulting, insulting and molesting women and young girls on public streets after dark.

All these places have a modified prototype of the White Chapel murderer. "Dick the Slasher." The announcement that *Dr. Tumblety* had come to New York and departed for a rural retreat, in the fancy of many timid females he has been located in Waterloo. And this is the more certain; since the veritable doctor spent a summer here *some ten years ago*. Moreover, during the past week, *a young lady was met* about seven o'clock, in the evening on a public street in the first ward *by a man who* said, "You are the girl I want," and *tried to seize her by the neck*, when she beat him in the face with an umbrella and he fled. Also, in the lower ward, a woman was followed for a long distance in a menacing manner, and sought safety in a neighbor's house and company home. If there is anything going on in this line more serious than trying to frighten timid females, the villain ought to be run down and punished. [Author emphasis added.]

Notice that the assailant surprised a woman walking the streets at night, then attacked her throat as a method of controlling her as he spoke to her. As the reporter also discussed, the ultimate intention of the assailant was clearly more serious than just intimidation.

There are a number of reasons why we can be certain that Tumblety was indeed in Waterloo, New York. First, Tumblety vanished from New York City on December 5, 1888, when he read in the December 4, 1888, New York newspapers that a Scotland Yard detective was just outside his window on a stakeout, him being the target of interest for the Whitechapel murders. He was no longer in New York City. Second, Tumblety's sister, Elizabeth Powderly, sixteen years his senior, lived in Waterloo, New York, in 1888 with her family. Elizabeth was Tumblety's fourth-oldest sister, who married a Thomas Powderly and had five children. According to sworn testimony in 1905 from her son, Thomas Powderly Jr., he recalled the time Tumblety was arrested in Toronto in 1880 for sodomy and then hid at the Powderlys' Waterloo home around 1880. The following newspaper articles report on this arrest, with Tumblety being incarcerated in October 1881 for indecent assault against a young man named Bulger:

AN UNNATURAL CRIME.
Francis Tumblety was arrested last night by Policeman Clark on a charge of having committed an indecent assault on a youth named Bulgar [*sic*]. He was detained at Court-street Station.

—*Toronto Globe*, October 15, 1880.

INDECENT ASSAULT.

Francis Tumblety was up on remand this morning charged with indecent assault on the person of a boy named Bulger on the night of October 14th. His Worship, after hearing the evidence of Bulger, was of the opinion that it could only be established as a common assault, and imposed a fine of $1 and costs, which the prisoner paid.

—*Toronto Globe*, October 19, 1880.

The phrase "unnatural crime" was a nineteenth-century euphemism for sexual assault or sodomy, and in fact, Powderly stated that Tumblety was, "in jail at Toronto; arrested for sodomy." It was reported that Tumblety spent the weekend in jail. According to the 1880 census, Thomas Powderly's mother lived in Waterloo, New York, which is about forty miles east–southeast of Rochester, located between Toronto and Tumblety's residence in New York City.

The *Waterloo Observer* even commented upon when Tumblety was in town years earlier, which not only conforms to the time Powderly recalled Tumblety being in Waterloo, but it also corroborates a positive identification of Tumblety in town in the previous week of December 1888.

A search through *Waterloo Observer* issues from the late nineteenth century makes it clear that this type of assault upon a woman walking alone at night in this small rural community was highly unusual. How coincidental—or not— that a valid Jack the Ripper suspect and well-known misogynist was in town as these evening outdoor assaults on women occurred.

Multiple sources stated under oath that Tumblety spent each evening roaming the streets, at the very locations of these assaults. We actually have sworn testimony of Tumblety roaming the streets of Waterloo: Thomas Powderly spoke in court under oath about this very activity. The attorney asked if there was anything peculiar as to how Tumblety dressed. Powderly responded, "Sometimes he would dress very neat, and then again two or three days he would put on old clothes and go out on the street."

THE TALL MAN IN A GRAY ULSTER, CHICAGO – DECEMBER 13, 1888

The Scotland Yard detectives based out of New York had no authority to apprehend him when he arrived in New York harbor, as reported in the *Sun*, December 4, 1888, "Inspector Byrnes said that no one has any right to bother him [Tumblety] for what occurred across the ocean, unless the Government becomes interested and issues a warrant for his detention. He is a tall fellow, with a sweeping dark moustache..." Although Tumblety knew full well that the Scotland Yard detectives, with the approval and assistance of the New York City Police Department, could not arrest him for the gross indecency charge, he also knew that they could easily drum up a felony charge just to extradite him back to England. Unsurprisingly, Tumblety vanished on December 5, 1888, making his way to Waterloo, New York. Upon the publication of the *Waterloo Observer*, December 12, 1888, Tumblety may have felt vulnerable to being extradited again. In his mind, local Waterloo authorities or reporters could easily cable the New York City Police Department. His choices were to stay in Waterloo and take his chances or leave. There is evidence that by mid-December, Tumblety left Waterloo. According to the *Cherryvale Champion*, December 13, 1888, an eyewitness told an Associated Press reporter on December 12, 1888, that Tumblety was thought to have gone to Chicago:

THE WHITECHAPEL MURDERER.
A Notorious Adventurer Suspicioned of the Crime, Believed to Be in Chicago.
Dr. Tumblety, who has become notorious through his detention in London under suspicion of being the Whitechapel murderer, is thought to be somewhere in Chicago. He is known to have friends there. He was in terror of his life in New York because of the bitter feeling against him among the English residents of that city.

Of significance, a Ripper-like assault on a young lady occurred one night. According to a Chicago newspaper, the *Inter Ocean*, December 14, 1888, a young Swedish girl named Hulda Johnson, aged twenty-two, was a domestic who was traveling in a cable car and got off at the corner of Cottage Grove Avenue and 55th Street. She noticed that the tall man who was sitting opposite her also got off, but she thought nothing of it. She waited for the Hyde Park Cable Car, but since it was not approaching, she stated that she decided to walk home along the tracks. According to the reporter:

> She had proceeded about a block when suddenly she was *grabbed by the throat* from behind. At the same time a gruff voice exclaimed: "I won't hurt you if you will let me walk home with you." [Author emphasis added.]

The young lady realized it was the tall man and yelled, "You are a bad man. Go away." The assailant then gripped her throat harder. She struggled and broke loose, and as she ran away screaming, she spotted "track repairers" in the distance working on the tracks. She immediately ran toward the repairers and continued to scream. She stated that, as she was running away, the assailant drew out a revolver and shot at her twice. The man then ran away, clearly realizing his intended nefarious agenda with the woman was not going to happen.

The woman later told the reporter, "The man tried to murder me, without doubt." She said she fought hard, and he even tore buttons off her cloak. She said the attacker was tall, rather good-looking, wore a dark mustache, and had no whiskers. He was dressed in a long gray overcoat or Ulster with a high collar, which was turned up. On his head was a dark gray cap.

According to the *Inter Ocean*, December 16, 1888, a man named Thomas Judge was arrested for the assault. Johnson was brought to the police station for identification and said that Judge fit the physical description of her assailant. Soon after, "half a dozen witnesses were found who declared that Judge was in McAndrews' saloon, at the corner of Wright and Halsted streets, at the time the assault was committed." The captain of police was satisfied with the witnesses' statements and subsequently released Judge. The assault remains unsolved.

This assault happened just as the assault on the nighttime streets of Waterloo had, just one week earlier. The attack occurred outdoors, and the victim was first grabbed by the throat and threatened verbally. Notice that the attacker in Chicago did not use his revolver to threaten the woman but instead decided to choke her. He only used the revolver when he felt the situation was getting out of his control.

We know Tumblety was in town during the Waterloo attack, though no eyewitness account of the assailant was given. In the Chicago case, the eyewitness description matches Tumblety perfectly, including wearing an Ulster coat, as reported when he arrived in New York Harbor on December 2, 1888. There is also an eyewitness account of Tumblety traveling within the United States wearing an Ulster coat. While in St. Louis in 1890, notice how Tumblety's attire is described:

> Jack The Ripper. The Mysterious Dr. Tumblety Now in St. Louis.
>
> But to his presence in this city. Last night at about 10 o'clock, while Donovan's Exchange, in the Chamber of Commerce building was crowded with billiard players, a large, massively built man strolled into the place. He was six feet and an inch tall, broad shouldered, dark skinned, with an immense jet black mustache that gave to his face a fierce, almost fiendish, expression; his apparel was of the finest quality, but of peculiar fashion; his head gear consisted of a delicately textured silk skull cap, with patent leather peak; he wore

a handsome *chinchilla overcoat*, broadcloth suit—sack coat—patent leather shoes, and cane; much jewelry adorned his person and altogether he was a man hard to place in any walk of life . . . He recognized no one, no one recognized him by word or sign. After a few minutes, he arose, walked deliberately across the hall, seated himself beside a youth and again relapsed into a study. Suddenly, and without speaking a word, he took a cigar from his pocket, gave it to the boy, and, still without a word, left the room, the boy following him. [Author emphasis added.]

—*St. Louis Republic*, April 18, 1890.

In the late nineteenth century, a popular Ulster coat was the Chinchilla Ulster. For example, in the *Portland Daily Press*, November 2, 1893, an ad for men's Ulsters had "Blue Chinchilla Ulsters, fast color, at $6.00, Blue Chinchilla Ulsters at $8.00." In the *New York Times*, October 28, 1891, another ad had "640 All-Wool Chinchilla Ulsters, usual retail price, $14 . . . $8. 275 Imported Chinchilla Ulsters, usual retail price, $18 . . . $10."

The victim of the Chicago attack said the tall man in the gray Ulster wore a cap. While Tumblety wore a derby hat while disembarking the *La Bretagne* on December 2, 1888, he admitted to wearing a slouch hat when he was walking the Whitechapel streets at night. This means Tumblety traveled with at least two different kinds of hats. The other type of hat Tumblety was known to have worn throughout his entire life was a cap. In an Associated Press article titled, "AH THERE! TUMBLETY. The Notorious Whitechapel Suspect and His Ways and Manners," as published in the *St. Joseph Gazette*, December 27, 1888, a picture of Tumblety was added, showing him walking with a greyhound; the article commented upon him owning a large dog in the 1860s. The image has him dressed in a double-breasted tweed short Ulster-like coat, complete with notched lapels, and wearing a dark cap. The proprietor of the Waverley Hotel in Hot Springs, Arkansas, stated under oath in 1905 that he'd known Tumblety "very well for many years," and said that Tumblety was generally in a "long coat." Dr. John B. Brooks, a physician in Hot Springs, stated that later in Tumblety's life he would wear "two or three coats" and these coats would be covered by an overcoat. Police Court "Judge" John W. Jones of Hot Springs stated he knew Tumblety for nearly twenty years and said that in the last few years of Tumblety's life, "sometimes he would wear three or four coats at one time."

On two separate occasions, Tumblety was reported to travel with a revolver; the first was in 1863. According to the *Evening Star*, April 1, 1863, out of Washington DC, on the night of March 30, 1863, Tumblety and his "colored servant" Rezin Alexander were robbed in the city by two men. They stole a ten and a five-dollar Treasury note and fifty cents of postal currency from Alexander and a flute and a revolver from Tumblety. The second record of Tumblety carrying a revolver was in 1882. A. Romaine Smith was the Hot Springs, Arkansas, mayor from 1882 to 1884. Under sworn testimony in 1905, Smith stated that in his first year as mayor, Tumblety asked him if he could carry his revolver on his person. At the minimum, Tumblety carried a revolver periodically in his travels.

The Chicago cable cars were part of an intercity mass transit system in Chicago that began in 1882 and replaced the older rail horsecar system. These cable cars were also called grip cars since they gripped onto an underground continuously running cable system. The system was run by the Chicago City Railway (CCR), which ensured travelers a smooth transition from the many railroads located through Chicago. The Hyde Park cable car that the young Swedish girl was attacked on traveled easterly, conveniently passing near the Hyde Park and Park Train Stations, which were connected to north–south running railroad tracks. These tracks directly connected to the Baltimore & Ohio (B & O) Railway System to the south.

The significance of the B & O Railway System is that it linked the major cities that Tumblety traveled to on a yearly basis. They were St. Louis, Chicago, Cincinnati, Pittsburgh, Buffalo, Rochester, Washington DC, Baltimore, Philadelphia, and New York City. Since the B & O Railway System was connected to hundreds of other train routes, Tumblety could easily travel to any city in the South, Midwest, and on the East Coast. The two major railroad companies that Tumblety used were the B & O Railroad and the Pennsylvania Railroad, which also operated in the Midwest and dominated on the East Coast.

There is a record of Tumblety using cable cars in New York City as well. According to the *Olean Democrat*, August 8, 1889, an Olean resident was traveling across the Brooklyn Bridge in a mass transit bridge car, which was a cable-hauled train car connecting the Park Row terminal in Manhattan and another terminal in Brooklyn. Tumblety was known to take the New Jersey Central Railway to Brooklyn, then use a cable car across the bridge when he traveled into Manhattan. The Olean resident stated:

> I had just finished my night's work, and was riding across the big bridge. I had barely secured a seat in the bridge car when a peculiar looking man entered. He was over six feet in height, his face was square and red, and his gigantic, wiry, black mustache . . . I immediately decided in my mind that he was Dr.

Tumblety, the alleged Whitechapel murderer.... Until at last I asked him his name. "Dr. Francis Tumblety, you may have heard it before," was the quiet reply... We parted at the Brooklyn end of the bridge.

Of further significance is that two women walking the streets at night were murdered in Chicago, one along the cable car tracks in 1884 and the other just a few blocks away in 1891—neither victim was raped nor robbed. While these murders will be discussed in detail later, it is worth noting here that a rash of assaults on women walking the streets at night in Buffalo, New York, occurred in nearly the same way as the December 1888 Chicago attack—all by a tall man in a gray Ulster coat with the lapels pulled up.

ASSAULTS BY TALL MAN IN A GRAY ULSTER, BUFFALO – DECEMBER 1886

According to the *Buffalo Times*, December 6, 1886, the wife of an "esteemed citizen" was walking down South Division Street between Chestnut and Pine Streets on "Wednesday evening," December 1, 1886, when a tall man in an Ulster with his collar up approached and faced her. As he blocked her from walking, she said, "What do you mean you miserable loafer!" The reporter then stated:

> ... he *grabbed her by the throat* and threw her to the sidewalk. She strove to rise and once fairly got upon her feet and struck at him when he again knocked her down. [Author emphasis added.]

He then reported, "... in fighting her way to liberty that her assailant becoming either frightened or infuriated drew a revolver from his hip pocket and placing it close to her face exclaimed: 'Damn you, I'll kill you.'" She continued to fight, and something caught his attention, so he ran away and "turned toward Swan." Just a few blocks away, at the end of the street he turned on, were the Union and Erie Train Depots. The *Buffalo Times*, December 14, 1886, reported the assailant as "a tall man in an Ulster," who knocked the woman down "and nearly garroted [strangled]" her.

Notice the uncanny similarities with the Chicago attack almost exactly two years later. An unknown tall man in an Ulster coat surprised a woman at night on the city streets, grabbed her by the throat, and threatened her. A fight ensued, and when he was not getting his way, he pulled out a revolver. While the Chicago attack came from a man who was riding with the victim in a cable car and ended with the incident on the tracks, the Buffalo attacker ran toward the train station. In both cases, his collar was up.

A second and a third woman were attacked in Buffalo by a tall man in an overcoat with the collar turned up, and in this case, just like in Chicago, the man was wearing a cap. According to the *Buffalo Times*, December 13, 1886, the assailant was ". . . a well-dressed . . . loafer who makes it his business to assault and insult women particularly the pretty ones . . ." Three nights later, a Mrs. A. Sutor was attacked outdoors in the same area, in this case on North Division, when a man grabbed her. She struggled and yelled, "Murder!" so he struck her in the face, causing her to fall to the ground. At that moment, a young man heard the commotion and yelled out his window, which caused the attacker to run away. Neither Mrs. Sutor nor the young man got a good look at the assailant. The reporter did interview "a young lady living on South Division" who claimed that she had seen this man around the neighborhood for the last two weeks. She stated he was, "6 feet tall, wears heavy boots with pants tucked in them, heavy long overcoat, the collar of which is generally turned up, wears a cap and pulls it down to his forehead."

Tumblety had a significant history in Buffalo and was known by multiple sources to cruise the streets at night. The *Buffalo Morning Express*, June 27, 1903, published recollections of Tumblety in Buffalo:

> Dr. Tumblety was a familiar figure in Buffalo about 1893. He was a tall, heavy man, who wore black sidewhiskers and a mustache. He appeared to have no occupation, and *spent most of his nights walking on Main and Washington streets*. Every detective knew him as a man who had been under suspicion of the Whitechapel murders. [Author emphasis added.]

Main Street and Washington Street in downtown Buffalo are only a couple of blocks away from all of the assaults that occurred. The locations and timing indicate that the attackers are the same person.

Recall that Tumblety was reported to be in Waterloo, New York, during the Waterloo attack, and he was reported to "have gone to Chicago" during the Chicago attack. Tumblety's whereabouts at the time of the Buffalo assaults in December 1886 are no exception. The *Catholic Union and Times*, November 25, 1886, reports:

> Dr. Francis Tumblety of Canada is spending some time in the city [Rochester]. He is at the National.

Buffalo is the neighboring city to Rochester, a two-hour train ride away. It was also the last stop before Tumblety entered Canada. Tumblety owned 3,000 acres of land just west of Toronto and visited Toronto regularly in the 1880s.

In the case of the Polly Nichols murder on August 31, 1888, the conclusion was that Jack the Ripper first strangled Nichols before mutilating her with the knife. Nichols's body had bruising along the lower part of the jaw and limited blood spatter, which conformed to this conclusion. This was also the case with the Annie Chapman murder on September 8, 1888. Chapman's tongue was protruding, and her head was swollen, which is consistent with someone first being strangled. The Buffalo, Waterloo, and Chicago attacks conform to the MO of Jack the Ripper as well. In all three locations, the assailant grabbed the woman by the throat first in an effort to strangle her. In each case, the woman successfully fought back, so we do not know what the assailant's nefarious plan was, other than it being callously against the will of the victim. The fact that he pulled out a revolver and threatened the victim's life clearly suggests a murderous intent.

THE RAHWAY MYSTERY, NEW JERSEY – MARCH 1887

In Rahway, New Jersey, on the evening of March 25, 1887, a woman was murdered on Jefferson Avenue. A farmer was driving into the city and noticed the body on the side of the road. Her throat was cut from ear to ear, and there were defensive wounds on her hands. According to the *Evening Star*, April 20, 1887, Dr. Victor Mraviag, of Elizabeth, performed the autopsy and stated the female was five feet two

THE RAHWAY VICTIM.

inches in height and around twenty-five years old with light brown hair and blue eyes. The cause of death was the cut to the neck, severing the jugular vein and windpipe. There was no evidence of criminal assault or rape.

Because there was no evidence of rape, authorities concluded that the motive was merely robbery; however, according to the *Sun*, March 27, 1887, there were three "gold finger rings" on the third finger of her left hand, and jewelry was still on her clothing. According to the *Morning Call*, March 31, 1887, detectives believed that the reason behind the murder was "to prevent disclosure."

To assist in the identification of the woman, the body was open for viewing at the morgue for ten days, and according to an Associated Press article in the *Semi-Weekly New Era*, April 9, 1887, over six thousand people viewed the body.

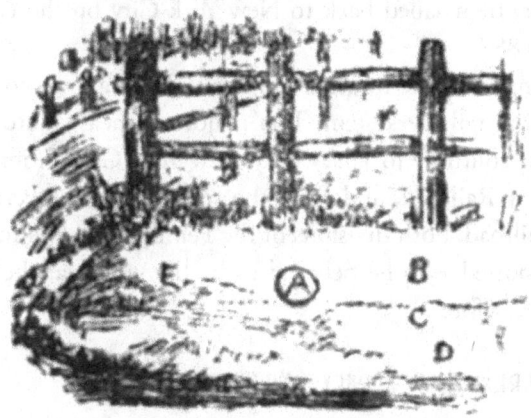

A. Where the body was found. B. The hat. C. The parasol.
D. The basket. E. The cloak. F. The knife.

Sadly, the woman was never identified. Law enforcement followed a number of clues, and a few arrests were made, but all suspects were released due to sufficient alibis.

According to the *Camden Daily Telegram*, March 30, 1887, two witnesses, John Savage and David H. Cox, claimed they saw a woman who resembled the victim arrive at the Rahway Train Depot at seven thirty P.M. Friday night. The woman asked them where Father Hofschneider, a German priest, lived. They told her and she left. Father Hofschneider stated that he was never visited by a woman. This woman arriving on the train and not living in the local area makes sense since such a large number of residents failed to recognize her. Since the murder occurred the very evening she disembarked, the killer may very well have followed the victim off the train.

A reporter from the *Morning Call* in Paterson, New Jersey, interviewed a number of detectives on the case and discussed motive in the April 1, 1887, issue. The detectives seemed to be confident that "the girl was murdered by someone who knew her. No total strangers would have pounced upon her and murdered her out of hand for murder's sake alone." The detectives and the reporter clearly had no understanding of serial offender motive.

Tumblety left New York for Liverpool, England, on May 25, 1887, onboard the transatlantic steamship *City of Rome*, which was the largest steamer traveling across the Atlantic at the time—meaning we know he was Stateside when the unidentified woman's murder occurred. Not only did Tumblety live within twenty miles of Rahway, New Jersey, but the city is the fourth stop along a train route between New York City and Philadelphia. He stayed in Europe for four months, then sailed back to New York City on the *City of Rome* on September 26, 1887.

It makes sense that the unusual murder in Rahway was committed by an assailant using the railway system. Two major northeast railroad lines merge in Rahway, then continue to Jersey City/New York City. From the southwest is the New Jersey Railroad, and from the southeast is the Perth Amboy and Woodbridge Railroad, both divisions of the Pennsylvania Railroad. Recall that an eyewitness spotted who he believed to be the victim at the Rahway Train Station the night before.

TRENTON SEX WORKER, NEW JERSEY - NOVEMBER 1887

Yet another unsolved murder of a sex worker occurred soon after Tumblety returned from Europe in 1887, one having similarities to both the Rahway murder six months earlier and the Moscowitch murder six months later. According to the *Morning Post*, November 19, 1887, the body of Ellen Quinn was found on Friday, November 18 in the cellar of an abandoned house along the New Jersey Central Railroad in Trenton, New Jersey, just feet away from the Delaware & Bound Brook Station. County Physician Lalor concluded that Quinn was strangled and had been dead for about forty-eight hours. The mutilation of the face was due to rats. Quinn was released from a three-month jail sentence on Thursday, November 17, so she must have been murdered Thursday night. On her body was a ring and a dime. Four local transients were arrested on suspicion, including James McDonald. All were eventually released, and the murder remains unsolved.

Just like the Rahway, New Jersey, murder, this murder occurred along the very same train route, between New York City and Philadelphia. Just like the Moscowitch murder, the victim was a sex worker whose body was found in a cellar. Note in November 1888 that an *Evening World* reporter stationed in Trenton, New Jersey, made a connection with the murder of Ellen Quinn and the Whitechapel murders:

> If the murder of Ellen Quinn had taken place in Trenton this year, instead of last, there would have been more attention given to it in the newspapers, because of its similarity to the Whitechapel murders that now startle the whole civilized world. Ellen Quinn was a poor unfortunate, who apparently fell victim first to the lust and afterwards to the brutality of a fiendish man. She was found in the cellar of an unoccupied house alongside the New Jersey

Central railroad, in this city, beaten to death and frightfully hacked about the face and person.

Because of the similarities the unsolved Quinn murder has with the Rahway murder, the Moscowitch murder, and even the Whitechapel murders, it deserves discussion, especially since we cannot eliminate Tumblety as having been in the area. The few newspaper reports available made no mention of Quinn being raped or robbed, however, they did publish the results of the post-mortem examination, discussing extensive details of the condition of the body. Since the results made no mention of rape, it does suggest that there was no evidence of rape. It is curious that unsolved murders and assaults of women occurred on the East Coast of the United States just before and just after Tumblety's extended stay in England in both 1887 and 1888, plus the fact that none were found when he was in England.

Tumblety was a transient, staying at most for weeks in one city but then traveling by train to the next city. This includes when he was in New York City, even though he considered it his home of record. Through the years, he did acquire possessions, but he stored them in Rochester, New York. Under sworn testimony in 1905, Tumblety's nephew, Michael Fitzsimmons, stated that he stored his possessions with his sister, Mary Fitzsimmons. The home had belonged to Tumblety's parents, but in 1883, it was passed down to Mary.

We have record of Tumblety temporarily renting a room in four New York City lodging houses during the late 1880s and early 1890s. According to the *New York World*, June 5, 1889, he lodged at 82 Clinton Place. Just one month earlier, the *New York Herald*, May 15, 1889, reported an eyewitness seeing him lodging at 17 Stuyvesant Street; in 1892, he lodged at 109 E. 9th Street; and lastly, 79 E. 10th Street was the location he lodged at once he arrived from London on December 2, 1888. This, though, seemed not to have been his first choice. According to the *New York World*, December 4, 1888, when Tumblety arrived on East 10th Street, the detectives stated he first tried to enter the Arnold House at 75 E. 10th Street. When that was locked, he tried to enter a lodging house at 75 East 10th Street. Finally, Mrs. McNamara's 79 East 10th Street door was unlocked. In January 1889, he did return to 79 E. 10th Street when he gave the "Tumblety Talks" interview with the *New York World* reporter. Tumblety was known to frequently switch lodging houses when visiting any particular city. Recall, in New Orleans in 1881, he even rented three rooms at one time. A *Times-Democrat* reporter stated on March 25, 1881, that Tumblety rented a room at the posh City Hotel. At the same time, he rented a room at the St. Charles Hotel, and in the slums, he rented a room at 190 Canal Street.

The four New York City rooms Tumblety rented have one thing in common: They are all located in a specific residential neighborhood filled with lodging houses for rent. All of these lodging houses are situated in the borough of Manhattan just east of Washington Square Park, conveniently located between two late nineteenth-century red-light districts, specifically neighborhoods. Immediately to the south was the Bowery and just to the north was the Tenderloin; both were within walking distance, and prostitution was rampant in both of these neighborhoods.

Tumblety's nightly pastime, even as far back as the early 1860s, was to slum in the red-light districts in every city he visited. For example, in the *Buffalo Commercial*, June 27, 1903, a Buffalo resident recalled Tumblety in that city, stating, "Dr. Francis Tumblety . . . was a familiar figure on the streets of this city back in the 60s. He usually walked about late at night." In New Orleans in the 1880s, Richard Norris testified under oath:

> . . . every night going through all the dark streets, walking like a Street Walker. He would take the darkest streets, and the darkest spots at night, and at one and two o'clock in the morning he would walk up Camp street, and all the dark streets and dark corners.

Specific to New York City, Tumblety was known to visit the red-light districts. In the *Buffalo Times*, June 27, 1903, an eyewitness stated, "In this city [New York City] he was one of the best known habitués of the Tenderloin streets after midnight, and was known as a 'night hawk' or 'masculine street walker.'" The Bowery was even closer, and Tumblety visited this neighborhood even during the day. In his 1889 autobiography, Tumblety claimed to have befriended a merchant named L. H. Schaukenberg, from 366 Bowery. According to the *Yonkers Statesman* newspaper, February 25, 1887, L. H. Schaukenberg was a store owner at 368 Bowery.

As the Scotland Yard detectives were scouring for damaging information in New York City in December 1888, it would be a surprise if they did not discover the unsolved Ripper-like murder of the Bowery sex worker in May 1888, just before Tumblety left New York for London.

These unusual assaults and murders in America between December 1886 and December 1888 were similar to the 1888 Whitechapel murders in important ways. Firstly, the offender approached the victim at night and on the street but murdered her in a separate, more private location. In the case of assaults, the assailant attempted to bring the victim to a separate location. Secondly, neither rape nor robbery was the motive for the murders. Thirdly, the method of attack was to the throat by cutting, strangulation, or both. Dellmus Colvin, aka the Interstate Strangler, a serial murderer and rapist active in New Jersey and Ohio in the late 1990s and early 2000s, called this type of attack personal. It doesn't take the mind of a murderer to understand why close-up assault—like strangling, slashing, or stabbing—is intimate: The attacker sees and feels the power and control over his victim as his rage is released. Lastly, Tumblety was known or reported to have been in the area of each and every assault and murder.

In view of the amended question, along with the murder of Bowery sex worker Minnie Moscowitch in May 1888, and that these mysterious and unsolved assaults and murders occurring across the pond just before and after the Whitechapel murders bear the hallmarks of a single serial killer, it can be argued that these unsolved murders of and attacks on women in the United States are connected to the London murders in the fall of 1888. Of note, Francis Tumblety, a Jack the Ripper suspect, cannot be eliminated as the offender in each and every case in the United States, especially when he fits so closely with the available eyewitness descriptions.

CHAPTER 6

A NARCISSIST'S SECRET

Why? If Tumblety was responsible for the 1888 murders on both sides of the Atlantic, *why* did he kill? What was his motive? Why would he have risked it all? His unusual and bitter hatred of women was commented upon even in his early years, so there must have been something that sent him over the edge at this particular time. We know that in December 1888, Tumblety began a public image campaign by updating his autobiography, and these updates had everything to do with his connection to the Whitechapel murders. The updates reveal a secret he had been hiding since around 1882.

New in the updated February 1889 version of his autobiography was his "My Vindication" section, which consisted of two chapters. He began the section with his vindication statement:

> Now let me say a word about the attacks which certain American newspapers recently made upon me, attacks that were as unfounded as the onslaught made on the great Irish leader.

Tumblety blamed the American newspapers for the libelous attacks but did not mention what the libel was about. These newspapers never discussed Tumblety's sodomy practices, only his connection to the Whitechapel murders. In view of this, the libel he was writing about being implicated in was his alleged involvement in the Whitechapel murders. However, nowhere in his updated autobiography does it mention anything about London or the Jack the Ripper murders, which leads to one conclusion: Tumblety purposely hid his connection to the murders, even when hinting at them, allowing the uninformed reader to overlook this connection. This contradicts a common claim that Tumblety concocted the whole story about being arrested for the Whitechapel murders, purposely attaching his name to the famous Jack the Ripper murders for publicity and notoriety. Tumblety could have easily refuted these claims, as he did in his autobiography specific to his 1865 Lincoln conspiracy affair. Case in point, Tumblety stated he was misidentified as Dr. Luke Blackburn, "of yellow-fever-plot notoriety," and then refuted it. In one case, he trumpets details of the experience, and in the other, he buries it, much like he buried the truth that he was an Indian herb doctor.

At this very time, as Tumblety was finishing up his February 1889 autobiography, he gave an interview to a *New York World* reporter on January 28, 1889. He told the reporter that the reason he was connected to the Whitechapel murders was because of the incompetence of Scotland Yard, specifically, it was the *English detectives* who believed he was involved in the murders:

> My arrest came about this way. I had been going over to England for a long time—ever since 1869, indeed—and I used to go about the city a great deal until every part of it became familiar to me. I happened to be there when these Whitechapel murders attracted the attention of the whole world, and, in the company with thousands of other people, I went down to the Whitechapel district. I was not dressed in a way to attract attention, I thought, though it afterwards turned out that I did. I was interested by the excitement and the crowds and the queer scenes and sights, and did not know that *all the time I was being followed by English detectives . . . My guilt was very plain to the English mind.* Someone had said that Jack the Ripper was an American, and everybody believed that statement. Then it is the universal belief among the lower classes that all Americans wear slouch hats; therefore, Jack the Ripper, must wear a slouch hat. Now, I happened to have on a slouch hat, and this, together with the fact that I was an American, *was enough for the police. It established my guilt beyond any question.* [Author emphasis added.]

Note the contradiction between what Tumblety stated in his autobiography and what he told the *New York World* reporter. In his autobiography, he blamed the New York papers for connecting him to the Whitechapel murders, while to the reporter he blamed the English detectives. The answer to this blame-game change makes sense in light of his decision not to mention what the slanderous attack was about—the Whitechapel murders. If Tumblety blamed the London police in his autobiography, then this would lead the reader back to the Whitechapel murders. Since he did not blame them in the updated autobiography, this is further corroboration that he was not looking for notoriety.

Chapter one of his "My Vindication" section is subtitled "Letters from Friends," while chapter two is subtitled "Farewell." A quick mention of chapter two: In this section, Tumblety announced his retirement, reminded the reader of his standing in high social circles, discussed his famed medical career, and ended the chapter with a poem about the libel of an honest man by certain newspapers being worse than the scourge of war.

Chapter one of his autobiography, "Letters from Friends," is a collection of short comments by acquaintances of Tumblety's sent to him soon after he returned from England. As he states, Tumblety published these letters to claim that his "social and professional standing" has been unimpaired. Most, if not all, may have been return letters with Tumblety making first contact, as evidenced by his banker Henry Clews stating, "I am in receipt of your letter of the 30th ult., and am much obliged for the comments contained." This suggests he solicited a response from these prominent New Yorkers in order to create the illusion that those in high social standing continued to accept him. A contemporary *New York World* reporter came to the same conclusion. Note the comments in a June 5, 1889, article:

> ... He showed a book purporting to give an account of himself as a physician. On the outside was printed that he had references from Gen. Sherman, Alexander Hudnut.... These references were printed in the book, but amounted to nothing. They were merely such letters as the gentlemen might write in response to an effusive and uncalled-for epistle from the doctor in the first place. He lives at 82 Clinton place.

Additionally, Tumblety spent time in numerous cities, so why did he not publish any of the letters from high society there? The likely answer is that there were no letters from others. If he had received them, it stands to reason that he would have published them.

In all, Tumblety claimed to have received letters from twenty-four New York City "friends," listing their names, but he only published "flattering" responses from ten of these letters in his 1889 autobiography. He merely name-dropped the rest. This New-York-City-only pattern in his correspondence testimonials can be used to ferret out his intentions. The autobiography was published in mid-February 1889, and the earliest letter was dated in January of that same year. It is quite apparent that as Tumblety was writing his "My Vindication" section, he was contacting acquaintances in hopes they would respond cordially. In so doing, he got to publish these responses to demonstrate that prominent New Yorkers considered him equal in social status—and innocent of the rumored offenses. The end of Tumblety's "My Vindication" section was his address for friends to send him letters, which was a general post to the New York City Post Office. This meant that Tumblety needed to be in New York City in order to collect these letters, hence, a reason why he returned there in late December 1888 or early 1889.

Seven of the ten letters were not only signed but also dated. These letters can be separated into three categories. First, one letter was dated before he arrived in Brooklyn, around January 18, 1889. Second, there were three letters dated nearly two weeks after he arrived in Brooklyn but before his initial publication of the 1889 autobiography around February 15, 1889. Third, there were three letters dated after the February publication and thus were later added to this edition. The letters in the second category were from Graeme M. Hammond, MD; National Hotel proprietor T. Halliday; and Dr. Cyrus Edson, dated January 23, January 24, and February 1, 1889, respectively. The letters in the third category were from Alexander Hudnut, Edward P. Doherty, Daniel J. Rooney, and Henry Clews, dated March 13, March 9, March 25, and April 2, 1889, respectively. Tumblety clearly added these to his February 1889 autobiography to create the perception of large numbers believing him to be a high-minded and noble gentleman.

The letter dated January 2, 1889, before Tumblety arrived in Brooklyn, around January 15, 1889, was from a Reverend W. H. De Puy, who states,

> F. Tumblety, Esq., M.D.
>
> Dear Sir:—I well remember the incident connected with our first acquaintance on board the City of Rome, on a trip a couple of years since, to the Old World. This acquaintance soon ripened into a sincere friendship, which has continued until the present time. I need not add that during your stay in this city I shall be glad to have you call at my office as often as may suit your convenience.
>
> I remain, my dear sir, very truly yours, REV. W. H. DE PUY, D. D., LL. D.

This particular reply letter is an excellent example of these actually being real letters, as opposed to Tumblety merely making them up. De Puy was a prominent Methodist priest but was also the editor of the *Christian Advocate* until 1888. Tumblety was a devout Catholic, so their religious affiliations would not have been where their lives connected. According to De Puy, they had met a couple of years prior to December 1888, while both were sailing to the "Old World" onboard the steamship *City of Rome*. A full-column article in the *New York Herald*, May 25, 1887, issue reported on the Hawaiian Queen Kapiolani sailing that day from New York City to Liverpool onboard the same ship. The article then stated, "There will be several 'honorable' on board, in whom she may find fine types of the American citizen, for among her fellow passengers are . . . W. H. De Puy . . ."

Although not mentioned in this article, Francis Tumblety was also onboard the *City of Rome*. This was likely the cruise on which the two first met.

These letters from apparent friends were acquaintances of Tumblety's in the mid-1880s, as evidenced by their content and that they were all from New York City. In his later 1893 autobiography, Tumblety added letters from friends in other cities. The fact that he had his 1889 autobiography published in just weeks, he likely used only New York City friends in order to rush publication. The letters can be useful in understanding what Tumblety was doing in New York City in the early- to mid-1880s. Tumblety was never known to have friends he would pal around with, except, of course, the young men he hired as travel companions. He was known to have cordial conversations with men he happened to encounter as he was by himself, such as during his travels or in a hotel lobby. Sworn testimony from eyewitnesses living in Hot Springs, Arkansas, shows that just after 1881, Tumblety changed his annual travel behavior to locations with hot baths, such as Hot Springs, Arkansas, and Saratoga Springs, New York. Corroborating this is an Associated Press article in the *New Ulm Weekly*, dated December 5, 1888, which stated, "Shortly afterwards he disappeared, and was not heard of again until 1883. In that year he went to Hot Springs, Ark., to be treated for rheumatism." In Tumblety's autobiographies, he writes about the benefits of hydrothermal treatments for ailments. Since Tumblety spent weeks, if not months, in New York City, it would not be a surprise that he spent time in the New York City hot bath establishments. Likely not a coincidence, four of the prominent New York doctors Tumblety mentioned were associated with hot baths. The homeopathic doctor, M. L. Holbrook, was not only a professor of hygiene at the Women's Homeopathic Medical College, but he also ran a Turkish bath establishment. Dr. E. P. Miller, an expert on Bright's Disease, ran a bath establishment at the Miller's Sanitarium. He also published articles on water cures and how to bathe. Dr. C. T. Ryan ran a Russian bath at Lafayette Place. Dr. Cyrus Edson was also associated with a hot bath facility.

One particular New York friend Tumblety added in the new "My Vindication" chapter may give us a window into a secret Tumblety kept. That person is Graeme Hammond, MD, a prominent New York City neurologist, or what was known at the time as an alienist. Hammond was editor of the *Journal of Nervous Mental Diseases*, chair of neurology at NYU School of Medicine, and future president of the American Psychiatric Association. Hammond was considered an expert on the diseases of the brain. He was also considered an expert in hypnosis, and in March 1889, he was questioned as an expert in a murder case where a young man named Willie Krulisch attacked a drug clerk named Gunther Wechsung with a hatchet. According to the *Evening World*, March 27, 1889, a claim was offered that Krulisch was under the hypnotic influence of an unknown person and thus was not under his own control. Dr. Hammond and a colleague, a Dr. Rockwell, were consulted, and after testing the boy they concluded he was not under hypnosis.

In the June 5, 1889, issue of the *Juniata Sentinel and Republican* out of Mifflintown, Pennsylvania, an article titled, "Strange if True," reports on Dr. Graeme Hammond teaching a class in medical school on hypnosis. After hypnotizing a student, he stated, "He is now under my control. I can do what I please with him. In his present state I could use this man as an instrument in committing a crime, and after I had withdrawn my influence and given him back his will he would remember absolutely nothing about it." Hammond controlled the student's actions with a number of verbal commands, such as having him ride an imaginary horse, then fall off and get injured. He then stated to the student, "You see that man leaning against the wall near the door? Look at him well. He is the murderer of your father." The hypnotized student became enraged and rushed forward. Hammond then caught the student and told him to "take him unaware." The student grabbed a pencil, crept along the wall, then thrust the pencil into the imaginary man's neck three times. Hammond then told the student that the police were coming so he should hide under the table. The student had fear in his eyes as he hid. Hammond then stated to the class, "Look at the man's face; guilt and terror are stamped upon it. You see a murderer, haunted by the fear of detection and the remembrance of his crime."

There is a curious connection between Graeme Hammond and the Whitechapel murders. Hammond's father was US Surgeon General Dr. William Hammond, who publicly gave his professional opinion on who Jack the Ripper might be. On November 19, 1888, a *Chicago Daily Inter Ocean* reporter spoke with William Pinkerton and asked:

"And what do you think are the probabilities of his being the man who committed the Whitechapel murders—murders committed, apparently, without any object in view? Do you consider that the Doctor was insane?" Pinkerton stated, "Yes, I do. I think a man guilty of such practices as those I have referred to must be insane; and Dr. Hammond—Surgeon General Hammond—some time ago, when asked as to whether or not he thought that the Whitechapel murderer was an insane man, said that when the murderer of those women was discovered he would undoubtedly be found to be a woman-hater and a man guilty of the same practices which I have described, and Twombley, or Tumblety, as being guilty of, and that such men were crazy and as likely as not to murder women."

The interview of Hammond that Pinkerton referred to was published in the *Williamsport Sunday Grit*, October 7, 1888. When asked what could cause "homicidal insanity," Dr. Hammond stated, "for some one of a dozen causes, disease, or drink, or what-not . . ."

William Hammond and his son, Graeme, worked closely together throughout the late nineteenth century, even publishing together on numerous occasions. In June 1889, William Hammond actually directed his son to take out the brain of a particular patient without permission, an act that made its way to court. An article subtitled, "Dr. W.A. Hammond to be Sued by the Widow of a Man whose Brains he Removed," states, "Ross died June 19 last. Word was sent to Dr. William Graeme Hammond, son of Dr. William A. Hammond, in obedience to what the wife considered her husband's agreement. Young Dr. Hammond came and removed the brain."

In his response in Tumblety's autobiography, Graeme Hammond claimed to have known him for several years, likely meaning 1886 to 1888: "Dear Sir:— I have had the pleasure of your acquaintance for several years, and have always found you to be an honorable and straight-forward gentleman." The other medical doctors Tumblety published as friends were involved with hot baths, so they likely knew him because he visited their respective hot bath facilities. Hammond, on the other hand, was not associated with a hot bath facility. This begs the question of how their paths crossed. There is evidence that Tumblety suffered from the very same disease Dr. Hammond claimed to be an expert in, so they may have had a doctor–patient relationship. A particular area of brain disease Hammond was considered by the legal community as an expert in was general paresis. In numerous New York City court cases, Dr. Hammond was used as an expert witness in diagnosing general paresis. On September 23, 1893,

Graeme Hammond examined a man named David Solomon, and according to comments in the *New York Sun*, September 23, 1893, Hammond certified he, "was suffering from paresis. On their certification an order was issued from the Superior Court for confinement . . . All the medical evidence taken in the case was to the effect that David Solomon was insane." In the December 19, 1900, edition of the *Brooklyn Daily Eagle*, Hammond testified in the Daniel Doody trial, stating Doody "was suffering from paresis." In the January 22, 1904, edition of the *New York Sun*, Hammond was recorded testifying in a court case about a man named Weber. It states, "Dr. Graeme Hammond testified that Weber was a sufferer from paresis . . ."

According to the US National Library of Medicine, general paresis is a problem with mental function due to damage to the brain from untreated syphilis, and it is one form of neurosyphilis, an infection of the central nervous system. Generally, neurosyphilis occurs about ten to thirty years after initially being infected with syphilis, and the patient is no longer contagious. Syphilis can lie dormant for ten or twenty years before progressing to neurosyphilis. While it can occur in the primary or secondary stages, it is generally associated with the tertiary stage. Cardiovascular syphilis, an infection of the heart and aorta, is often associated with neurosyphilis.

In an article in the February 4, 1892, edition of the *Daily Leader* titled "Have You Paresis?," famous New York neurologist Dr. Allan McLane Hamilton stated that general paresis is also called general paralysis of the insane, paralytic dementia, and softening of the brain. In the very same 1892 article, Hammond's father, Dr. William Hammond, stated, "The patient becomes regardless of his personal appearance. Neglects to change his linen and appears in public half dressed. His memory fails rapidly and his acts are eccentric and absurd." In the last few years of Tumblety's life, he dressed as a bum, rarely changing his clothes, and he was very dirty. In an article in the *Arizona Weekly Citizen*, November 13, 1886, titled "Paretic Dementia," Dr. William Hammond stated that paresis was a new form of insanity, "termed *paresis*, general paresis, *general paralysis*, progressive paralysis, paretic dementia, *softening of the brain*, and brain wasting." [Author emphasis added.]

John B. Brooks, a surgeon in the Civil War and Hot Springs physician, was interviewed under oath in 1905 about his interactions with Tumblety. Brooks testified that he knew Tumblety from about 1882 to 1902, with Tumblety visiting him at least once a year. He gave his medical opinion on Tumblety's physical and mental condition and stated that he was, "a man suffering from softening of the brain." The attorney asked if it was progressive, and Dr. Brooks replied,

"Yes sir." Upon cross-examination, Brooks stated, "I judge from his manner and seeing him that he was in a diseased condition." Brooks was a physician and would have known that softening of the brain meant paresis. Brooks was also a physician at Hot Springs, Arkansas, which in the late nineteenth century was considered the mecca for patients suffering from syphilis. Hot Springs became federal property in 1832, called Hot Springs Reservation (HSR), and physicians began coming to Hot Springs in the 1850s due to the growing belief that bathing in hot springs had curative properties. Hot Springs became known nationally in 1877 when the US Congress financed direct supervision of the HSR with the first supervisor, Civil War Union General C. W. Field. In an extract from the Register of Departments from Government Free Bathing Pools at Hot Springs, Arkansas, September 1885, Superintendent Field produced numerous testimonials on the success of the hot springs treatment of diseases, especially syphilis, such as in the case of Albert Hudson. Hudson stated, "Condition on arrival at the Springs: Syphilis, eyeritis, full of sores, and crippled from use of mercury. Condition now: Have taken 60 baths; good condition; able to work, and no particular illness." In the case of J. E. Todd, the patient stated, "Syphilis had full control of me . . . and after taking 50 baths I must say that life came in my leg and all indication of syphilis has disappeared from my system."

The reason Dr. Graeme Hammond was used as an expert is because it was extremely difficult to diagnose syphilis before they could directly test for it, which occurred in 1906 with the Wasserman test. Syphilis was known as "the great imitator," since it causes symptoms similar to many other diseases. Tumblety claimed he had taken his hot baths for rheumatism and would never have admitted he suffered from syphilis. Tumblety, though, was likely using rheumatism not as a disease but symptomatically. According to IPUMS-USA, an interdisciplinary research center at the University of Minnesota, in the 1880s, the term 'rheumatism' was still used as a symptomatic description of conditions rather than as a clinical diagnosis: "The designation of 'rheumatism' appears to have included any condition which prohibited free movement, such as rheumatoid arthritis, coxalgia (scrofula, or tuberculosis of the joints) and syphilis."

It should not be a surprise that Tumblety contracted syphilis since his hypersexual habits placed him in a high-risk category for contracting syphilis. Tumblety sought out services from young male sex workers in the slums of every city he visited, and he did this for decades. The earliest account of Tumblety visiting the slums at night was in 1860 in Boston. Norris admitted to prostituting himself for extra money in 1881 and stated that Tumblety wanted Norris to penetrate him. Not only was Tumblety having sexual contact with multiple unknown young men, but the percentage of male sex workers infected with syphilis was—and is—much higher than the average male.

There is evidence that Tumblety may have known he had contracted syphilis by the writing of his 1893 autobiography. He added two chapters that he did not include in his earlier autobiographies, in which he singled out only three diseases. The first chapter is titled, "A Few Remarks on Two Leading Diseases, viz. Paralysis and Bright's Disease." The modern name for Bright's Disease is nephritis, and this is what was on Tumblety's death certificate as the cause of death. Chapter two is titled, "Causes of Heart Disease." Recall, in January 1888, Tumblety stated to the Toronto reporter that he was constantly in dread of sudden death because of kidney and heart disease. Was Tumblety also afflicted with the third disease he created a chapter for: paralysis? We know of numerous occasions where Tumblety would pass out, and the Hot Springs surgeon, Dr. John Brooks, stated that Tumblety would occasionally drag one of his feet, that ". . . he walked lame. He seemed to drag one foot after the other." There is a reason why Tumblety would never have admitted to having paralysis: He would have had to admit he had syphilis. Tumblety claims in his autobiography that paralysis is a leading disease, thus, he can only be referring to the prevalent disease of the nineteenth century, general paralysis of the insane, i.e., neurosyphilis. Tumblety does indeed discuss this disease as progressive, its first condition being "gouty diathesis," followed by "cerebral congestion" causing *"general paralysis"* [emphasis added] with a "cutaneous affection." (Tumblety was reported having a cutaneous affection, namely, a red face.)." Recall, Dr. William Hammond referred to the disease as general paralysis. About the third stage Tumblety states, ". . . all of which ends in a crippled nervous system and brain." This is exactly what neurosyphilis attacks. Additionally, neurosyphilis is often associated with cardiovascular syphilis, so Tumblety having heart issues makes sense.

Also in Tumblety's 1893 autobiography is an omission pattern, a pattern he used in the past when he purposely kept information away from readers. In his 1866 autobiography, there are over twenty references to Tumblety being an Indian herb doctor, including in the title, but in his 1872 autobiography, he omitted all references to Indian herb doctoring. Tumblety clearly took these references out because he was attempting to erase this part of his history and replace it with being a surgeon. In the *New York World*, December 5, 1888, Young Martin H. McGarry stated that when he worked for Tumblety in 1882, Tumblety told him he was a retired surgeon; he also told Richard Norris in 1881 that he was a retired surgeon. He even stated in his autobiographies that he was a "disciple of Abernethy." John Abernethy was a late-eighteenth/early nineteenth-century English surgeon.

A second example of omission: Tumblety told the *New York World* reporter on January 28, 1889, that the reason he was creating his 1889 autobiography was to vindicate himself from the slanderous claims of the English detectives about his connection to the Whitechapel murders, but when the autobiography came out two weeks later, there was absolutely no mention of what the slander was about. A third omission: What Tumblety left out of his 1893 autobiography allowed him to distance himself from the leading nineteenth-century disease of syphilis. Instead of stating the cause of general paralysis was syphilis, Tumblety merely states, "whatever the determining cause."

The suggestion that Jack the Ripper was a person who blamed sex workers for infecting himself or a loved one with syphilis has been an accepted plausible motive behind the murders for quite some time. There is the well-known rumor of Prince Albert Victor, or Prince Edward, the grandson of Queen Victoria, having syphilis and being Jack the Ripper. In *The Mystery of Jack the Ripper*, Leonard Matters suggested Dr. Stanley, a Harley Street surgeon whose son died from syphilis contracted by a Whitechapel sex worker, took out his revenge upon them. While the story is likely fictitious, it shows that the idea was around. Guy Logan, the late-nineteenth/early twentieth-century London journalist who reported that Inspector Andrews crossed the Atlantic in December 1888 "in search of the Whitechapel fiend on the strength of important information, the nature of which was never disclosed," alluded to "a certain terrible disease, contracted in that neighbourhood, probably spurred him on to vengeance, remorseless and implacable." Logan clearly meant a venereal disease, like syphilis. When William Pinkerton discussed Dr. William Hammond's expert alienist opinion that Jack the Ripper was insane, he connected this to Tumblety because of his "habit of indulging in certain vices," meaning, his practice of sex with unknown young men. A recent explanation claims that Pinkerton had a flawed nineteenth-century belief that homosexuals were insane. In view of this, since Dr. Hammond said Jack the Ripper was insane, then Tumblety fit the insane profile. Actually, Hammond never connected homosexuality to homicidal insanity in the article Pinkerton referred to, but Hammond did with disease. Recall that Hammond stated syphilis is also referred to as general paralysis of the insane, in other words, disease-induced insanity. It is equally likely that Pinkerton did not mean Tumblety was insane because of his homosexuality but because he had disease-induced insanity. Pinkerton stated that Tumblety was in the habit of, at a high volume, having unprotected sex with unknown young men. Someone with this kind of habit was clearly in a high-risk category for contracting a venereal disease such as syphilis.

Even if a person blames women for their syphilis, to then commit multiple murders requires a special kind of ruthlessness; someone with a complete lack of remorse.

According to modern psychology experts studying abnormal violent behavior, serial offenders as a whole are not insane—meaning they know right from wrong—but simply do not care. Based upon decades of study, modern psychologists now understand that serial killers have personality developmental disorders. One such developmental disorder is antisocial personality disorder (APD), fully expressed by violence and a lack of remorse. It is labeled as a cluster B personality in the *Diagnostic and Standard Manual of Mental Disorders, Fourth Edition*, and is connected to psychopathy. Not all individuals with APD are considered psychopathic, but those who have minimal empathy and feelings of grandiosity are likely psychopathic. According to the *DSM-IV*, a characteristic of APD is a "pervasive pattern of disregard for, and violation of, the rights of others that begins in childhood or early adolescence and continues into adulthood." Individuals with APD fail to conform to social norms and instead engage in deviant behavior, such as sexual assault, and many have criminal records and repeated arrests. Included with the lack of remorse are consistent irresponsibility, impulsivity, irritability, and aggressiveness.

Narcissistic personality disorder (NPD) is a personality disorder characterized by "a pervasive pattern of grandiosity, need for admiration, and lack of empathy that begins by early adulthood and is present in a variety of contexts." Those diagnosed with NPD show signs of selfishness and a lack of interest in and empathy for others. Dr. Anthony Benis, ScD, MD, states in his book, *Toward Self & Sanity*, that aggressive narcissists "love to travel." The criteria in the *Diagnostic and Statistical Manual of Mental Disorders* gives the following features for NPD:

- *Having an exaggerated sense of self-importance;*
- *Expecting to be recognized as superior even without achievements that warrant it;*
- *Exaggerating your achievements and talents;*
- *Being preoccupied with fantasies about success, power, brilliance, beauty or the perfect mate;*
- *Believing that you are superior and can only be understood by or associate with equally special people;*

- *Requiring constant admiration;*
- *Having a sense of entitlement;*
- *Expecting special favors and unquestioning compliance with your expectations;*
- *Taking advantage of others to get what you want;*
- *Having an inability or unwillingness to recognize the needs and feelings of others;*
- *Being envious of others and believing others envy you;*
- *Behaving in an arrogant or haughty manner.*

It is often difficult to differentiate between antisocial personality disorder and narcissistic personality disorder since they share many characteristics. For example, seventy-three psychologists from the APA Division participated in a study on the personality structure of serial killer Ted Bundy. Psychologists Samuel and Widiger reported in the *Journal of Abnormal Psychology* in 2006 that 96% of the psychologists gave Bundy a diagnosis of APD; however, 95% also saw Bundy meeting the criteria for NPD.

The term Malignant Narcissism is occasionally used to refer to NPD but is also used for a person exhibiting both APD and NPD. In an article titled, "The Malignant Narcissist," April 21, 2008, Pamela Kulbarsh, RN, BSW, a psychiatric nurse who is a member of San Diego's Psychiatric Emergency Response Team, states that a narcissist's fundamental problem is the lack of empathy. They are intrinsically grandiose. They are extremely manipulative, complain and criticize, and will do something illegal, immoral, or violent if they believe they can get away with it. They do not feel responsible for their actions because they believe they are the victims of injustice, discrimination, or prejudice. Malignant narcissists are predators who hunt easy prey and are serial bullies, serial adulterers, gold diggers, pedophiliacs, rapists, child molesters, terrorists, and serial killers. Cambridge psychology professor Simon Baron-Cohen also stated in his book, *The Science of Evil: On Empathy and the Origins of Cruelty* (Basic Books, 2012) that those with NPD have no empathy for others, which suggests prefrontal and limbic abnormalities.

Another name for Malignant Narcissism is Aggressive Narcissism. The following is the Hare Psychopathy checklist for traits of an aggressive narcissist along with comments about Tumblety:

1. *Glibness/superficial charm*: Effective for Tumblety in acquiring wealthy patients.

2. *Grandiose sense of self-worth*: Decades of examples in Tumblety's case.
3. *Pathological lying*: Lying was a tool for Tumblety.
4. *Cunning/manipulative*: Tumblety's attorneys and banker referred to him as cunning. Judge J. Jones called him shrewd.
5. *Lack of remorse or* guilt: Many cases, such as hiring young Joseph Mitchell for four months promising pay and inclusion in his will but never following through on either.
6. *Shallow affect*: Expressed in autobiographies.
7. *Callous/lack of empathy*: Exploited patients for money.
8. *Failure to accept responsibility for own actions*: Always blamed others.

The following are Sandy Hotchkiss's Seven Deadly Sins of Narcissism, matching each "sin" with Tumblety's behavior:

1. *Shamelessness*: After sexually molesting a young boy in Baltimore, his only concern was to not be arrested as opposed to the welfare of the boy.
2. *Magical thinking*: Tumblety wrote in each version of his half dozen autobiographies that he was a highly esteemed medical doctor occupying the highest of social circles.
3. *Arrogance*: Countless examples, such as writing in his 1889 autobiography that the libelous attacks against him were like the attacks made against "the great Irish leader" (the famous British Member of Parliament Charles Stewart Parnell).
4. *Envy*: Tumblety carried in his travel chest a surgical kit in order to prove he was a retired Army surgeon (verified lie). He also carried with him a gold medal, claiming that he received it from the citizens of Montreal (verified lie).
5. *Entitlement (defiance of their will is a narcissistic injury triggering narcissistic rage)*: Tumblety told a reporter that thinking about how he was treated in London by being arrested on suspicion and then jailed made him so angry that he lost all control of himself.
6. *Exploitation*: Cornerstone of his Indian herb doctor business.
7. *Bad boundaries (societal norms do not pertain to them)*: Continuously arrested for sexually assaulting young men against their will.

According to Adam Blatner, psychiatrist and author of *Creating Your Living: Applications of Psychodramatic Methods in Everyday Life*, the definition of rage is "losing one's temper and flying into fits of aggression." Blatner explains that this is generally considered the last stage of anger, the first six stages being stress, anxiety, agitation, irritation, frustration, and anger. For a person diagnosed with NPD, there are no stages; they go straight from feeling stress to full-blown rage. Not only does Tumblety's behavior fit a person diagnosed with NPD, but there are also examples of his narcissistic rage throughout his life. Recall in the January 9, 1875, issue of the *Liverpool Leader*, an article that was published warning readers of the Great American Doctor:

> There comes to us a tale of a decent woman from the Isle of Man who sought his advice respecting a bad leg. He told her it was due to the immorality of her parents, but would cure it for 3 pounds. This she declined, whereon he [Tumblety] ordered her to get out legs and all or else he would kick her out! Other women young and unmarried, have fled in alarm from his premises, and say his language and conduct suggested danger.

Tumblety's Baltimore lawyer, Frank M. Widner Jr., swore under oath in 1905 a recollection of when he had witnessed Tumblety's rage. Tumblety gave him a cigar, and Widner stated that he accepted the cigar but never smoked it, fearing his client may have tampered with it. Widner then recalled another incident.

> I remember one day he came into my office in the period from May 1902 to July 1902, sat himself on the edge of the chair, as he usually did, in an attitude that was really threatening. He was talking excitedly about, I should say, to the best of my recollection, the papers that Simpson had retained in this case of the United States Engraving Co., and the attitude he assumed toward me was such that I drew back my chair from my desk and assumed a position of defense, in case he should spring upon me. I was very much afraid that the man would make some movement, his attitude was so threatening, and he was so nervous... He had worked himself up to a state of mind that was not at all compatible with the amount involved, or with the importance of the case, because I knew I could procure the papers for him by process.

As mentioned, Tumblety himself said that it was a real possibility when he was stressed that he just might lose control of himself, i.e., rage. A *New York*

World reporter interviewed Tumblety, and that interview was published in the January 31, 1889, issue. In it, Tumblety talked about losing control.

> His [Tumblety's] long black mustache has been trimmed close and reaches down in the shape of a thick growth of beard around his chin, which he keeps smooth shaven. His face is ruddy and he has blue eyes. If he ever dressed sensationally in the past, he does not do so now. Yesterday he wore a dark suit which was by no means new, and a little peaked traveling cap. Altogether, he gave the appearance of a prosperous Western farmer. He wore no jewelry.
>
> Dr. Tumblety talks in a quick, nervous fashion, with a decidedly English accent, and at times, when describing his treatment by the English police, he would get up from his chair and walk rapidly around the room until he became calm . . .
>
> "How long were you in prison?"
>
> "Two or three days; but I don't care to talk about it. When I think of the way I was treated in London, *it makes me lose all control of myself.* It was shameful, horrible." [Author emphasis added.]

Forensic scientist and criminal profiler Dr. Brent Turvey stated that behavioral patterns of violent offenders identified at the crime scene are relatively consistent and classified as Behavioral-Motivational Typology. The patterns found at crime scenes resulting from violent offenders are power reassurance, power assertive, anger-retaliatory, sadistic, and administrative behaviors. Dr. Turvey studied the Whitechapel murders, specifically the crime scenes and victims from Polly Nichols to Mary Kelly, and interpreted the offender's behavior as non-sadistic, observing a lack of sexual assault to the victims, lack of torture while alive, postmortem humiliation through mutilation, and display. Turvey observed experimental behavior, as opposed to ritualistic, and a need to instill fear or terror in the public. Turvey states, "they [offender behaviors] describe an offender who evidences both anger-retaliatory and reassurance-oriented behaviors." Specific to anger-retaliatory, the offender attacks the very identity of a woman, indicative of misogyny. Reassurance-oriented behaviors come from a feeling of personal inadequacy and are intended to restore self-confidence and self-worth. Collecting souvenirs, such as the organs or Chapman's rings, is a "token of remembrance." Turvey states that this is commonly associated with reassurance-oriented needs.

While the ruthlessness of the attacks can easily be explained by anger-retaliatory behavior, the collection of organs can be explained by reassurance-oriented behavior. There is, though, another possible explanation that is supported by evidence: the obsession with creating an elixir of health or life.

Tumblety was ill before he died—an event he deeply feared but which was preceded by both public and private symptoms, instilling within him a profound preoccupation with curing himself. Neurosyphilis is a tertiary stage of syphilis, which can manifest itself years after the initial contraction of syphilis. When did Tumblety discover that he contracted this incurable progressive disease? Tumblety took an unusually long trip to Europe, arriving in England on May 2, 1878, and returning to New York City in April 1880. He spent a fair amount of time in France. According to the *Evening Post*, October 16, 1878, Tumblety was registered at the banking house of Drexel, Harjes & Co. in Paris "for the week ending September 28." In the October 28, 1878, edition, Tumblety was still in Paris "for the week ending October 12." Soon after Tumblety returned from Europe in April 1880, he began his periodic trips to watering holes and health spas, such as Hot Springs, Arkansas. This means that Tumblety abruptly changed his decades-long lifestyle of traveling to cities, opening up an herb office, and publicly advertising. The very last time he advertised was in California in 1878. Changing his entire lifestyle and travel behavior first in Europe and then in the United States by including trips to watering holes suggests he knew about his syphilis. One possibility as to why Tumblety took the unusually long trip to Europe was to find a cure for his syphilis. In the nineteenth century, the University of Paris was at the forefront of medical research. In his 1872 autobiography, Tumblety even claimed medical credentials from Paris, France.

Tumblety being aware that he had syphilis is a perfect motive for anger-retaliatory behavior. If he did release his rage upon those whom he believed were responsible for his exposure to this incurable disease, then on or about 1880 would have been the time he began his assaults and murders in the United States. Corroborating this assertion is an eyewitness account of Tumblety's threatening mindset against sex workers in 1881. Young Richard Norris started an annual relationship with Tumblety, which went on for twenty years, in New Orleans during Mardi Gras season in 1881. Norris admitted in a sworn deposition in 1905 that he made extra money as a young man by being a sex worker but claimed he merely accepted Tumblety's offer to come to his room to write a letter. It was at this time that he saw Tumblety's collection of surgical knives in his travel chest, and a few weeks later Tumblety put one of those knives to Norris's throat to sexually molest him. Before the molestation, Tumblety pulled a cigarette out of Norris's mouth and gave him a cigar. According to Norris,

Tumblety then said that there are two things wrong with young men: cigarettes and streetwalkers. Tumblety then added,

> "They [streetwalkers] should all be disemboweled."

Norris made a curious comment to the attorney deposing him when he met up with Tumblety just after the Whitechapel murders in February 1889. Tumblety admitted to him that he was in the Whitechapel District during the murders. It was evident that Norris, a man who likely knew Tumblety better than almost anyone, especially his secretive side, was convinced Tumblety was Jack the Ripper. The attorney asked, "During your acquaintanceship with Dr. Tumilty, of over twenty years, you had occasion to notice his peculiarities and habits?" Norris replied:

> It seems to me he had peculiar habits, every night going through all the dark streets, walking like a Street Walker. He would take the darkest streets, and the darkest spots at night, and at one and two o'clock in the morning he would walk up Camp street, and all the dark streets and dark corners. I used to watch him very close because I did not know what kind of fellow he was.

The attorney also asked, "You had occasion to judge as to his mind?" Norris replied:

> Well, I am no doctor, but from his manner—his hobby was that women should be killed; that is, honestly, why I was afraid to go with him.

The term, "hobby," is not a word one would use to refer to a person who only murdered in one particular year but to refer to a person who continuously killed. It suggests that Norris suspected Tumblety fit the profile of a serial killer. Coincidentally, we see unsolved cases of women being brutally murdered without being raped, in a nighttime hit-and-run fashion, on the streets in locations where Tumblety was known to be beginning in 1882. Additionally, it was common knowledge among Tumblety's acquaintances that he walked the slums at night, staying on the darkest side of the street.

Another habit that Tumblety changed around 1880 was how he dressed. His nephew Thomas Powderly was asked in court under oath in 1905 about Tumblety visiting Powderly's mother in Waterloo, New York, and he recalled the time his uncle spent two weeks with them in 1880. Powderly stated that he had met Tumblety forty to fifty times. When asked by the attorney how peculiar his uncle dressed, Powderly remarked on a change in appearance before the two-week visit in 1880 and after:

> Sometimes he would dress very neat, and then again two or three days he would put on old clothes and go out on the street . . . Previous to that time he used to dress awful neat, and always looked well, always had fine clothes with him, all the time.

Thomas Powderly was family, so he likely knew Tumblety better than mere acquaintances. Recall, Tumblety stated to the *New York World* reporter in January 1889 that he was walking the Whitechapel streets at night and dressed so as to not bring attention to himself. It seems this habit of dressing down for walks on the street at night in order to blend in began about the same time he knew he had syphilis. It was also around this time when women were being assaulted and murdered at night on the streets in America without being raped or robbed.

An apparent contradiction to Tumblety having NPD, specifically, lacking remorse, are the times he graciously wrote self-help essays for the public in major newspapers and the times he gave money to certain charities, as published in the *New York Herald*. This, though, can be viewed as evidence not of his concern for others but of the selfish motive of repairing his public persona.

An example of the self-help medical/philosophical essays Tumblety published was in the *Burlington Weekly Free Press*, June 9, 1892, titled, "A Parent's Duty to the Young," where he passed on advice in parenting. He signed the article, "Dr. F. Tumblety," letting the reader know that his advice was professional but also free.

The second supposed selfless activity Tumblety participated in was donating financial gifts, handled by the *New York Herald*, which began in 1891 and ended in 1893. In the July 22, 1891, issue of the *Herald*, an article reported that Tumblety donated a check for $323.75 to assist an American stowaway named Frank Sherman. It was a donation applauded by the paper. On August 22, 1891, the *New York Herald* published an article titled, "Dr. Tumblety's Kindness," covering Tumblety's donation to another cause:

> He sends to the Herald Money to Pay for Baths for Four Thousand Persons
>
> To the Editor of the Herald: I cordially indorse the Herald's opinion that cheap baths are a blessing to the poor. Enclosed please find my check for $200. Please purchase tickets and supply the needy with them, and oblige—Francis Tumblety, M.D.—Bar Harbor, August 19, 1891.

In the *New York Herald*, June 6, 1893, was an article titled, "Help the Ice Charity." It was the *New York Herald*'s appeal for funds for the Free Ice Charity. In the article, "Francis Tumblety, MD" was listed as giving $100:

> Late Sunday evening Dr. Francis Tumblety gave notice that he would have $100 at the Herald office on Monday morning and he was as good as his word. It is interesting to note in this connection that Dr. Tumblety was also the very first subscriber to the fund last year. He is a firm believer in the efficiency of charity to save life and refresh the sick, and consequently doubles his subscription for the work of the coming season.

While on the surface it looks like Tumblety was merely being altruistic, curiously, the only time he ever wrote for the papers and ever gave to charity was between 1891 and 1893. If Tumblety was truly magnanimous, then it begs the question as to why his generosity was never extended throughout any other time in his life. The answer to this clearly lies in what he published immediately after his last donation: his 1893 autobiography. In it, he goes into detail about every essay he wrote and every charitable gift he gave. He even published responses to these charities in his autobiography. For example, Tumblety stated, "Extract of a letter received from Dr. F.E. Shepardson: Dear Doctor, I am pleased to see the good that you are doing. There is no doubt but what your money was well spent, and that the recipients of your generosity appreciated your kindness" (p. 98). Another example, "Extract of a letter . . . July 21, 1891: Dear Dr. Tumblety, I was delighted in reading in today's Harold [sic] your manly and democratic letter, enclosing your check for the amount of $323.75 for the release of the young man Sherman" (p. 99).

Tumblety's charitable donations ended abruptly in 1893, yet he maintained his wealth of over three million dollars in today's value up to his death in 1903. He was wealthy enough to continue to give to the underprivileged, yet he did not. While only donating to charity for two years of his life does not conform to being a charitable person, it does conform to a narcissist exploiting the press and packing his 1893 autobiography with "selfless" activities. Recall that his abruptly written 1889 autobiography was an attempt to repair his reputation from the scandalous Jack the Ripper murders by publishing testimonials from prominent friends. Republishing his autobiography only four years later with his many noble deeds would further improve the reputation of his public persona for the very same reason.

CHAPTER 7

A TASTE FOR RELEASING RAGE UPON WOMEN
1880 TO 1882

When?

If Tumblety was assaulting and murdering women in the United States, the motive behind the crimes most certainly would have been anger-retaliatory due to a combination of having a lifelong bitter hatred of women, convinced that they were the curse of the land, and he himself contracting one of those curses—the incurable and progressive disease of syphilis. As defined by experts, "A trigger is a short happening in the life of a serial killer, which activates the underlying killer instinct and towards the first murder." Tumblety would have been ripe for murder, being easily triggered to kill by any relatively small yet unwanted event. Because of this, we should expect to find homicides around the year 1880. Changes in Tumblety's travel behavior, specifically traveling to Hot Springs, Arkansas, for the medical treatment of hot baths, suggests he knew of his affliction. Recall that, in the late nineteenth century, Hot Springs was the mecca for syphilis patients. There is sworn eyewitness testimony that Tumblety began his trips to Hot Springs in 1880 or 1881. In the court case in 1905 contesting Tumblety's will, John Geary, a resident of Hot Springs "for thirty years" and owner of a lodging house, the Geary House, was questioned. The attorney asked Geary if Tumblety was a frequent visitor to Hot Springs, and Geary replied:

> Well, yes; I think something like twenty years; he told me last winter [Note: The last time Tumblety visited Hot Springs was the winter of 1902/1903] that he had been coming here for twenty two years. I don't know that I was acquainted with him for the first year or so, but I knowed him about twenty years.

Geary specifically said "twenty two years," which means the first time Tumblety visited Hot Springs was the year 1880 or 1881. Indeed, it was in 1880 that Thomas Powderly noticed an abrupt change in the style of clothing Tumblety wore as he walked the streets. Before 1880, Tumblety wore his flashy, expensive clothing; after 1880, he wore plain clothing to not bring attention to himself. According to numerous eyewitness testimonies of Tumblety out on the street at night, over his plain clothing he always wore an overcoat.

There is another small window into Tumblety's feelings about women in the early 1880s, thanks to an eyewitness account of a young man Tumblety had a relationship with, Martin H. McGarry. As published in the *New York World*, December 5, 1888, a *World* reporter stood outside 79 East 10th Street the night previous in hopes of speaking with Tumblety, who had recently arrived back in New York after jumping bail in London and hiding out in the lodging house. McGarry arrived at the location with the same intentions, but he was also rebuffed by the proprietor, Mrs. McNamara. Upon striking up a conversation, McGarry told the reporter that he was hired by Tumblety in 1882 as a travel companion. Tumblety had told McGarry that he was a retired army surgeon, the son of a wealthy Irish gentleman, and went to medical school at the University of Dublin. He also told McGarry that his father died and "left him a big lot of money." These, of course, were all lies to ensnare McGarry, which clearly worked. The reporter asked McGarry about Tumblety's "aversion to women," and McGarry said:

> He always disliked women very much. He used to say to me: "Martin, no women for me." He could not bear to have them near him. He thought all women were impostors, and he often said that all the trouble in this world was caused by women.

Considering Tumblety had just discovered he was inflicted with an incurable, progressive disease, his condition would clearly be included in "the trouble in this world." Since the evidence shows that he knew he had syphilis around the year 1880, it was appropriate to search through digitized US newspaper archives for women being murdered or assaulted beginning around that time with the following restrictions in mind. If a murder or assault ended in the apprehension and conviction of a suspect, I excluded it even though there was certainly a high percentage of innocent people being convicted. If the motive of an assault or murder was clearly sado-sexual or robbery and not anger-retaliatory, I ignored the case. Additionally, if the victim was raped, then I dismissed the case. Even though rape certainly fits into anger-retaliatory behavior, it was impossible for Tumblety to have raped due to his condition of having an unusable micropenis the size of the tip of a person's thumb.

If Tumblety was clearly not in the area, such as being overseas on his trips to Europe, I also discounted murders occurring in America during that time. Between 1878 and April 1880, Tumblety spent most of his time in Europe. In view of this, plus his knowledge of his affliction around 1880, searching for assaults and murders in the United States that Tumblety was potentially involved in should begin no earlier than April 1880.

Determining his annual travel locations and patterns can be used to establish whether or not to consider a case attributable to Tumblety, thus, possibly excluding it from consideration. Even after 1880, there were times Tumblety was not in the United States. McGarry stated that he traveled with Tumblety throughout the United States and the United Kingdom beginning in July 1882, stating:

> One day he told me he wanted to see Boston, and off we started for Boston, and then visited New Haven and Philadelphia, when we stopped at the Girard Hotel in Philadelphia. It took us three weeks to see the sights in Philadelphia. The Doctor showed me everything. We came back to New York and the Doctor took it in his mind to go to Glasgow. I wouldn't go with him and he went alone. He was back in a month, and went to Mrs. McNamara's No. 79 East Tenth street to live. He telegraphed for me to come there and I lived with him for three weeks. We knocked about New York during that time and he then persuaded me to go to Queenstown with him.

What McGarry's recollections show is that Tumblety was a constant traveler and sometimes traveled alone even when he had a young male travel companion. It also shows that Tumblety would stay at 79 East 10th Street throughout the 1880s and would sometimes stay for up to three weeks before traveling again.

Tumblety constantly traveled by train, only staying in one city for a few weeks at most. Although a transient, he was relatively consistent in his annual travels. For example, he made annual, or bi-annual, trips to locations such as Hot Springs, Arkansas; St. Louis, Missouri; New Orleans, Louisiana, during Mardi Gras season; Rochester, New York; Chicago, Illinois; New York City; Washington DC; and Boston, Massachusetts. The numerous train stops between these cities also guaranteed his presence in other cities and towns, such as Cincinnati, Ohio, and Pittsburgh, Pennsylvania.

Lastly, if there was a clear physical description of the offender and it did not match Tumblety, those cases were eliminated. The suspect must be considered tall and wear clothing such as an overcoat or hat, which Tumblety was known to have owned.

The newspapers at the time rarely used the word "rape," however, often referring to it as the victim being "outraged" or "sexually assaulted." For example, a rape/murder in Denver was reported in the *Philadelphia Inquirer*, May 5, 1890:

> DENVER, Col., May 4. – Mrs. Butler, a widow lady, residing on South Eleventh street, was found lying on the floor of her room this morning dead. Her clothes were torn off, the body badly bruised and there were other indications of a desperate struggle had taken place. The physicians say the woman had been outraged and then murdered.

On numerous occasions, officials told the reporter that the killer first raped his victim and then murdered her to avoid being discovered. In their mind, the only person to get them put in prison and/or have them executed can never speak. In an Associated Press article published in numerous local newspapers, a young woman from Macon, Missouri, named Emma Rachels was murdered and then thrown into a well:

> She [Emma Rachels] had been missing for two days when her father's well was searched, and there she was found dead, with indications that she had been murdered and thrown in the well. A coroner's inquest was held and it was decided that she came to her death by being murdered by unknown parties. It is believed that she had been betrayed, outraged, murdered and then her body was concealed in the well.
>
> —*Manhattan Mercury*, February 5, 1890.

Most murder stories of women also reported an arrest and a conviction of someone local, such as a male acquaintance, farmhand, or townsperson. Case in point, according to the *St. Joseph Weekly Gazette*, August 13, 1891, a wife and daughter were murdered in Severance, Kansas, "Mrs. D. J. Smith, the daughter of the woman murdered here last evening by her husband, died to-day of hemorrhage of the brain." Sadly, over two hundred women were reported to be murdered—often raped first—in the United States in the late nineteenth century. There were *at least* twenty-three in the year 1891 alone, many others either not discovered in the search or never having been reported in the newspapers. In order to give them one last voice, their names (as reported) are included here: Mary Munson, Laura Burnell, Mrs. Smith & daughter D. J. Smith, Miss Wellesley, Agnes Laurence, Miss Goodson, Nellie Ryan, East River Hotel victim, Mary Hensoldt, Fannie Bell, Carrie Humphreys, Mrs. Greenwood, Mary Hensoldt, Emma Hoskins, Blanche Mckey, Mrs. William Nibch, Mrs. Barnaby, Mrs. Nelson, Mrs. Belle of Denmark, two daughters of William Smith, and Mary Tobin.

Of the hundreds of these murders of women in the late nineteenth century in the United States that were reported in the newspapers, thirty-nine unsolved murders fit into the strict restrictions stated above, meaning Tumblety cannot be eliminated as having committed the crimes. If we add the hundreds of assaults on women that did not end up in a homicide, the total number of unsolved murders and assaults that successfully fit into these restrictions is at least seventy! The details of these cases will be discussed. None of these cases showed a motive of rape or robbery, the two most common motives reported. Reporters and police officials used the term "mysterious," for these cases since a motive was not apparent to them. A link that was revealed in comparison, and which connects nearly all of these sixty assaults and murders, is close proximity to train tracks or having happened near a train station.

The following are the mysterious, unsolved murders and assaults of women that occurred between 1880 and 1882—the period when Tumblety's syphilis had yet progressed into the tertiary stage (a progression about which he may have been ignorant until he began his acquaintance with Dr. Graham Hammond, just a few years before the Whitechapel murders). Otherwise generally healthy, Tumblety's life certainly changed from working on his business to visiting watering holes to soothe his aches and pains. During this time, there were vicious, unsolved, mysterious murders in the United States, as well as a number of assaults, that bore the hallmarks of disorganized and sudden rage attacks from a transient stranger getting a taste for murder.

DID TUMBLETY FINALLY PULL THE TRIGGER? – AUGUST 1880

As compared to other years in the 1880s and 1890s, 1880 had a low number of assaults and murders of women in the United States as reported in the newspaper archives. Most of the murders and assaults that did occur involved the victim being raped and are therefore excluded from examination here. Also, most of these cases were solved, ending in a conviction, and thus are excluded. One particular unsolved murder was different, and coincidentally, it was quite similar to the Jack the Ripper murders. The offender invested extra time and energy on overkill, nearly severing the girl's head with a large knife along with mutilating her body. This is exactly what to expect in a rage killing, exhibiting anger-retaliatory behavior. According to the *Boston Evening Transcript*, August 19, 1880:

> Wednesday [August 18] forenoon, about eleven o'clock, as Captain Joel Sargent of West Hill, Barnstable, Mass., was going through the Kelly woods, about a mile from the village, he saw something white in a brush heap on the side of the road, directly opposite the old Cody Schoolhouse, which aroused his curiosity. Proceeding to the spot and removing some of the brush, he beheld the body of a young girl, terribly mutilated, the head being nearly severed from the body, and a large butcher knife sticking in her left side. . . . The body was recognized as that of Mary Cassidy, fifteen years old, daughter of Mrs. Hannah Cassidy, a respected widow of Barnstable.

Sadly, there were no eyewitness accounts of anyone in the area. Since the village of Barnstable is only a quarter mile from the beach to the north and a half mile from the beach to the south, this would put the location of the attack within walking distance to the railroad tracks traversing on an east–west course just south of the village. The reports made no mention of Cassidy having also been raped, suggesting there was no evidence to support that crime. Further, the overkill and ferocity of the attack are what is seen in a rage murder as opposed to a sado-sexual murder.

Tumblety was back on the East Coast of the United States at the time, and it was at this time that Tumblety lost a court case, along with thousands of dollars. After Tumblety had arrived in New York City in April 1880, he was soon involved in a court case where he claimed a young man named Joseph Lyons and his mother stole from him. According to the *Rochester Democrat and Republican*, December 3, 1888, Attorney William Burr told a *New York World* reporter the details. Burr stated that he met with Tumblety in July 1888:

> I met him in July, 1880. He brought a suit against a Mrs. Lyons, charging her with the larceny of $7,000 worth of bonds, and I was retained to defend her. It seems that several years before he met the son of Mrs. Lyons [Joseph Lyons] while walking on the Battery. The lad had just come from college and was a fine looking young man. He was out of employment. Tumblety greeted him and soon had him under complete control. He made him a sort of secretary

in the management of his bonds, of which he had about $100,000 worth, mostly in governments, locked up in a downtown safe-deposit company. He employed the young as an amanuensis... On April 23, 1878, the "Doctor," as he was called, started for Europe by the Guion line steamer Montana. See, here is his name on the passenger-list, "Dr. Tumblety." He gave a power of attorney to the young man, and under that some South Carolina railroad bonds were disposed of, as it was claimed and shown, under an agreement that they were to be taken as compensation. When Tumblety got back the young man had disappeared and the mother was arrested, charged by the "Doctor" with having taken the bonds... I remember well how indignant he became when I asked him what institution had the honor of graduating so precious a pupil... He refused to answer, and I thought he would spring at me to strike. There was quite a commotion in court. The case fell through and the lady was not held...

The *New York Herald Tribune*, July 2, 1880, stated that the young man's name was Joseph J. Lyons, and the elderly lady was Mary Lyons, living at 257 West Houston Street, but there was a slight mistake. Researcher Roger Palmer used the address and discovered that Mary Lyons was Joseph's mother and the elderly lady Tumblety sued was Mary's mother, Catherine. The *New York Tribune* stated that the elderly lady's daughter accompanied her to the Tombs Police Court, so it is clear the reporter mixed the mother's name with the daughter's name.

If Tumblety had to release his rage, it would have been at this time. Losing a court case to a woman may have been the trigger that caused him to finally step over the line and brutally murder fifteen-year-old Mary Cassidy. Burr even commented that Tumblety was filled with enough rage in court to possibly attack him. Also, it is not beyond reason to see him releasing his rage upon those whom he hated most, unmarried women. Tumblety was then in Toronto, Canada, in October 1880, when, according to his nephew Thomas Powderly, he was arrested for sodomy. Tumblety stayed with the Powderly family in Waterloo, New York, at the end of October into November 1880.

DRAGGING HER TO A DARK, EMPTY LOT – MAY & AUGUST 1881

There were two similar assaults on women in May and August 1881 that involved a man surprising them grabbing them then attempting to drag them to a more secure location. While there is no physical description of the offender, the nighttime attacks were very similar to the attacks made by the tall man in the gray Ulster coat in Buffalo in 1886 and Chicago in 1888, and the physical description in those attacks matches Tumblety. The first was reported in the *Brooklyn Daily Eagle*, May 2, 1881, involving a thirteen-year-old girl named Minnie Sneideker, near a vacant lot on DeKalb Avenue in Brooklyn:

> [Minnie Sneideker] . . . was suddenly seized by an unknown man, who put his hand over her mouth and tried to drag her into the lot. Her screams attracted the attention of Officer Skelton, of the Fourth Precinct, and her assailant ran off and made his escape.

The second assault was reported in the *Brooklyn Daily Eagle*, August 15, 1881, stating:

> On Saturday night the wife of G. Ross Cary, the manager of Western Union Telegraph office in Exchange Place, Jersey City, was attacked on Montgomery avenue about 9 o'clock, as she was on her way home from visiting some friends. She is 50 years of age. A man sprang out upon her from behind a large wall, and attempted to drag her to the roadside, threatening her with instant death if she cried out. She screamed for assistance and struggled violently, and at this the ruffian struck her a powerful blow in the face. Her cries attracted three men, who came running down the road, and the ruffian fled. She suffered no injury, save from the blow and the fright.

In both cases, an unknown man surprised the female victim out on the street at night and then attempted to forcibly drag her to a dark empty lot. While there is not enough information to reasonably connect these assaults with Francis Tumblety, especially since there are no reported physical descriptions of the assailant, keep them in mind when we discuss a March 1896 murder along the same train route as Jersey City, when a tall man in a gray Ulster coat murdered a young woman at night by grabbing her and dragging her to an empty lot.

THE VICTIM OF A QUACK – MAY 1881

Thanks to a portion of the coroner's inquest having been published in contemporary newspapers, we have a unique opportunity to review the details of a May 1881 unsolved murder and mutilation of a young woman on Long Island, New York. According to the *Brooklyn Daily Eagle*, September 4, 1881, the remains of a young woman were found in the woods near Freeport, Long Island, on Friday, August 26, 1881:

> The head, arms and legs were cut off, and the internal organs removed. The head and arms were wrapped in one bundle, and the body and legs in another.

Coroner J. H. Denton, of Hampstead, began a coroner's inquest on Saturday, August 27, 1881. Denton's opinion was that the woman had fallen victim to malpractice; the product of an abortion gone wrong where the parties involved attempted to dispose of the body. Because an abandoned wagon was found near the area, Denton believed that the victim was attacked "a few miles from where the butchered body was found." He also concluded that the remains were brought from Manhattan and then deposited in the woods of Long Island:

> The bundle must have been carried across the fields, or along the railroad track, for a considerable distance, as there is no public thoroughfare within a quarter of a mile of the woods in which the bundles were deposited.

At the inquest, the young man who found the body, Joseph Ritchie, testified that the woods were owned by Mrs. Raynor R. Smith. He also stated that the location where the remains were found was only four hundred feet from the railroad tracks of the Montauk Railroad and just three-quarters of a mile from the Freeport Depot.

A Dr. Raine testified as to his inspection of the remains, stating that the victim was a female of about thirty years of age. After extensive detail of the condition of the remains, he stated that the skin of the throat had cuts from a sharp instrument. He also saw no fractures to the skull.

According to the *New York Times*, October 30, 1881, in an article titled, "The Victim of a Quack," the police revealed the identity of the woman. Her name was Ella, or Ellie, Clark, aged twenty-seven, who had formerly lived in New York City but had moved to Stamford, Connecticut, where she had worked as a domestic servant for the wealthy Brooks family for the last five years. The Long Island detective in charge, Detective Steven Payne, determined that she had come to New York City specifically to get an abortion. The *New York Times* article continues:

> It is known that here [New York City] she sought the assistance of a notorious quack. It is believed that he killed her by his quack treatment, and then

cut up her remains, packed them in the manner in which they were found, and caused them to be removed from the City in the hope that the crime would never be brought to light. Coroner Denton says that this man is now under the constant surveillance of the New York Police, and that his arrest on the charge of malpractice in only a question of time... How the body was removed from this City is still a mystery.

According to the *Brooklyn Daily Eagle*, November 27, 1881, Ella Clark was involved in a love triangle with the family's coachman, John Spencer, and another domestic servant, Ellen Mills. While Ella Clark was intimate with Spencer and wanted him, Spencer decided to marry Ellen Mills. Ella Clark had gotten pregnant, then decided to have an abortion.

The comments in the *New York Times* article about a quack doctor in New York City that Clark went to see immediately bring up the possibility that this man was the quack doctor Francis Tumblety. However, it was not. The physician Clark sought out was Dr. James C. Thomas, whose office was at 107 W. 47th Street. Thomas lived in what was, and is, the Diamond District of Manhattan. In the early nineteenth century, diamond merchants established themselves on 47th Street. Immediately west of the Diamond District is the Theater District of Manhattan, where most of the established theaters were. In fact, 107 W. 47th Street is at the northern border of the Tenderloin District and could be considered part of the Tenderloin.

Soon, the inquest determined the series of events from when Ella Clark left Stamford, Connecticut, to when she went missing in New York City. According to the *New York Times*, November 27, 1881, and the *Brooklyn Daily Eagle*, December 11, 1881, Ella Clark came to New York City on May 2, 1881, and arrived at her brother's Manhattan home at 740 3rd Avenue, which was a few blocks from Grand Central Station. Her brother's name was Lawrence Clark. According to the New York Transit Museum, New York City banned soot-belching steam engines south of 42nd Street, keeping the pollution away from the major population area. The magnificent Grand Central Train Depot opened on 42nd Street in 1871, which connected all rail traveling north and northeast to locations such as Albany, New York, and Boston, Massachusetts.

Lawrence testified at the inquest stating that he brought Ella to a friend of hers on May 2, a Mrs. Kennedy of 327 E. 27th Street. Ella never told Lawrence that she was pregnant; just that she needed to see Dr. Thomas. Lawrence stated that he never saw Ella again and contacted Mrs. Kennedy nine or ten days later.

Kennedy told him she had not seen Ella since May 5. Lawrence then reported her missing to the police.

Mrs. Kennedy testified to the jurors that Ella stayed at her home from May 2 to May 4 and then left to visit Dr. Thomas at his office. She brought with her a satchel and a bundle. Kennedy then stated that Ella returned that same day, telling her that Dr. Thomas was not home. Kennedy noticed that Ella no longer had the satchel and bundle. Kennedy then stated that Ella left for Dr. Thomas's office the next morning on May 5, never to see her again.

A *New York Times* reporter spoke directly to Dr. James C. Thomas, who stated:

> I will tell you very gladly all that I know about the matter. Something like five years ago the girl was in the habit of calling to see my cook and the latter one day asked me if I could not find a place for her friend Ella. I replied that my business was not hunting places for servants, but that I would see if I could not secure a situation for her. The wife of Mr. Thomas Brooks, now of Stamford, Conn., but who at that time was residing on East Forty Fourth Street, between fifth and Madison avenues, was in need of a servant and took the girl into her family and she became a great favorite, and Mrs. Brooks, I learned, regarded her as her best servant. Before I proceed further I will say now that I never saw the girl professionally, and I never saw her to my knowledge after the family of Mr. Brooks left New York.

Dr. Thomas then told the reporter that, in May or June, Ella Clark's brother approached him on the street and told him that his sister had said she was coming down from Stamford to be under his care. He told the brother that he had never seen her at all. Dr. Thomas then told the reporter that the first time he heard that Ella Clark went missing and then was murdered was from reading the newspapers. He then said that Mrs. Kennedy—although he did not know her name—approached him on the same day he read about the murder in the papers:

> . . . a woman came to my house and asked to see me. She was crying when I entered my office. She inquired "Are you Dr. Thomas?" I told her that I was, and she surprised me by exclaiming, "I'm going to be arrested and so are you." I asked what for and she said on account of the Ella Clark affair. The woman said that the girl came to her house and stayed a week. She told the woman that I had treated her and was very kind to her. When she left the woman's house she said she was going to my house to stay. I informed the woman that

I was not in the habit of admitting patients to my house. In fact it was a thing that I never had done and what was more I never would do it . . . It is quite evident that the girl Ella Clark used my name as a cloak and a cover to her acts and movements.

Even though the Dr. Thomas lead for investigators was promising at first, it was a dead end. Police became convinced that Ella Clark never met up with Dr. Thomas. Still, an Associated Press article, as published in the *Buffalo Morning Express*, November 18, 1882, reported that the verdict rendered by the coroner's jury was that Ella Clark was the victim of malpractice.

Once all leads from New York City dried up, Detective Payne's attention was then on Long Island where the dismembered body was found. Payne continued to believe that Clark died from an abortion gone wrong and became convinced it must have been a Long Island physician. He was first convinced it was Dr. Charles R. Smith, of Freeport. An article in the *New York Times*, March 8, 1882, began:

> On Saturday last Stephen Payne, a local detective, residing at Baldwins, Long Island, made a complaint against Dr. Charles R. Smith, of Freeport, before Justice Losee, of feloniously placing the dead body of Ella Clark in the woods at Freeport with the intent to conceal the murderer.

Dr. Smith, though, insisted on his day in court to clear his name. Smith went to the justice, gave himself up, and demanded an examination. After reviewing the arguments and evidence, the justice discharged him from custody.

Curiously, Detective Payne, who was completely convinced Dr. Smith had killed Clark, became just as convinced that it was a different physician from Long Island one year later. According to the *Brooklyn Union*, May 4, 1883:

> Detective Payne, who has been long working on the case, claims to have secured proof that the remains were those of Ella E. Clark, of Bridgeport, Conn., who was missing from her home in April or May 1881, and that she was brought to the house of Mrs. Morgan Carman, at Milburn, now accused of causing the death of Mrs. Sidney S. Smith, of Oceanville, by malpractice, and that Ella Clark died at Mrs. Carman's from the effects of criminal medical practice.

Morgan Carman was never charged with the murder of Ella Clark, and the murder remains unsolved to this day. Detective Payne was consecutively convinced that Dr. Thomas was the cause of Clark's death, then Dr. Smith, and finally Morgan Carman. What all three failed leads have in common is that Detective Payne, along with the coroner, assumed—as fact—that Ella Clark died during a failed abortion. It may have been true, but recall that the organs were missing from the corpse. There was no physical evidence that Ella Clark had received an abortion. Also, Payne and the coroner believed that the offender wrapped the body parts and threw them into the woods to keep them from ever being discovered. This leads to a problem. If someone, especially a physician who had an office near the woods where the body parts were found, was attempting to dispose of the body parts in order not to be connected to Ella Clark, why leave the head with the rest of the body? If by chance the corpse was discovered, only the head (at that time) could be used to identify the victim. A physician would have known this. Once the victim was identified, detectives could piece the puzzle of her known whereabouts together, as they did with Ella Clark. Chances of getting caught rise exponentially with the head in the picture. Burying the head in a separate location, or even burning it, would have been so easy.

There is another possibility that matches the evidence: Ella Clark had a fatal encounter with a serial killer after leaving Mrs. Kennedy's home. Ella Clark left her home on the morning of May 5, 1881, with the full intention of getting an abortion. Mrs. Kennedy recalled that when Clark returned to her home on May 4, she did not have the satchel and bundle and said that she would be *returning* to the quack doctor's office for the next few days. A logical answer is that Ella Clark met up with someone on May 4, whom she believed was going to give her an abortion, then left the satchel and bundle at their office. If it was not Dr. Thomas who Ella Clark met up with, which quack doctor, or so-called abortion expert, did she ultimately encounter? Clark had lived in New York City for over twenty years of her life and, thus, would have known the area, including people and businesses. There were likely very few quack doctors in that particular section of Manhattan, and less than one square mile from Mrs. Kennedy's home was the location of Francis Tumblety's office at 77 E. 10th Street. Attorney William Burr recalled Tumblety still having an office in Manhattan just seven months earlier, in the late summer of 1880, as reported in the *Rochester Democrat and Republican*, December 3, 1888. In Burr's comments, he said:

> At this time [beginning in July 1888] he [Tumblety] kept an herb store, or something of that sort, at No. 77 East Tenth street.

Tumblety's office was also within walking distance due south on Park Avenue from Dr. Thomas's office and was actually one-third the distance closer to Mrs. Kennedy's home than Dr. Thomas's office. While we cannot be certain that Ella Clark met up with Francis Tumblety the quack doctor—and future Jack the Ripper suspect—the coincidences are intriguing. Tumblety had promoted his skills in dealing with medical issues, such as abortions, in the past. He had given a young Protestant woman medicine to abort in Montreal, Canada, many years earlier. Further, Tumblety was known to have been in New York City in May 1881. According to the *Leavenworth Times*, May 25, 1881, Tumblety filed a lawsuit against the *New York Times* for not retracting its report on his arrest and incarceration in New Orleans for allegedly pickpocketing the pocketbook of Henry Govan just two months earlier. He had to have been in New York City to file the lawsuit.

There is even the possibility of a chance encounter of Ella Clark meeting Tumblety just on the street because this was Tumblety's backyard. Ella's brother, Lawrence, lived next to Grand Central Station, a location the transient Tumblety was constantly at when taking a train to Boston, Albany, or any location to the north. Dr. Thomas's office was in the Diamond District, and we know Tumblety always had on his person multiple diamonds. Additionally, just a few blocks west of Dr. Thomas's office was the Theater District, and Tumblety loved theater. When young Martin McGarry was hired by Tumblety to be his travel companion, McGarry told a reporter that Tumblety took him to the theater in Manhattan. According to the *New York World*, December 5, 1888:

> He took a liking to me, and that day I was employed by him. My duties were not hard. I was always to be near him. He got up at 11 o'clock when he would usually send out his jug for a pint of old ale. He breakfasted in the house and then walked around town. Usually he went up to the Morton House, where he pointed out the actors to me and told me who they were and what they did. Sometimes in the afternoons we would drop in to the matinees.

The Morton House was at 19 East 16th Street next to Union Square. Union Square was within walking distance, a few blocks to the west of Mrs. Kennedy's home. Lastly, Dr. Thomas's office was in the northernmost section of the Tenderloin, where Tumblety was known to prowl. Francis Tumblety had any number of reasons to encounter Ella Clark on the streets of New York City—planned or otherwise.

Recall that Ella Clark's corpse was found near the railroad tracks in Long Island, just east of Brooklyn. Clark's corpse had to have been moved south past the Brooklyn Bridge, which would have had to pass the last-known address of Tumblety's office (documented just months earlier) at 77 East 10th Street.

Even the condition of the corpse coincides with Tumblety's MO, not to mention that it was found near a railroad, Tumblety's preferred method of travel. The organs were missing. Because of Tumblety's interest in human organs, such as the time he attempted to steal the organs of James Portmore in St. John in 1860, it can be argued—if he was the killer—that just before or just after he dismembered the body, he kept them.

Tumblety was also interested in dismemberment, or amputation. Dr. J. H. Ziegler was the young physician with whom Tumblety spoke each night at St. John's Hospital in St. Louis in 1903 from May 2 to May 28—the latter being the day of Tumblety's death. Dr. Ziegler stated that Tumblety would discuss medicine with him daily and that Tumblety would quiz him on how to handle patients in an office setting in the country. He then pointed out that the questions Tumblety asked required medical knowledge. Ziegler stated that they talked about surgery, and Tumblety asked him what kind of operations he had seen. Ziegler stated, "He [Tumblety] would ask about an amputation; if I had seen any amputations, and I told him I had."

Note the surprising coincidence between Mary Cassidy and Ella Clark in connection with Tumblety. Just days before the Cassidy murder, Tumblety was wronged (in his mind) and lost the subsequent lawsuit case; just before Clark's death, Tumblety, who was wronged two months earlier, filed a lawsuit near the time of her death. Serial killer Andrew Urdiales admitted that when he was wronged in January 1986, he then went out searching for a woman to kill with a knife in order to release his rage. He found Robin Brandley, aged twenty-three, and stabbed her forty-one times. This rage attack was very similar to the attack of Whitechapel murders victim Martha Tabram, who was stabbed thirty-nine times in the early evening of August 7, 1888.

Even though the coincidences are numerous and intriguing, there is no direct evidence that the quack doctor Ella Clark likely went to on May 5 was Jack the Ripper suspect Dr. Francis Tumblety. Still, we *cannot eliminate* Tumblety as possibly having been the killer; therefore, Ella Clark's unsolved murder is worth considering in the list of possible murder cases attributable to Francis Tumblety. Either way, at least the Ella Clark case is no longer hidden from history.

SLAUGHTER OF THE INNOCENT – MARCH 1882

On March 2, 1882, a young Black woman named Anne Moorman was murdered in Lynchburg, Virginia, near Yellow Branch. According to the *New York Times*, March 4, 1882, Anne Moorman, or Estha/Eddie Anne Moorman, was murdered two days earlier. She was found in a thicket near the road after dark with her throat cut and two pistol wounds through the head. She was not reported to have been raped, especially since clothes were still on her body. Early suspicions were on a Black man named Jesse Slaughter, the intimate friend of Anne Moorman's mother. He was released for insufficient evidence, however, but they kept their suspicions on him. Two years later, he was rearrested, since some overalls covered with blood stains were found near the murder site that resembled overalls Slaughter wore. The belief was that Jesse Slaughter had an argument with her mother earlier that day and supposedly threatened her life. He then noticed who he thought was the mother walking down, so he shot her. The inference is, he slit her throat to ensure her death. According to the *Norfolk Virginian*, April 24, 1884, young Anne Moorman was wearing the mother's clothing, which caused Slaughter's confusion. There is no record that the case went to trial, likely because the evidence was weak.

Neither the police nor the press ever reported the possibility that the killer may have been someone who did not know Moorman, such as a transient making their way through the area. It is not surprising; they thought they already had their guy. While local law enforcement accepted that offender motive was neither rape nor robbery, they had little understanding of serial killer behavior. Anne Moorman's brutal murder by being shot and having her throat cut does indeed fit into the category of anger-retaliatory. The woman's slashed throat and the fact that she was outside is Ripper-like, but the two gunshot wounds are not. The December 1886 Buffalo assaults of women on the streets at night and the similar December 1888 Chicago assault, both in locations inhabited by a tall man in a gray Ulster coat, involved the suspect carrying a revolver. If the offender was Tumblety in all three cases, this makes sense. Recall, Tumblety was known to carry a revolver while he was traveling in the United States.

Curiously, Moorman was murdered near a railroad, which was part of a railway system Tumblety likely took if he did not take a steamer to New Orleans. In 1881, the Norfolk and Western Railway was formed from the Atlantic, Mississippi, and Ohio Railroad, which had a direct route from Cincinnati to Lynchburg and then to Washington DC. After his visit to New Orleans during Mardi Gras around February of each year between 1881 and 1902, he would then travel north on the Mississippi to his annual watering hole, Hot Springs, Arkansas. This naturally brought him to St. Louis, which connected to Cincinnati, and then to Lynchburg on his way back to New York City.

The second railway that connected New Orleans to Lynchburg and then to New York City was the Virginia Midland Railway. The significance of this railway is that the railroad travels directly through the Yellow Branch location of Moorman's murder before arriving at Lynchburg. Trains ran along the Appalachian Trail to Lynchburg, or Tumblety could have traveled to Hot Springs and then traveled through Memphis, Tennessee, to Lynchburg. Lawyers Road Train Station was within walking distance of the murder site.

Under sworn testimony, Richard Norris stated that Tumblety was in New Orleans each Mardi Gras season from 1881 to 1901. In 1882, Mardi Gras was on February 21, which means Tumblety passing through Lynchburg around March 2, 1882, was a definite possibility, even if he stopped at Hot Springs.

Sadly, there were no eyewitnesses to the murder, so we have no physical description of the killer. Still, we *cannot eliminate* Tumblety as the possible offender since the motive seems to have been anger-retaliatory, the murder was near the railway, and there is the possibility that Tumblety was in the area.

WICKED BRUTAL ATTACK ON THE WELCOME MAT – MARCH 1882

On March 7, 1882, a thirty-five-year-old woman was murdered in Boston with her throat deeply cut. On this occasion, an eyewitness saw the assailant. The *Boston Globe*, March 7, 1882, stated, "A few minutes past 8 o'clock this morning the neighborhood of Kirkland and Pleasant streets was in a perfect blaze of excitement. 'A woman murdered at 5 Kirkland street!' was the cry which quickly brought hundreds to the house." She rented the first floor of a three-story home with her thirteen-year-old daughter. At about eight A.M., the young woman yelled to her daughter to not be late for school. She then left the home for the corner store, Brown's Bakery, at 83 Pleasant Street for milk.

On her return, she was followed by a man. An eyewitness, a carpenter living at 9 Kirkland Street, stated that as the woman neared her front door, he heard the man yell, "Get in there!" The woman then replied, "Get along, I don't know you." As she opened the door, the man struck her on the right side of the neck with the blade of a large knife, causing a deep cut. She fell in the front hallway entry near the foot of the stairs. The daughter heard her yell, "Help! Murder!" The daughter helped her mother into the back room and called to the landlady for help. The woman soon died from the wounds. The daughter got a glimpse of the man and stated, "His back was turned towards me, but I saw the side of his face and part of his mustache. It was a thick mustache. He was a big man." In the *Boston Globe*, March 16, 1882, they gave further details of the wounds the woman received. The paper noted that the officer's statement had the first wound as a deep stab to the thigh penetrating about four inches. There were two cuts "on the left side," with one of those cuts penetrating the lung. The left arm was also cut in three places. In total, there were nine wounds.

In the *Boston Globe*, March 11, 1882, the carpenter described the assailant as a suspicious person of six feet tall to six feet two inches, with very broad shoulders, about forty-five to fifty years old, with sandy side whiskers and a mustache tinged with gray. His chin and cheeks were clean-shaven. He wore a dark-blue smooth overcoat with a velvet collar; a high, round crowned derby hat, black in color and somewhat worn; and dark pantaloons. In the *Hartford Courant*, March 8, 1882, a witness stated that this man was following her, attacking her, then following her into the house. He then waited for the assailant to come out, and as the man passed him, he followed. He stated that the man walked up Kirkland and then turned onto Pleasant Street. He continued to follow. At the corner of Pleasant and Tremont Streets, he met two police officers and told them, "That man has just now assaulted a woman on Kirkland street." One of the officers stated, "I guess it's only a family quarrel," and then asked if the carpenter was drunk. The carpenter stated, "The man, all this while, was going along quietly with both hands in his overcoat pockets. He looked around once and then passed on until he was lost sight of beyond the bridge."

According to the *Boston Globe*, March 12, 1882, at around seven thirty A.M., a man "about 40 years of age, tall and spare, about six feet in height, weighing about 170 pounds, wearing a round top hat and long blue overcoat buttoned up to the chin, and apparently under the influence of liquor, went to a well-known cutlery store on Washington street and asked to see some knives." The man then paid for a pocketknife. Then, at around seven fifty A.M., and about twenty-five minutes before the murder, a man fitting this description "rudely assaulted" another woman on the streets. In the *Boston Globe*, March 16, 1882, the woman stated that the man grabbed her by the arm and threw her down as if to get her out of his way.

In the *Boston Globe*, March 15, 1882, the report on the murder states that another woman claimed she was also assaulted: "The number of persons who were assaulted by the alleged murderer are increasing at an alarming extent. Now, a lady who lives on Shawmut Avenue, says that she was roughly spoken to by a man answering to the description of the murderer, on Tuesday noon."

Additionally, the article added, "Between 8 and 9 o'clock a man answering to the description was seen at the Know-nothing crossing, near the Boston & Providence railroad station, inquiring the time of the departure of trains for New York, and when told that the last one for some length of time had gone seemed quite disappointed, and disappeared."

There were a number of arrests, but in every case, it was a man who knew the victim. When the murder victim was attacked, the carpenter clearly heard her say, "I don't know you." All who were arrested were eventually cleared. The case remains unsolved.

According to Tumblety himself, he was six feet tall. While Tumblety was known to have dark hair, in the 1880s he waxed it and his thick mustache black. Upon his death in 1903, the undertaker stated Tumblety's hair and mustache were white. In this case, the murder was witnessed, and the offender's description fits Tumblety very well. If the man who rudely assaulted the lady on the street less than a half hour before the murder is the same man, his actions conform to misogynistic behavior very similar to what has been reported from Tumblety.

A man who fit the description of Tumblety was at the train station one hour after the murder, seeking to leave quickly for New York City, the city Tumblety called home. There is no direct evidence that Tumblety was in Boston in March 1882, but Boston was a city Tumblety visited in 1882 during his constant travels. Recall, in July 1882, Tumblety hired Martin McGarry to be his travel companion. McGarry told the reporter that his 1882 travel route included Boston, saying, "One day he told me he wanted to see Boston, and off we started for Boston, and then visited New Haven and Philadelphia, when we stopped at the Girard Hotel in Philadelphia. It took us three weeks to see the sights in Philadelphia. The Doctor showed me everything."

Tumblety's preferred mode of travel within the United States and Canada was by rail. If Tumblety was the killer and attempted to get back to New York City as quickly as possible, he would have gone to the train station, which is exactly what happened with the offender in this case.

According to an article in the *Chicago Tribune*, November 23, 1888, an old Boston resident recalled that Tumblety came to Boston in 1859 and opened up his quack doctor business in the Horticulture Building, which was at 211 Tremont Street. Notice that Tumblety's old office was within walking distance of the murder site. How interesting that the killer was last spotted on Tremont Street. The Boston & Providence Train Depot was around in 1859, so he likely used it. It is also quite close to the murder site, so the killer may very well have arrived at the Boston & Providence Train Depot.

DUMPED INTO A WATERY DITCH – MARCH 1882

According to the *Morning Post*, March 24, 1882, the body of Alice Faulkner, aged fourteen years, was found by two boys under the New York Central Railroad in Syracuse, New York, her body very decomposed. She was brutalized and dumped into a ditch filled with three feet of water. The *Evening Gazette*, March 27, 1882, gives greater detail:

> Thursday afternoon the body of a girl, about 14 years of age, was found floating in three feet of water in a ditch just outside of the city limits of Syracuse, and in the town of Salina. It was taken to an undertaker's room, where it was identified as that of Alice Faulkner, daughter of a farmer living in the vicinity of where the body was discovered. When found, the body was neatly clothed in a wine colored waisted dress and dark sacque [*sic*]. A brown felt hat with feathers was imbedded in the mud. There was a large wound in the temple and a discolored circle about the neck, denoting the pressure of a rope or hand. The wound on the temple was evidently inflicted by some blunt instrument but was not of a nature to cause death. Investigation showed that the girl, who is said to have possessed more than ordinary physical beauty, left her parents, and the mother had applied to the police for her recovery...

The *Ogdensburg Advance and St. Lawrence Weekly Democrat*, April 6, 1882, gives further information:

> The body of Alice Faulkner, aged 14, was found by boys floating in a ditch near the Central railroad crossing of the Liverpool road a mile from Syracuse, Thursday afternoon. She left home after a dispute with her parents four weeks ago.

While it was assumed that the young woman was raped, her body was decomposing in the watery ditch for a month, so there was no proof either way. Notice how similar the attack was to the attacks in Waterloo and Chicago in December 1888 and the Buffalo attacks in December 1886.

Faulkner's body was found near the railroad tracks, which may not have been a coincidence. Tumblety's nephew, Michael Fitzsimmons, stated under oath that Tumblety would periodically visit Rochester, New York, and his method of travel was by rail. Syracuse, New York, is situated between Rochester, New York, and Saratoga Springs, New York. In the *New York World*, December

5, 1888, Martin McGarry stated to a *World* reporter that this was exactly the route they took in the second half of 1882:

> After we saw everything about Rochester we went to Saratoga. The Doctor took rooms at No. 151 Congress street. It was the finest suite of rooms at the Springs . . .

Tumblety then made a second trip with McGarry to Rome, New York, which neighbors Syracuse immediately to the east:

> After a trip to Rome N.Y. we returned to New York and went to the Hygeia Hotel on Laight street, although the Doctor still kept his rooms on University Place.

Tumblety was the epitome of a transient, never staying in one location for more than a few weeks. This constant traveler, especially in the northeast, would have traveled through Syracuse numerous times each year.

In 2005, the FBI's Behavioral Analysis Unit-2 (BAU-2) at the National Center for Analysis of Violent Crime (NCAVC), the unit created to research serial murder, held a symposium composed of a hundred thirty-five subject-matter experts in the law enforcement field, mental health, academia, and the criminal justice community in order to put their heads together and better understand serial offenders. A general list of serial offender motives discussed and agreed upon were anger/rage, criminal enterprise, financial gain, ideology, power/thrill, psychosis, and sexually based. It was the consensus of the experts that the motives behind serial offenders may be a combination of motives and that an offender's motive can change even after the first murder. Take, for example, thirty-three-year-old serial killer Aileen Wuornos, who began murdering White, middle-aged men in December 1989, paused for six months, then murdered six more men in relatively quick succession from June 1990 to November 1990. The only reason she stopped was because she was arrested in January 1991. In each case, Wuornos was engaging in sex work along Florida's Interstate 75 corridor and was picked up by the victim. When the victim parked the vehicle in a secluded location, Wuornos shot him multiple times in the chest and head with a .22 caliber handgun and then robbed him. When discussing the murder of her first victim, Richard Mallory, aged fifty-one, Wuornos first claimed self-defense, although she later recanted. Why did Wuornos murder Mallory when she had never shot a customer before? While Wuornos may have simply murdered Mallory for financial gain, the motive of anger and rage may have played a role, especially since she was known to be short-tempered and prone to violence. Wuornos then stopped murdering for six months, likely realizing she was literally getting away with murder. Once she started up again, she murdered weeks apart and never stopped until she was arrested. This change in the frequency of murders suggests Wuornos had an additional serial offender motive, possibly power/thrill—receiving a sense of empowerment and excitement after each kill. She got a taste for blood. If Tumblety did indeed begin killing women once he realized he had caught a progressive, incurable disease, further similar unsolved murders from this time forward hint that he may very well have gotten a taste for it too.

CHAPTER 8

UNSOLVED MURDERS & ASSAULTS BETWEEN 1883 AND 1886

A common pattern of assaults and murders of women in America who were neither raped nor robbed for financial gain seems to become more consistent and periodic between 1883 and 1886. It is as if a transient serial killer was formulating an MO for achieving both a violent personal rage attack on women—either by bludgeoning, choking, and/or cutting—and also a quick getaway at opportune times. Women were the victims of surprise attacks mostly at night by an unknown man either randomly encountered on the street or from having first been followed. When someone arrived for assistance, the assailant vanished in the darkness. The attacks, frequency of attacks, and getaways are quite similar to that of the Yorkshire Ripper, Peter Sutcliffe. The murders and attempted murders by Sutcliffe occurred on the street at night and were very personal and brutal, first bludgeoning the woman over the head with a hammer and then repeatedly stabbing her. Of Sutcliffe's known assaults and murders, he committed between one and five crimes a year.

Coincidentally—or not—the attacks in late nineteenth-century America were always near a railroad, either for steam engines or cable cars. The pattern suggests a transient serial killer taking advantage of the railways—arriving, attacking, then quickly leaving on the train.

With regards to MO, there is actually a modern-day equivalent to a nineteenth-century transient railway serial killer, yet it was not discovered until three decades after women were being murdered by a Ripper-like serial offender: the truck-driving serial killer or long-haul trucker serial killer. Terry Turner, a criminal analyst from the Oklahoma State Bureau of Investigations, began spotting similarities in murders along the interstate. She realized that some long-haul truckers were picking up sex workers at truck stops, killing them, then dumping them. Author and journalist Ginger Strand studied many of these cases and published her results.

Over a dozen long-haul truckers have been identified as serial killers. Recall Dellmus Colvin, the Interstate Strangler, who claimed to have killed over fifty sex workers. He admitted to being a misogynist and once said, "She gave me some lip and I just strangled her." He said that sex workers were easy since they freely entered the truck. When asked by Ron Swanson on his *The Darkest Net* podcast in February 2021 why he strangled, Colvin said, "It was personal, and it was clean." He also said that, in most cases, he did have sex with them, and he never kept trophies. When asked why he killed, he said, "Because I could." He was also asked, if he were free, would he kill again? He said, "Absolutely." Colvin also claimed that he sold one of these women to another truck-driving serial killer who has not been caught.

A second long-haul trucker serial killer was Robert Ben Rhoades, the Truck Stop Killer, possibly also having killed over fifty women. John Robert Williams, the I-40 Truck Stop Killer, murdered sex workers with his girlfriend, Rachel Cumberland. Wayne Adam Ford claimed God told him to murder sex workers. Joe Methany was known to eat parts of the women's bodies. The Vampire Trucker, Timothy Jay Vageades, actually wore fangs as he killed. A seventh trucker serial killer was Edward Surratt. The Redhead Killer has yet to be identified. There was also Bruce Mendenhaull; James Robert Cruz; and Canadian Keith Hunter Jesperson, aka, the Happy Face Killer. Jesperson confessed to killing 160 women. An eleventh Trucker serial killer was Adam Leroy Lane. There were also Oscar Ray Bolin and Robert Rembert Jr. This list is not exhaustive, but it does show how many identified transient serial killers there are in modern history—further supporting that Jack the Ripper being a transient would not be unusual.

Dellmus Colvin said that truck-stop sex workers were easy targets. These women, a group of people who purposely work on the outskirts of society, willingly entered his truck—a perfect secluded area to commit murder. Colvin stated that he was even stopped by a state trooper for speeding, yet the trooper was unaware that in Colvin's cab was a dead female body.

Modern-day long-haul trucker transient serial killers were active for decades before anyone realized women were being murdered. This was at a time when the FBI existed. It is not a surprise that a nineteenth-century version of the long-haul trucker serial killer, a railway transient serial killer, preyed upon innocent women walking the streets at night and hid under the radar of history.

A Man Wearing a Slouch Hat – March 1883

One year after the Welcome Mat murder in Boston was another shockingly similar murder in that same city—a violent attack on a young woman at the entrance to her home. According to the *Boston Globe*, March 19, 1883, Etta B. Carlton, aged thirty-one, was murdered on the evening of March 18 in the greater Boston area "just over the line between Watertown and Cambridge, in the former place, on Mount Auburn street, near Norwood park." At seven thirty P.M., Etta Carlton—reportedly a "most handsome" woman—had just put her children to bed and was speaking with them. The doorbell rang. According to her daughter Fanny, Etta went downstairs to answer the door. Fanny then heard yelling coming from the entrance hallway, so she went downstairs. She discovered her mother lying on the floor in a pool of blood. Fanny ran in hysterics out of the house and to a neighbor. The neighbors noticed a "ragged wound extending nearly across her forehead," although, she was still alive. They took her to her bedroom and went for a doctor. The *Boston Evening Transit*, March 19, 1888, stated that Doctors Morse, Hosmer, and Wyman arrived but were helpless to save her life. She soon died of her wounds. Just before eight P.M., Officer George Barrington of Cambridge arrived at the house accompanied by a Special Officer Carroll. They discovered a bloodied six-inch-long paving stone in the hallway and determined that the offender hit Etta over the head with it, crushing her skull.

The medical examiner, Alfred H. Holt, completed an autopsy and reported several ragged flesh wounds about the face and scalp and a contusion on the right side of the abdomen. Holt concluded that the cause of death was the result of these injuries. The motive was neither robbery nor rape.

Detectives also noted that railroad tracks were near Carlton's home. The Carlton home was "near Norwood Park," which is the location of the East Watertown Railroad Station. According to the *Boston Evening Transcript*, March 21, 1883, Etta Carlton was employed at Casey's Saloon at 149 Cambridge Street, so detectives theorized that Carlton was followed home from work. Cambridge Street paralleled the Fitchburg Railroad tracks that had train stations along the way. The Watertown Railroad tracks joined into the Fitchburg Railroad tracks in Cambridge on the northern border of East Watertown.

A man named Joseph Bird was passing by the house around seven P.M. and noticed a middle-aged man sitting on the opposite side of the street. He was wearing a slouch hat, but Bird could give no other description.

A reward of four thousand dollars was offered for the arrest of the murderer, however, nothing came of it. Although a number of people were arrested, indicted, and even held in pre-trial confinement for months, none were taken to trial due to a lack of evidence.

In the eyes of local inspectors, a motive for the murder was elusive. In the *Boston Globe*, March 24, 1883, investigators were asked about the case:

> "The whole thing is a blank," said a City Hall inspector. "You can make a half dozen theories as to who put up the job or killed the woman, and either one will be as near right as the other. I might work on the idea that the husband was at the bottom of it. Or I might theorize that a tramp or housebreaker, intending to commit robbery, finding that he had killed Mrs. Carlton, fled in terror without stealing even the necklace upon her neck. Again, I might suppose that the murdered woman had been slaughtered in a fit of jealousy, or that some acquaintance of the husband could have done it without his knowledge. I might theorize till I am gray, and be just as near right then as now. See?"

Notice in the following opinion in the same article how unaware nineteenth-century investigators were of the motives of serial killers:

> A special officer attached to one of the most important police divisions in this city said: "What do I think of it? Well, I'd like to know what is at the bottom of it. No man, or woman either for that matter, would kill a person in cold blood, as was the case here, unless there was a good reason for it. There is a motive, and mark my words, it will come out yet . . ."

The fact that the motive was not the usual robbery or rape clearly confused the authorities in 1883. Because the victim was ruthlessly stabbed and beaten, it is difficult not to see this was a rage murder. The Associated Press article in the *Harrisburg Daily Independent,* March 20, 1883, even stated this: "The crime is one of a mysterious nature, no possible motive except that of revenge being probable."

Two years later, in November 1885, as reported in the *Saint Paul Globe*, November 24, 1885, a prison inmate named Frasier Cunliff confessed to the murder, while also implicating the victim's husband, Frank Carlton. This, though, was a hoax. The *Republican Journal,* November 26, 1885, stated, "An investigation showed the alleged confession to have been a hoax." The murder remains unsolved.

While Bird recalled seeing a middle-aged man wearing a slouch hat sitting on the opposite side of the street within one hour before the murder, he could not determine his height, given the man's seated position. Tumblety admitted in a January 1889 interview that he was arrested on suspicion for the Whitechapel murders partially because he often wore a slouch hat. Recall, in the article titled, "Tumblety Talks," in the *New York World*, January 29, 1889, Tumblety explained why he was arrested. He told the reporter that while in the Whitechapel District, the "English detectives" were following him. The reporter asked, "Why did they follow you?" In Tumblety's reply, he stated,

> ... Then it is the universal belief among the lower classes that all Americans wear slouch hats; therefore, Jack the Ripper, must wear a slouch hat. Now, I happened to have on a slouch hat, and this, together with the fact that I was an American, was enough for the police. It established my guilt beyond any question.

While Tumblety generally wore his military-style cap, he was reported as wearing his slouch hat later on in his life. In the 1905 Missouri Probate Court trial transcript, a witness named Daniel O'Donovan stated he knew Francis Tumblety in 1901. The attorney asked, "Will you state briefly the condition of Dr. Tumblety's clothes when you knew him, during the period you knew him?" Under oath, O'Donovan replied, "On two or three occasions during the period of time that I saw him last, he wore a slouch hat, and on one particular occasion I remember he wore a pair of cutting shoes; both the slouch hat and the cutting shoes seemed to brace up his appearance considerably..." Tumblety clearly owned—and wore—a hat matching the description of several aforementioned and subsequent offenders—including the Ripper himself.

DUMPED INTO THE RIVER - MAY 1883

Yet again in 1883 a young woman was brutalized and then thrown into water, but this time it was a river. According to the *St. Louis Post-Dispatch*, May 28, 1883, the decomposed nude body of an unknown woman was discovered late Saturday afternoon, May 26, at the southernmost point of Coney Island, New York. Manhattan Beach Company watchman Louis Smith spotted the body bobbing in the water. As the tide came in, the body advanced toward the shore. Her throat was "cut from ear to ear." The woman's age was thought to be between twenty and thirty years. Marks on the ankles suggested that weights were attached to the feet. No one ever identified the body, which means the investigation hit a dead end.

Tumblety lived just a few miles away in Manhattan but was also known to room in Brooklyn just north of Coney Island. Brooklyn and Coney Island make up the western edge of Long Island. When Tumblety returned from hiding to New York City in January 1889, he first roomed in Brooklyn. He came back to finish his February 1889 autobiography, which has Brooklyn, New York, listed as the city of publishing. The Coney Island Railroad travels from Coney Island straight into Brooklyn. If the murder did occur near Coney Island, Brooklyn was just minutes by train for a quick getaway.

Nothing more was reported on the case, meaning it remains unsolved. It is clear that if the body was never identified and there were no witnesses, then the chances of solving the case are slim. Even though it received very little attention, it can be argued that a dismembered body of a woman with her throat cut was more ruthless than even the Whitechapel murders—and the result of an anger-retaliatory motive.

IN THE COMPANY OF A TALL MAN - SEPTEMBER 1883

According to the *San Francisco Examiner*, October 7, 1883, on September 2, 1883, Rose Ambler of Stratford, Connecticut, had visited a man she was having a relationship with, William Lewis. Lewis claimed Rose left his house at nine P.M., where she began her dark, two-mile walk back to her father's house. The next morning, her lifeless body was discovered along Oronoque Road near the Housatonic River. She was "laid on the broad of her back, with her hands under her hips, and her bonnet on the back of her head."

ROSE AMBLER.

Her dress was drawn up to her waist, but there was no evidence of rape. The cause of death was strangulation. Recall that the bodies of Whitechapel victims Polly Nichols and Annie Chapman showed evidence of first being strangulated.

Rose Ambler was neither raped nor robbed. According to the *New York Times*, September 7, 1883:

> In the absence of evidence of an outrage [rape] it has been the generally accepted theory that the only motive which could prompt the crime would be either that of robbery or revenge. It was certainly not the former. Neither valuables nor money were taken from the body.

The location of the body convinced the authorities that the killer was unfamiliar with the surroundings since it was in a location commonly used by walking traffic. Initial suspicion lay on William Lewis, but his alibi was convincing enough to eliminate him as the offender. The case remains unsolved to this day. The *Meriden Daily Republican*, September 8, 1883, reprinted an article from the *New Haven Morning News*, which published an interview with a Detective Fuller, who stated:

> People have been found who swear that she, Rose Ambler, was in the company of a *tall man* that evening after she left Lewis . . . [Author emphasis added.]

Additional details about the tall man from the eyewitness account given at the coroner's inquest by an Edward Bartram and Julia Roberts are reported in the *Democrat and Chronicle*, September 9, 1883. Neither Bartram nor Roberts recognized the tall man, however, Bartram recognized Rose Ambler:

> The evidence of Mrs. Julia Roberts, of Stratford, and Edward Bartram, of Bridgeport, was taken next. Mr. Bartram is a young man who is to be married to a lady residing near Stratford Green, not far from the home of William Lewis. He visited his betrothed on Sunday. For some reason he left Stratford to return to Bridgeport at an early hour in the evening, not later than 9:30 o'clock. As he passed down the highway he overtook two persons, a woman and a man. The woman was Rose Ambler. She was going toward her own home from the home of her lover, William Lewis. Mr. Bartram did not recognize the man with whom she walked. He did recognize Rose Ambler. The man was tall and heavily built. An animated conversation was in progress. There was no reason to suspect that the woman was on any but good terms with her companion, and Mr. Bartram passed rapidly by, supposing that young lady had accepted the escort of some friend over the dark and lonely highway. When he was asked if he thought he would be able to identify the man, the witness was in much doubt. He did not think it would be justifiable to attempt to fasten any crime upon the evidence so slight as must be his memory of Rose Ambler's companion, seeing him only for a moment, and then only casually. Mrs. Robert's testimony was accepted as going far to corroborate that of Mr. Bartram. Mrs. Roberts, whose brother it was that first discovered the murdered girl's body, is the daughter of one of the most respected citizens of Stratford, and no one questions her veracity. Returning with a gentleman friend from church on Sunday evening, she passed a man standing alone on

the Oronoque road foot-bridge; he acted very nervously and seemed to be anxious to escape observation. He was tall and heavily framed. She and her escort went through the maple path some time previous to the hour when Bartram started home. Rose Ambler, going from her lover's house to her own home had to pass over this foot-bridge.

If Mrs. Roberts's opinion that the man attempted to escape observation, along with the authorities' opinions that the offender was unfamiliar with the area, are true, then this matches an opportunistic transient killer stationing himself at a favorable location: the entrance of a dark road. If Bartram did indeed see the killer, it was likely the tall man purposely engaged in conversation with Rose Ambler. In the Chicago and Buffalo assaults, the tall offender(s) threatened, or conversed, with the victims first, as opposed to executing a surprise attack, which conforms to Bartram's account.

An article in the *Yorkville Enquirer*, September 20, 1883, stated that Rose Ambler's home was about a mile northwest of the New York and New Haven Railroad bridge across the Housatonic River. Her body was found along the popular section of Oronoque Road, which followed the Housatonic River, which paralleled the railroad just hundreds of feet away. This is yet another similarity to the Jack the Ripper murder of Polly Nichols, the murder site being hundreds of feet away from the Whitechapel Train Station and the tracks near the murder site. The *Daily Telegraph*, September 1, 1888, stated, "A bridge over the Great Eastern Railway is close at hand [the Nichols murder site on Buck's Row], and the railway line was also fruitlessly searched for some distance."

Stratford, Connecticut, is situated between Boston, Massachusetts, and New York City, so the train route taken by Tumblety certainly stopped in Stratford. There is evidence that Tumblety was in Boston just over one month earlier. The *Boston Globe*, July 16, 1883, reported on a "Thomas Tumblety" being fined in the Boston Municipal Court for one dollar and costs for drunkenness, and five dollars and costs for assault and battery. Neither the 1880 US Census nor the 1885 Boston City Directory shows a Thomas Tumblety living in Boston. Francis Tumblety was, however, on a number of occasions, referred to as Thomas Tumblety. The *New York Tribune*, February 22, 1861, reported on a court case Tumblety was involved in where the court records stated his name was Dr. Thomas Tumblety. On another occasion, in the *Baltimore Sun*, December 25, 1861, a letter was at the Baltimore post office for T. Tumblety, MD.

Just one year earlier, Martin McGarry traveled with Tumblety, and he stated they visited Boston, followed by New Haven, Connecticut, and then

Philadelphia, Pennsylvania. If Tumblety followed the same travel pattern, something he was known to do, he would have visited New Haven, Connecticut, after his Boston visit. He then would have traveled through Stratford, Connecticut, on his way through New York to Philadelphia.

BETWEEN ST. LOUIS AND CHICAGO – OCTOBER 1883

According to the *Chicago Tribune*, October 16, 1883, the body of Zora Burns was found in a deserted lane in the north part of Lincoln, Illinois, on October 15, 1883. Lincoln, Illinois, is situated directly between St. Louis, Missouri, and Chicago, Illinois, along a train route that connects the two major cities. Burns's throat was cut from ear to ear, and her forehead was crushed. She was found lying on her face. The postmortem examination revealed that she was pregnant and was not raped. According to the *Inter Ocean*, October 18, 1883, there was also a cut over her left eye and a bruise over the right. Her hair was filled with burrs and weeds. There were slight traces of an attempt at an abortion. On the evening of Sunday, October 14, 1883, at eight P.M., she was at the Lincoln House, where she paid her bill and left. She went to the office of a grain merchant named Orrin A. Carpenter, for whom she worked as a domestic servant. Carpenter, the supposed richest man in Lincoln, was suspected early in the case, arrested, and even tried for her murder. On March 22, 1884, twelve jurors unanimously acquitted Carpenter. The case was never solved. Neither robbery nor rape was considered the offender's motive.

According to multiple eyewitness accounts in sworn depositions and testimonies, Tumblety was known to visit St. Louis, Missouri, each year or more beginning around 1882 and up until six months before his death in May 1903. St. Louis was very profitable for him during the Civil War. Traveling by train from St. Louis to Chicago linked him up with what was known as the panhandle route of the Pennsylvania Railroad line, which included Chicago, Cincinnati, Pittsburgh, Philadelphia, and numerous routes through New Jersey. This connected Tumblety to multiple cities, each one containing his favorite evening pastime: soliciting young men in the city slums. Tumblety then extended the panhandle route to Brooklyn and New York City, where he considered his home.

According to his nephew, Michael Fitzsimmons, Tumblety also visited his brother in Rochester, New York, each year or two, which meant he could arrive from the west by train from Chicago to Cleveland to Buffalo to Rochester, or from Pittsburgh to Buffalo to Rochester. Coincidentally, an unsolved murder of a young woman occurred in Rochester just weeks after the Burns murder, following the same geographical line as Tumblety's favorite travel routes.

ERIE CANAL - OCTOBER 1883

Two weeks after the murder of Zora Burns, parts of a dismembered body of a woman were found floating in the Erie Canal in Rochester, New York. According to the *New York Times*, October 26, 1883, "a forearm and left leg was in the canal at Lock 65, just outside the limits of the city of Rochester." The next day, the right leg was discovered, followed by the discovery of additional body parts. A "prominent physician" who was used by the authorities to examine the body pieces stated that the absence of decomposition both discounted the theory that a grave was robbed and that the death occurred less than a week ago. The physician's professional opinion was that the woman was murdered.

A common theory of why murderers dismember their victims' bodies and then throw them into the water is to disguise the victims' identities. In so doing, the investigation goes nowhere, so the killer is not caught. Dismembering a body would likely not have been the result of a train passenger killer quietly exiting a train stop, murdering, then quickly escaping back on a train. In Tumblety's case—if he was the killer—Rochester was not a mere train stop but the home of his brother and other family members. His nephew, Michael Fitzsimmons, stated under oath that Tumblety would visit Rochester nearly every year and stay for a period of time. Dismembering a body would make sense in this instance since he was likely not quickly leaving the city and would have ample time to dispose of remains.

Tumblety was known to travel on the canal and also walk the slums at night in each city he visited. We actually have sworn testimony of Tumblety roaming the Rochester streets at night and acting unusual. In Eleanor Elsheimer's sworn deposition, she stated that one evening in downtown Rochester sometime between 1895 and 1898 she spotted Tumblety hiding in a dark stairway:

> Elsheimer: "I was going to downtown Saturday evening, and on the right hand side of Main Street as I passed the doorway I saw this man; he was tight against the wall as he could be, with his hands down at his side looking furtively out."
> Attorney: "Doorway or stairway?"
> Elsheimer: "Stairway."
> Attorney: "Light or dark?"
> Elsheimer: "It was a dark place but the light shone in."

Attorney: "Was his posture one of concealment?"
Elsheimer: "I couldn't just tell, he looked so queer."
Attorney: "His hands were down at his side?"
Elsheimer: "Yes, and his head back against the wall."

According to the *Toronto Mail*, November 22, 1883, Tumblety was in Toronto, an eyewitness stating, "At this time his [Tumblety's] arm was in a sling." The significance of this Toronto sighting in November is that he was likely in Rochester, New York, during the murder of the young woman at the canal. Tumblety would first visit his family in Rochester, then travel through Buffalo, New York, and enter Canada. Recall, Tumblety owned three thousand acres just west of Toronto in Guelph.

LOOKING FOR A TALL MAN – NOVEMBER 1883

According to the *Courier-Post* (Camden, New Jersey), November 26, 1883, on Saturday, November 24, 1883, young Phoebe Paullin was walking from West Orange, New Jersey, to Orange, New Jersey, to do some shopping for her mother. She was well-dressed in a black velvet suit and was wearing a gold watch and chain. She was last seen on Eagle Rock Road. A man and his fourteen-year-old boy were walking along that same road, strayed from the road, and came across her body. Her throat was cut from the windpipe to the left ear. Her body was bloody and bruised. It was clear that her body was dragged from the road a hundred feet to where she was found. None of her jewelry was taken. There were reports that Paullin was raped, however, the official answer states otherwise. According to the *New York Herald*, December 5, 1883, when asked as the Coroner's Inquiry if Paullin was "outraged," the county physician admitted he could not tell conclusively, but he thought there was an attempt. This, though, was only concluded because the offender did not rob the victim. In the physician's nineteenth-century mind, the only remaining motive for a murder such as this had to be attempted rape.

In an article in the *New York Times*, December 1, 1883, titled, "Looking for a Tall Man," it was revealed that local authorities were looking for a tall, well-dressed, man who was spotted walking down Eagle Rock Road "the night she was killed." Curiously, some witnesses stated that he wore a light-colored overcoat and others stated he wore a dark overcoat, but all admitted that it was dark outside. An eyewitness stated he saw a six-foot man at about six P.M. wearing a dark overcoat and who looked to be twenty-eight years old. Two witnesses,

Mart and Chet Williams, stated they saw a young lady walking down Eagle Rock Road, then saw a tall man in a light overcoat "coming out of the park below the stone-cracker as he came down the road."

Still another witness, George Franks, an Orange saloonkeeper, stated he saw Phoebe Paullin near the stone crusher shortly after six P.M. The *St. Louis Post-Dispatch*, November 28, 1883, continues with Franks's account:

> A tall man, who wore a long overcoat, was on the opposite side of the road. As the girl turned north towards Eagle Rock from the stone crusher the man crossed over to her. Then a sharp curve in the road hid them from sight.

While arrests were made, no one was convicted of her murder and, thus, it remains unsolved. The case was thoroughly investigated, as evidenced by the Pinkerton Agency being involved. Both sets of eyewitnesses were convinced of the overcoat color, so it seems that they may very well have identified two different tall men, or perhaps one witness was mistaken in that detail. A witness named Frank Hardy may have even seen a different set of assailants. Hardy stated that he saw a tall man and a short man following the woman up Eagle Rock around six P.M.—perhaps the men were together, perhaps not. Nor do we know why this man was (or these men were) following Paullin. Of significance is that because the victim's jewelry was not taken and she was not raped, a solid motive was never determined. This opens up the possibility of Tumblety being involved. Not only was his residence less than twenty miles away from Orange, New Jersey, but the crime scene was also situated along a train route regularly used by him, which easily connected him to this location.

ALONG THE CABLE CAR ROUTE - JANUARY 1884

According to Chicago's *Inter Ocean*, January 17, 1884, the body of Amelia Olson, aged nineteen, was found in the morning of January 16, 1884, in an open prairie lot bounded by Leavitt, Chicago, and Western Streets, only yards from her home and along the cable car route. A veil was wrapped tightly around her neck. The police were convinced that robbery was not the motive, since money and jewelry, such as gold earrings and a finger ring, were found on the body. The county physician, a Dr. Bluthardt, assisted by Dr. Kroat, concluded that Amelia Olson was not outraged and died of asphyxiation. Olson ended work "at the sewing machine" at 239 West Indiana Street at six thirty P.M., Tuesday, January 15. A person answering the description of Amelia Olson got off the train at Leavitt Street, crossing at about eight P.M., and so was likely murdered soon after this since the murder site was between the train station and her home. It also suggests the possibility that the offender spotted her at the train station and followed her. Over half a dozen arrests were made, but in each case, the suspect had a solid alibi.

Amelia Olson was murdered along the same train route as Zora Burns just three months earlier. While it is well known that Tumblety took the panhandle train route having a stop in Chicago, there is also evidence that he occasionally stayed in Chicago for a short period of time. In the *Inter Ocean*, November 20, 1888, the famous William "Billy" Pinkerton of the Pinkerton Detective Agency had his office in Chicago. He commented to a reporter about seeing Tumblety in Chicago in 1869: "In Chicago, along about '69, he was detected in indulging in the vices to which I have referred, and he had to fly that city." In the *Pittsburgh Daily Chronicle and Telegraph*, November 27, 1888, a reporter interviewed a man claiming to have "seen him [Tumblety] a hundred times in Chicago." A report in the *Chicago Tribune*, February 27, 1890, stated, "Dr. Francis Tumblety, the famous Whitechapel suspect, is here fresh from his travels." Tumblety's former Rochester neighbor, Eleanor Elsheimer, stated in a sworn deposition in 1905 that her brother, James McMullen, lived in Chicago and recalled seeing Tumblety in a Chicago bookstore. According to the 1880 census and Rochester City directories, James McMullen lived in Rochester, New York. The last time he was in the Rochester City Directory was in 1893, so this was likely when he moved to Chicago. He died before the 1900 census was taken, meaning McMullen saw Tumblety in Chicago sometime between 1893 and 1899.

If the killer did indeed follow his victim off the Chicago cable car, then the Olson murder may have something in common with another attack: this is exactly what would occur in December 1888 to the twenty-two-year-old Swedish girl who was traveling in the cable car and got off in downtown Chicago. Recall, she noticed a tall man with a dark mustache, no whiskers, and wearing a gray Ulster coat exit the cable car when she did. He then attacked her by the throat and threatened her with violence if she did not walk with him, clearly an effort to get her into a more secluded area and commit a heinous crime. Luckily, she fought him and escaped. The Swedish girl was convinced the man wanted to kill her. Olson may very well have acquiesced to his demand, and for that, she was murdered.

Three Assaults in Brooklyn – October 1884

The *Brooklyn Daily Eagle*, October 4, 1884, reported on an assault of twenty-three-year-old Mary Hatton. As she was walking to County Hospital at Flatbush on October 3, she was attacked by a stranger:

> When she reached the corner of Drummond street and Bedford avenue, a man suddenly sprang from the side of the street near the open field and caught her by the throat, striking her at the same time a violent blow on the face. Fortunately in answer to her screams Miss F. Horton and Mrs. J. Oborglock rushed down the road. The rascal fled, leaving Miss Hatton fainting in the arms of her rescuers . . . This is the third assault that has been made within a short time upon women in this locality.

While none of the reports gave a physical description of the assailant, a number of facts are very similar to the Buffalo and Chicago assaults by a tall man in a gray Ulster coat in 1886 and 1888, respectively. The attack was on the street by a stranger who first grabbed the victim by the throat. Just like the Buffalo assaults, the offender spent time in the area attacking women.

As mentioned, while Tumblety generally rented rooms in Manhattan, he was also known to rent rooms in Brooklyn. For example, when Tumblety arrived from England in December 1888, he rented a room in Manhattan at 79 East 10th Street, but within two days he left the city. When he returned in January 1889, he rented a room in Brooklyn. When he finished his February 1889 autobiography, a Brooklyn publishing company published it. The *Brooklyn Citizen* even called Tumblety a Brooklynite in their November 23, 1888, issue, which stated in the subtitle, "Is He The Ripper? A Brooklynite Charged With the Whitechapel Murders."

One more fact the Brooklyn attacks have in common with the Buffalo attacks in December 1886: Multiple women were attacked on different nights in a relatively short period of time. It is definitely not a case of the assailant arriving by train, committing a crime, then quickly leaving the area by train. It demonstrates that the assailant was staying in the area, and when the assaults abruptly ended in a week or two, it suggests that the assailant had left the area. This would not be the last time a pattern of multiple assaults occurred at a particular location and then abruptly ended. This second pattern conforms perfectly with Tumblety's travel behavior. Tumblety was constantly traveling from city to city, but in cities such as New York, Brooklyn, Buffalo, St. Louis,

Pittsburgh, and New Orleans, he would stay for a few weeks, and in some cases for a few months. Transient in the short and long term, Tumblety's travel habits conform to both patterns of attack.

REFUSING A VENGEFUL TRAMP – OCTOBER 1884

Covington, Kentucky, borders the Ohio River with Cincinnati, Ohio, a city in which Tumblety maintained an office for years. It is also a train stop between St. Louis, Missouri, and New York. According to an Associated Press article published in numerous newspapers, such as the *Philadelphia Times*, October 18, 1884, on October 17, 1884, Annie Madison's twenty-nine-year-old lifeless body was found at her home. She had been choked with a rope and her throat had been cut deeply with an ax. The thirty-year-old husband was arrested on suspicion, but according to the *Courier-Journal*, October 18, 1884, the eight-year-old son, Albert Madison, said an old man with gray whiskers committed the crime. It was reported that a few days earlier, a tramp was refused help by Annie Madison, and the tramp said, "You'll hear from me again in a few days." The case remains unsolved.

While the weapon was an ax and not a knife, as in the case with the Whitechapel murders four years later, the murder was clearly the result of anger, or rage. If it was indeed the tramp who murdered Annie for not helping him a few days earlier, then the motive was anger-retaliatory. Further, there is clear evidence that some—or all—of the Whitechapel victims were strangled first before their heads were nearly decapitated. Annie was not raped, nor was any theft involved, which conforms to possibly being murdered by Tumblety. Also, Tumblety was aged fifty-four, and when he was not waxing his mustache, it was gray, so the boy's eyewitness description of the killer *does not eliminate* Tumblety.

There is evidence to suggest that Scotland Yard heard about this unsolved near decapitation of a young woman in the Cincinnati/Covington area and may have been attempting to link it to Tumblety. The *Cincinnati Enquirer*, as reported in the *Union Record*, January 24, 1889, revealed that detectives were inquiring about Tumblety in Cincinnati:

> It has been known for some days past that detectives have been quietly tracing the career in this city [Cincinnati] for Dr. Francis Tumblety, one of the suspects under surveillance by the English authorities, and who was recently followed across the ocean by Scotland Yard men . . . The investigation in this city is understood to be under that direction of English officials now in New York, and based upon certain information they have forwarded by mail.

This information may have been about potential murders Tumblety may have been involved in in the United States. In the *Oakland Tribune*, December 8, 1890, Tumblety's brother, Lawrence, was interviewed about Francis Tumblety's antecedents. The subsequent story Lawrence told to the reporter about another man stealing his brother's identity—thus, claiming his brother's innocence—was a complete lie, but the reason he lied is significant. Lawrence Tumblety's story has all of the hallmarks of being a smokescreen. Scotland Yard was investigating Tumblety's antecedents: "The London police could not learn much of Tumblety's antecedents, and to the present they are trying to identify him with other crimes."

We do have a record of Tumblety traveling by train in the Cincinnati area as part of his usual travel pattern. According to the *Union Record*, January 24, 1889, a Cincinnati private detective named James Jackson claimed to have befriended Tumblety between 1870 and 1875. He recalled to the *Cincinnati Enquirer* reporter that Tumblety had a bodyguard named Jack. He stated, "In 1875 I was at Aurora, Indiana, and boarding a train found the doctor and Jack occupying seats." Jack was "a tall giant fellow."

TALL MAN IN A LONG GRAY OVERCOAT – DECEMBER 1884

Just west of Rahway, New Jersey, the site of the soon-to-be Rahway Mystery, a number of assaults occurred at night on the streets of Plainfield, New Jersey. An Associated Press news cable in the *Dunkirk Evening Observer*, December 20, 1884, stated,

> PLAINFIELD, N.J., December 20. – Mrs. John O. Stevens and a female servant were assaulted on Evona Avenue about eight o'clock last night by an unknown man. The assailant knocked a lantern from the servant's hand and then threw the two women down. The servant's cries brought help from a house nearby and the man was frightened away. Mrs. Stevens has been in convulsions since the attack and is in a precarious condition.

The women were out on the street at night when a complete stranger attacked them, and only because of fear of being caught did the attacker run away. The *Courier-News*, December 22, 1884, gave further details:

> The condition of Mrs. John O. Stevens, of Evona, is somewhat better, she being able to be about the house. A New York detective is working up the case of

the assault. A man answering the description of the assailant got off the train from Jersey City that reached the Evona station at 7:40 P.M. that evening. He was tall and wore a long gray overcoat.

The report states that a New York detective, a police official with no authority in the Plainfield, New Jersey, jurisdiction, took over the investigation. This begs the question as to why. The only logical conclusion is that an eyewitness identified the tall man in the gray overcoat either arriving at a local train station from New York City just before the attacks or departing for New York City just after the attacks. This is exactly where Tumblety lived at the time, *and* Tumblety would travel by train from New York through Plainfield, New Jersey.

This particular attacker seems to not have been done with Plainfield, New Jersey. Three days later, two more assaults on women walking the streets at night occurred by a tall man. An article in the *Sun*, December 24, 1888, "Seized By a Strange Man," stated:

> PLAINFIELD, Dec. 23. – The woman assaulter who appeared in Evona last week seems to have turned up in Plainfield. On Monday evening, between 7 and 8 o'clock, while Nellie, the eleven-year-old daughter of Mrs. Kate M. Overbaugh, a widow, of 109 East Second street, was returning from a rehearsal for a Christmas entertainment, she was addressed by a tall, slim man, who asked her the name of the street. On receiving an answer, he passed on but, turning, he grasped the girl about the waist and, putting his hand over her mouth, forced his fingers down her throat. She was thrown to the ground in the struggle . . . She described the man as wearing a soiled light overcoat and a cap or low derby hat . . . Soon after 7 o'clock on the same [Monday] evening, as Mrs. Annie Buist, a widow, of West Front street, was passing along Central avenue in the vicinity of West Third street, a tall man attacked her . . . The places where the two assaults were committed are less than five minutes walk from the center of town . . . All three are tall and slim, and in two instances the overcoat is described as light in color.

Recall, in December 1886, in Buffalo, New York, a tall man in a gray Ulster overcoat assaulted multiple women who were walking the streets at night, and in December 1888, a young woman was attacked on the tracks by a tall man with a black mustache wearing gray Ulster overcoat. Also in December 1888, a tall man in a gray Ulster with a black mustache attacked a woman in the same manner. This is almost exactly what the tall man in a gray overcoat was doing in

Plainfield, New Jersey, in December 1884. Further, this is yet again a pattern of multiple assaults upon women on separate days, just like Buffalo in 1886, and Brooklyn just two months earlier.

DISMEMBERMENT IN THE RIVER YET AGAIN – JULY 1885

On July 23, 1885, parts of a dismembered female body were discovered packed in a bag drifting in the Charles River in the Boston area. According to the *Boston Globe,* July 24, 1885, a janitor of the Union Boat Club, Alexander Cormack, looked out the window of his boathouse and spotted a brownish-gray bag clinging to the slip where he was moored. When he opened it, he discovered the dismembered body parts of a woman. The medical examiner, Dr. Stedman, performed an autopsy and concluded that the woman was about forty years of age and approximately five feet and eight inches tall and that she was likely thrown in the river three days earlier, meaning July 20. There was a knife wound that started just below the sternum and into the abdomen, then down the ribs, making two semicircular gashes. The victim's tongue protruded with finger bruise markings on the neck, suggesting she was first strangled. A bicuspid tooth was missing. The trunk was dressed in a sleeveless chemise. The forehead had received a severe blow. No evidence of rape was reported. Ring markings "on the third finger of the left hand" suggested that the killer may have stolen her wedding ring, eerily similar to the wedding ring and keeper ring stolen from the body of Annie Chapman in East London as trophies.

According to the *Boston Evening Transcript,* August 11, 1885, it was determined that the mutilated body was Mrs. Nellie, or Ellen, Mitchell, who had been missing since Monday, July 21. While many "positive identifications that were made" were "proven false," the fact that Ellen Mitchell had the same bicuspid tooth extracted by a dentist on January 23, 1884, a similar body freckle pattern, and a similarly owned chemise convinced authorities the victim was Mitchell. According to the *Boston Globe,* January 15, 1887, the husband, Frank Mitchell, was arrested on suspicion one month later and held in pre-trial confinement for a full seventeen months. Frank Mitchell confidently and continuously maintained his innocence, and his daughter stood stoutly by his side. Additionally, his neighbors and the local community were convinced of his innocence. In January 1887, State Supreme Court Judge Holmes released him, and soon after, the charges were dropped.

The case remains unsolved. Boston was certainly one of Tumblety's stops as he traveled in the 1880s. While the victim did not have her throat cut, she certainly was strangled, and her abdomen was attacked with a knife. It may not be a coincidence that the dismemberment and discarding of the body in the river is nearly identical to the murder of the unknown woman in Rochester, New York, two years earlier. As in the case with Rochester, Tumblety spent time in Boston, so if he was the offender, hiding evidence makes sense, as opposed to killing and leaving on the next train.

Recall also the dismembered body of Ella Clark in New York City in 1881. Although the remains were not found in a river or canal, they were discarded quite a distance away from where Clark was last seen.

Followed from the Train Station – December 1885

The *Boston Evening Transcript*, December 8, 1885, reported on the body of Carrie Whitney, aged thirty-five, which was discovered on a highway on Saturday, December 5, 1885, near Lake Massapoag, Sharon. The *Boston Globe*, December 7, 1888, stated the body was found on Lake View Street. Sharon is ten miles south of Boston, Massachusetts, and has been connected to Boston by train since the early nineteenth century. The medical examiner stated that Whitney's neck was broken, which was the cause of her death. Bruises on the body were inflicted before death. According to the *Boston Globe*, December 8, 1885, Whitney was a sex worker "well known in the low life west end" of Boston and "known amongst her sisters of sin as Carrie Lee." One year earlier, Whitney was afflicted with softening of the brain—what today is known as neurosyphilis. Medical Examiner Holmes identified the brain as being swollen, which corroborated Whitney having had neurosyphilis. Besides a broken neck, there were bruises on the face and neck. Even though the papers claimed she was raped, the examiner did not report this and would have, since this determines motive.

The *Boston Evening Transcript*, January 15, 1887, reported on a supposed deathbed confession of Edward Greenleaf, as claimed by Mary E. Wilbur. She claimed Greenleaf confessed that he, Harry Peach, and Hiram Beals were connected with Whitney. State detectives investigated the claim and were satisfied that Wilbur's statement had no foundation; specifically, there was no deathbed confession. The case remains unsolved.

Detectives did find men who believed they saw a woman walking alone Friday afternoon down the train tracks away from Boston and toward Sharon. The agent at the Sharon train depot stated he saw her walking there and noticed she was walking toward Sharon Heights slowly and wearily. If the killer was on the train, he would have seen a lone female ripe for the taking. Sharon Train Station is a stop along the Boston & Providence Railroad, which was the same train route Tumblety took when he traveled between Boston and New York City.

A GIRL'S SINGULAR STORY – JANUARY 1886

At nine P.M. on January 21, 1886, an eighteen-year-old woman named Annie Doran was walking along a railroad bridge on Waldo Avenue in Jersey City, over what was known as the Pennsylvania Railroad cut, and was attacked by someone she did not know. The cut was a fifty-foot drop to the railroad tracks. According to the *New York Times*, January 22, 1886, in an article titled, "A Girl's Singular Story," the girl says that the man threw a canvas bag over her head, tied a rope around her neck, and was about to throw her into the cut when approaching footsteps were heard. The man, she claims, then ran away, and she started for her home, about two blocks distant. Detectives are investigating her story.

While the report did not give a physical description of the assailant, a number of facts about the crime have similar patterns to other crimes discussed. First, the attack was at night by a complete stranger. It was not a case of a vengeful boyfriend or acquaintance. Second, the attacker clearly had intentions of murdering the young woman, and doing so without robbing or raping. He planned to hang her, then drop her onto the tracks fifty feet down. Third, the attack was along railroad tracks. Fourth, the railroad line, belonging to the United New Jersey Railroad & Canal Company, a subsidiary of the Pennsylvania Railroad Company since 1872, was the same line Tumblety traveled on to and from New York City. In fact, the very next stop was the terminus to board a ferry into Manhattan, where Tumblety considered his residence.

Lastly, this particular railroad track traveled through Rahway, the location of two mysterious murders in the next few years. Recall, the Rahway Mystery murder, which would occur in the next year, happened less than twenty miles from the location of the attempted murder of Annie Doran. Every single time Tumblety traveled by train through Jersey City on his way to Philadelphia, Hot Springs, etc., he traveled through Rahway.

MURDERED BY PERSON OR PERSONS UNKNOWN – APRIL 1886

According to the *Courier-Post*, April 12, 1886, the body of a woman in her mid-to late-thirties was found on April 11, 1886, in a thicket of woods between Merchantville and Camden, New Jersey. Two men, George Bachelor and Charles Schlitz, were training their hunting dogs, then came across the body lying facedown with the jacket pulled over her head. A hood, a scarf, a basket, and some food were scattered in a radius of about twenty feet. The woman had a stained and crumbled letter dated March 21, 1886. According to the *Morning Post*, April 15, 1886, Bachelor stated at the coroner's inquest that one week earlier they were training their hunting dogs and saw a woman lying on the ground. She was drunk, so they lifted her and set her beside the path. He then stated that about one hour later he remembered two men walking together toward the place where he and Schlitz had left the woman. One was a tall man and the other was shorter and stout. They appeared to look like vagrants.

An article in the *Courier-Post*, April 13, 1886, stated that on April 12, County Physician Gross performed a postmortem exam and determined that she was beaten about the face and that the cause of death was strangulation. He estimated the time of death was about one week earlier. According to the *Philadelphia Times*, April 15, 1886, the victim was identified as Annie Dugan, a vagrant. The *Times* also stated that a coroner's inquest was held on April 14, and twelve jurors rendered a verdict that the deceased "was murdered by some person or persons unknown." There was no evidence for the common motive of theft or rape, which caused some officials to doubt that the deceased was murdered.

Camden and Merchantville are about 3.5 miles apart. Besides a road, connecting the two cities was the Camden and Mt. Holly Railroad, which paralleled the road about three hundred yards to the north. According to the National Register of Historic Places, the Merchantville Train Station was built in 1881. This route became the Philadelphia & Long Branch route, which proceeded directly east to the coast and then north along the New Jersey beach towns. Not only were there at least six similar murders along this route in the next few years but Tumblety was known to be at one of these beach towns. It is also where Tumblety claimed to have been in 1892, demonstrating that Tumblety took this train route.

NEAR CARLISLE TRAIN STATION – JULY 1886

On July 23, 1886, thirteen-year-old Mary, or Mamie, Holweger was clubbed and mutilated in Franklin, Ohio. According to the *Dayton Herald*, February 7, 1887, Mamie was murdered near the Holweger home "one mile north of Franklin." While initially it was assumed and reported in the papers that Mamie was sexually assaulted, Detective Kuntz rejected this. According to the *Dayton Herald*, August 18, 1886, "The detective [Kuntz] makes the startling assertion that he can prove that the child was not outraged, as was reported." The case was never solved.

Franklin, Ohio, is also located just north of Cincinnati, Ohio, and was a train stop between Cincinnati and Cleveland, a route Tumblety would have taken beginning with his annual/biannual Hot Springs, Arkansas visit, then onward to St. Louis, then to Cincinnati, followed by Cleveland, and finally, Rochester, New York. This virtually guarantees that Tumblety commonly made stops in Franklin, Ohio. George H. Lower, a resident of Hot Springs, Arkansas, testified under oath in 1905 that he had a friendship with Tumblety in Hot Springs beginning around 1885. He considered their relationship a friendship because Tumblety had written over a hundred fifty letters to him throughout the years as Tumblety traveled. The attorney asked Lower if Tumblety met up with him in the last four or five years [1897 or 1898] as much as he did before this. Lower replied:

> No, sir; he would come in and go out of the City, and I never would know where he was. Before that period he would write from St. Louis, *Cleveland, Ohio*, Baltimore, New York City, New Orleans, Atlanta, Georgia ... [Author emphasis added.]

Lower's testimony corroborates Tumblety's train route as he left Hot Springs, Arkansas, between 1885 and 1898. Not only did Tumblety travel through Cleveland, but he stayed there for at least enough time to write and post a letter.

From Cincinnati, the train line was the Cincinnati Hamilton & Dayton Railroad, which had a train stop one mile north-northwest of Franklin called the Carlisle Train Station. Recall that Mamie Holweger was murdered one mile north of Franklin, which means the murder site was within walking distance of the Carlisle Train Station.

At a time when there was no centralized, organized federal law enforcement in the United States, if a serial killer was using the railways to commit murder at any location, then vanish from the area by rail, not only would they have been able to kill with near impunity, but no one might ever know of their existence. There was simply no official governmental body to track such things back then. The papers were clear that local law enforcement in any given city was appropriately attempting to identify a local killer, but no one was attempting to identify patterns of similar murders along the railways.

CHAPTER 9

JACK THE TRIPPER AND POST-1888 US MURDERS & ASSAULTS

Unusually similar unsolved murders and assaults, after the assaults and likely attempted murders of the women in Waterloo, New York, and Chicago, Illinois, in December 1888 near the railways may suggest that this was just a continuation of one or more nineteenth-century serial killers, not unlike transient serial killers of today. The next two murders, one in September 1889 and the other in September 1890, occurred just across the river from Philadelphia in Camden, New Jersey. The central railroad system that connected Chicago, St. Louis, and Pittsburgh to the major cities in the northeast, including Philadelphia/Camden, was the Pennsylvania & Ohio Railroad. This was the railroad line Tumblety always took, which guaranteed that he was in Camden each year.

THE FIRST SUSPICIONS OF FRANK LINGO – SEPTEMBER 1889

Within a day of the one-year anniversary of Annie Chapman's murder on September 8, 1888, Annie Leconey, or Laconey, was brutally murdered in Camden, New Jersey, which borders Philadelphia, Pennsylvania. As in the case with Chapman, Leconey's throat was cut from ear to ear. According to the *Camden Daily Telegram*, Monday, September 9, 1889, the

THE MURDERED GIRL.

murder was committed at Leconey's Mill, which was one mile from Merchantville, New Jersey. Annie was the housekeeper of her cousin, Chalkley Leconey. Annie's uncle, Chalkley's father, had died just a few weeks earlier. That morning at five A.M., Annie had breakfast with Chalkley and a farmhand named Garrett Murray. By seven A.M., Annie was murdered. Her body was found in the kitchen on her back while her clothing was up to her knees. A bloody butcher's knife was near her body.

Detectives quickly arrested a Black man named Francis, or Frank, Lingo, who had served time for robbery in the past. Lingo had been working at the farm for two and a half months and was last on the farm the previous Thursday. Chalkley Leconey claimed that Frank Lingo was their farmhand and was supposed to eat breakfast with them but did not show. Chalkley asked Annie to save Lingo's breakfast. Not only did Lingo miss breakfast but he did not show up for work in the field either.

Lingo was brought to the kitchen to see the victim. According to the *Camden Daily Telegram*, September 10, 1889, he told the police, "If these were the last words I had to say, I would tell you that I know nothing about this affair. The last time I saw Miss Annie was last Thursday. She invited me to stay to supper, saying that if I did so I would have company up to the camp-meeting grounds." He was asked why he did not come to work for Mr. Leconey. He said, "Because the people around here are all the time teasing me."

Coroner Stanton empaneled a jury of twelve men, which was composed of farmers from the local area. The inquest began with the jurors viewing the body. The county physician, Dr. William H. Iszard, stated that there was no doubt of her virginity. He believed rape had been attempted but not accomplished and added, "it was as if the villain had not succeeded in accomplishing his dastardly purpose of ravishing his victim." He gave no evidence of his assertion since her clothing only showed signs of a struggle and she was not exposed. According to the Camden County Courier, September 14, 1889, the jury heard evidence that footprints leaving the house toward a creek nearby and along a bank measured ten and a half inches long, however, Lingo's shoes measured eleven and three-quarters inches. Bridget Smith, the washerwoman, told the jury that Lingo had attempted to assault her on one occasion, but she prevented him from doing so.

And then a bombshell testimony to the prosecutor seemed to absolve Lingo and implicate Chalkley Leconey. According to the *Passaic Daily News*, September 17, 1889, Leconey's chief hired hand, Garret Murray, a Black man, told Prosecutor Jenkins that he accompanied Leconey to the house just before the murder: "Murray says that Leconey went into the house and a few minutes later he heard groans from within. Soon after this Murray says he went away. Later he was met by Leconey and William Smith, who threatened to fasten the crime on Murray if he attempted to squeal." Part of the plot was to pin the murder onto Lingo. In the Sentinel, October 3, 1889, William Smith corroborated the story at the habeas corpus proceedings in front of the Supreme Court. The article stated, "Smith is a white man, a veteran of the war, who lives in a little shanty on the Cooper property not far from Leconey's place . . . He swore that on the morning of the 9th, about day break, he heard Chalkley Leconey calling outside his house. He went over and Leconey said, 'Smith, I've had a fuss with Annie over at the house and I'm afraid I've hurt her.'" The motive offered by the detectives was that Richard Leconey's estate was about to be settled, and Chalkley wanted Annie's share of the will.

In court, Annie's father, Richard's brother, sat by his nephew's side, convinced he did not kill his daughter. Ultimately, Chalkley was acquitted on March 4, 1890, largely due to many inconsistencies in Murray's testimony. For example, the defense attorney pointed out that if Murray's testimony is true, then Annie died just before five A.M., but the physicians examined the body at nine A.M., and it was still warm. The estimated time of death was approximately seven A.M. If truly innocent, this means the offender murdered Annie after Chalkley and Garret Murray left the house. If the physicians are correct that the offender must have been interrupted, then we do not know what his true agenda was.

Recall that McGarry stated he not only visited Philadelphia with Tumblety, but they stayed for three weeks. McGarry said, ". . . and then visited New Haven and Philadelphia, when we stopped at the Girard Hotel in Philadelphia. It took us three weeks to see the sights in Philadelphia. The Doctor showed me everything." Tumblety was clearly very familiar with the Philadelphia area and traveled through Camden by train on his way to or from New York City. There was a train station in Merchantville. According to the *Brooklyn Daily Eagle*, August 9, 1889, a three-month-long New York City court case that Tumblety was involved with was recently adjudicated. According to the *Olean Democrat*, August 8, 1889, an Olean resident was traveling by cable car on the Brooklyn Bridge on August 1 and stuck up a conversation with fellow passenger Francis Tumblety. They parted ways on the Brooklyn side of the bridge. This means that Tumblety's unusually long stay in New York City had ended, and he was now, at this time, in transit; thus, we cannot exclude him.

LINGO'S BAD LUCK – SEPTEMBER 1890

The Annie Leconey murder may very well have been from a local person attempting to rob the farm, but the attack was vicious, suggesting rage. Additionally, there was a second murder the very next year and close to the first anniversary of the Double Event murders. An Annie Miller was murdered on September 26, 1890. According to the *Philadelphia Times*, September 28, 1890, Annie Miller had "the same ghastly wound which had been found upon the throat of Annie Leconey and there was also the stab wounds which had been inflicted before the throat was cut." She was mutilated along a lonely road, then thrown into the woods. According to the *Philadelphia Times*, October 7, 1890, the Miller farm was three miles from the Leconey farm. Francis Lingo was again suspected and arrested, witnesses coming forward claiming to have seen him in a patch of woods near the murder site.

The county physician, Dr. Iszard, initially stated that the victim was sexually assaulted but soon recanted this. The *Passaic Daily News*, September 30, 1890, reported, "County Physician Izard says the announcement that the post mortem examination revealed that Mrs. Miller had been criminally assaulted was premature." In order to maintain his claim that the motive was rape, notice how Dr. Iszard explained it, as reported in the *Courier Post*, September 27, 1890:

> Rape Believed to Have Been the Motive.
>
> The first impressions that the motive for the deed was rape is confirmed in the minds of the authorities by the development made in the case to-day, and while County Physician Iszard's opinion, as given to a Courier reporter this morning, was a guarded one, it was to the effect that rape had been attempted and the resistance of the woman had led to the murder.

Recall that this was the same explanation that Iszard gave for Annie Leconey's murder one year earlier.

The case went to trial, and according to the *Monmouth Inquirer*, March 26, 1891, Lingo was convicted of the murder in the first degree. The case against him was based on circumstantial evidence. The jurors also knew Lingo was suspected in the Laconey murder the year before.

In the *Courier-Post*, March 8, 1892, the Supreme Court granted a new trial based upon new evidence.

In the *Courier-News*, November 14, 1892, Supreme Court Justice Garrison ordered the jury to acquit the prisoner. The defense attorney, "cited several principles of the common law protecting the rights of persons accused of crime . . . He cited as his third principle the rule of law in homicide cases which relate to motive. He held that so far the crime alleged against his client showed no motive." Even though Dr. Iszard guardedly concluded rape was the motive without rape having to have occurred, the Supreme Court justice disagreed.

The citizens of Merchantville demanded action, and even though both Lingo and Chalkley were acquitted, they wanted an execution. An article in the *Berkshire Eagle*, November 14, 1882, stated:

> The good people of Merchantville are in arms because of the acquittal in Camden of Francis Lingo (colored), the alleged murderer of Mrs. Annie Miller. Their anger knows no bounds, and is intermingled with fear that someone else may be murdered in that vicinity and the perpetrator go unpunished.... As soon as it was learned that Lingo was a free man threats of lynching him, should he return to the community, were freely made, and the threats grow in earnestness and volume.... The citizens argue that as the murders of Miss Annie Leconey and Mrs. Annie Miller, both of which occurred within their midst, are unavenged; there is no safety for them ... they fear that the acquittal of Chalkley Leconey and Francis Lingo of the respective murders (the latter was also arrested for the first crime), will set a lawless precedent that may result in another mysterious killing. They also feel that someone should be hanged for each murder, but as there is no probability of either mystery ever being cleared, the best they can do is to take, in a measure, the law in their own hands and protect their homes by aggressive methods.

Notice how the truth took second fiddle to their community's protection. If Lingo was indeed murdering these women, then we might expect to see more from him. But there was nothing ... until 1897.

According to the *Morning Post*, December 11, 1897, Frank Lingo was arrested for attempting to lure a Philadelphia resident named Katherine Berry "to a lonely spot" near Merchantville, New Jersey, in order to rape and murder her. Berry advertised in the newspaper "for a position as companion to an aged lady or invalid." Berry received a reply from a "Mrs. Mabel Cooper," of Merchantville inviting her to a location two miles from Pennsauken station. In the letter, Berry "was told that a colored man servant would meet her" at the station. Berry became suspicious and told her brother, Robert Berry, who went to Merchantville. Robert Berry discovered there was no Mrs. Cooper, and with the help of Police Chief Linderman, they discovered that Frank Lingo wrote the letter. Linderman then arrested Lingo.

Frank Lingo admitted to writing the letters but claimed he wrote them for "a colored man who gave his name as William Jones and a light complexioned colored woman who he understood was Miss Mabel Cooper." He then continued:

I saw the couple driving in Merchantville twice and wondered who they were. One day I was sitting on a coal box when the couple drove up and the man asked me if I was Frank Lingo. I told him I was and we talked about the murder cases. He said he would see me again. One day right afterward I saw him on the street. He shook hands with me and said "Excuse my glove." A day or two afterward he came and asked me if I would write a letter for him for Miss Cooper, who lived out near Ellisburg. I wrote the letter and he gave me a quarter. Then I wrote the other letters and read the answers to him. He got me to get the mail, and I got a bundle for him one day. That is all I know about the case that I've been drawn into.

The charge before the jury was forgery, and forgery only, so the defense team made the decision only to fight that. While they proclaimed that the story of Lingo attempting to lure Miss Berry was untrue, they put all of their energy into dismantling the forgery charge of faking letters signed by a Mrs. Mabel Cooper. It seemed very winnable in their eyes since there was no Mrs. Cooper to be found. How can you forge a person's letters and signature if they do not exist? The problem, though, was the jurors were so appalled by why Lingo supposedly wrote the letters, that he was attempting to lead the woman into the woods to rape and murder her. Not only was Lingo convicted but the judge awarded Lingo twenty years in prison and a $3,000 fine.

Corroborating the point that Lingo was effectively being retried for the Annie Miller murder was a fast-spreading rumor that Lingo confessed to the Miller murder while in prison just days after being jailed, as reported on the *Morning Post*, December 28, 1897. A *Post* reporter asked Prosecutor Jenkins if it was true, and Jenkins "laughed it to scorn." The reporter then interviewed Lingo in his cell, who expressed astonishment and replied, "No! I never done that and I haven't seen nobody but Dave Corbett who come to see me last night, and you . . . What things they do say about me. Everybody's agin me, and that's what sends me up for twenty years. They lied about me." The reporter asked if there was any Mrs. Mabel Cooper. Lingo stated, "If there ain't I've been the victim of some of them black enemies of mine out to Matchtown. I didn't never see Miss Berry till I see her in Camden. Somebody else has gone there and she thought it was me."

Even though the newspapers and many of the citizens of Merchantville were convinced of Lingo's guilt in the Miller murder and the Leconey murder, the reason why they should still be considered unsolved crimes is twofold. First, there was not enough evidence to bring charges against Lingo in the

Leconey murder, and Lingo was ultimately acquitted of the Miller murder. The reason why there was insufficient evidence may very well have been because Lingo was telling the truth. Lingo lived in the area, so when Miller was murdered, he certainly would have been near the murder site. The fact that the press published the idea of residents lynching Lingo for the Miller murder even if he was innocent shows how far people were willing to go. The truth was secondary. Merchantville residents who were convinced Lingo was the murderer and then saw him walking freely among them were likely living in constant fear. Another murder may happen that very night or in five years, for all they knew. In view of this, it is not out of the question that a number of residents may have plotted against Lingo in 1897 and framed him in a forgery conspiracy. Why in 1897? Curiously, in a local newspaper, the *Camden Daily Telegram*, April 22, 1897, the reporter opened old wounds and recalled both murders and Lingo's supposed connection to the murders, stating, "During the trial evidence was produced which pointed to Frank Lingo, a colored man, as the guilty party."

Second, neither Annie Leconey nor Annie Miller were raped, while Lingo's supposed agenda against Miss Berry in 1897 was to rape her and then kill her. He apparently was so obsessed with someone, not local and whom he'd never met, that he attempted to lure her to Merchantville. If Lingo was a serial killer, meaning, murdering more than one person at separate times, we should expect a similar motive. But the motive in the murders was not rape. Additionally, a rage murder makes sense if Lingo felt wronged in his daily life, i.e., being wronged by a local woman. There was no reported incident that Miss Berry was near Lingo to get him angry.

These are actually the second and third mysterious murders of a young woman only a few miles from Merchantville. Recall, in April 1886, Annie Dugan was murdered "between Camden and Merchantville," in a stretch of about 3.5 miles. It seems that the connection between her murder and the others was that Dugan was not from the area. The only possible suspects in the Dugan murder were two White men, one tall and the other stout. No one saw a Black man, such as Lingo, near the murder site.

There is a separate answer to all three murders: an offender not from Merchantville but only transiting through. Connecting the two cities was the Camden & Mt. Holly Railroad, which paralleled a road about three hundred yards to the north. Additionally, the Merchantville Train Station was along the Camden & Mt. Holly Railroad. While local authorities were looking for a local offender, the facts also fit the possibility of a killer who passed through the area.

Tumblety used to take this train route as he traveled on the Baltimore & Ohio Railroad system on his way back to New York City multiple times per year. This means Tumblety was near all three murder sites in the same year of each murder.

THE PITTSBURGH RIPPER AND THE GUNSAULIS MURDER – MAR/APRIL 1891

The March 5, 1891, issue of the *Pittsburgh Daily Post* reported upon a street assault with a large knife on young Kate McGarvey, the article titled, "May Be Another Ripper. A Young Woman Assaulted by a Strange Man With a Knife":

> Kate McGarvey, a young woman, was murderously assaulted about 8 o'clock last night on Second avenue. She was on her way to her home at No. 334 Second avenue, and as she passed the pork packing establishment of Rea & Co. near Try street, a man jumped out from the shadow and slashed at her several times with a large keen-edged knife. She ran screaming out the avenue, attracted the attention of Officers Roach and Devlin, but her assailant had secreted himself before they arrived. Miss McGarvey was fortunately unhurt, although the clothing on her back was slashed into shreds. The police are looking for the local "ripper."

Likely because Kate McGarvey was neither injured nor killed, there are no other accounts of the attacks yet discovered. If the murder had been successful, it most certainly would have made national news since the Jack the Ripper murders were just a few years earlier. While there is no description of the assailant, the account of the attack matches so many accounts of the attacks and murders reported in this book.

Interestingly, the Baltimore & Ohio Train Depot was just yards away. Tumblety's habit to travel from Hot Springs and/or New Orleans to St. Louis, then on the Baltimore & Ohio railway system, connected Tumblety to either Buffalo and Rochester or to Philadelphia, through New Jersey, and then to New York City. Alternatively, Tumblety would leave Manhattan at Grand Central Station, travel by train north to Boston, Massachusetts, or Albany, New York, west to Rochester and Buffalo, New York, south to Pittsburgh, Pennsylvania, and ultimately to Hot Springs, Arkansas.

A murder occurred in Pittsburgh one month after the attack on Kate McGarvey, and this time eyewitnesses saw a tall man with a mustache wearing a gray overcoat in the vicinity of the crime scene. This murder, though, was that of a young man. While not a young woman, there are a number of curious coincidences that lead to considering the possibility that Tumblety perpetrated the crime. According to the *Pittsburgh Dispatch*, April 7, 1891:

> John W. Gunsaulis was murdered at the lonely falls on the West Liberty road at a few minutes after 10 o'clock on Sunday night. Less than five minutes before he had left his sweetheart, Miss Maggie Smith, at her home, and her kiss was still warm on the lips. He was scarcely past his 21st birthday, and on Thursday he was to have been married. As he left the home of his fiancée he had laughingly showed her the money with which to make the first payment on their home. The amount was $1,250, and beside that he had a gold and a silver watch. The robber left only the silver timepiece . . .

John Gunsaulis was found dead Monday morning with a bullet hole in the back of his head. He was lying on an embankment alongside the road he had to travel from West Liberty. Gunsaulis's fiancée, Annie Smith, was quoted in the *People's Register*, April 10, 1891, stating:

> John came to our house yesterday afternoon. He took supper and spent the evening with us. He left a few minutes after 10 o'clock. He told me that he had been followed by a dangerous looking man when he came out to see me on Saturday evening, and he said he had seen the same man walking after him that afternoon . . . While he was with me in the evening he spoke several times of the man he had seen following him. He described the man as being tall and heavy, wearing a gray overcoat and having a mustache. Just before leaving, he said, "Well, I suppose I'll meet my man to-night." . . . He also told me that the same man had come up to him one evening a week before, and asked him for the time. He pulled his revolver, and said, "Now I have got the drop on you, get away from me."

The *People's Register* then stated that Gunsaulis's body was found facedown, clutching his revolver in his left hand. There were three empty chambers in the revolver.

A fifty-year-old vagrant named Holmes Anderson was quickly arrested and charged with Gunsaulis's death. The *Pittsburgh Press*, March 23, 1896, stated:

> Anderson was arrested the next day [after Gunsaulis's body was discovered] at the home of his brother-in-law in Allentown. After a tedious trial, in which it was proved that he was near his home all that night, Anderson was acquitted.

The case remains unsolved to this day, and just as with so many women who were murdered or assaulted, the suspect in this case was a tall man wearing a gray overcoat. Also, notice that the physical description Gunsaulis gave to his fiancée matches the physical description of Tumblety; both being tall and having a mustache. Even though Gunsaulis believed the motive of the tall man was robbery, it may also have been the tall man making aggressive sexual advances. Tumblety's evening activities in multiple cities in the United States match the encounters Gunsaulis told his fiancée. Richard Norris stated under oath that Tumblety was relentless, even coming to his work and speaking with his boss. When Tumblety was arrested in March 1881 in New Orleans for pickpocketing young Henry Govan, Govan stated that Tumblety was relentless in his advances toward him. In the case of Gunsaulis, the tall man was hounding him for a full week with Gunsaulis even believing he would encounter the very same man the night he was murdered.

Recall, this is why Tumblety was arrested in New York City two months later, in June 1889, when he attempted to "engage in a conversation" with George Davis. Young Davis was angered by what Tumblety had implicated and then called Tumblety a vile name. Enraged, Tumblety hit him with a cane. Notice the similarity, not to mention the events occurring less than two months apart. Not only did Tumblety approach Davis at night as the tall man did with Gunsaulis, but Tumblety also responded violently after being rejected, as the tall man may have done. Gunsaulis did put a gun to the head of the tall man.

Two months after the Pittsburgh Ripper attacked young McGarvey and one month after Gunsaulis was murdered and robbed of his $1,250 and gold watch, Tumblety was in Hot Springs, Arkansas, where a burglar entered his room and robbed him. Shockingly, notice what he reported stolen, as published in the *Times-Picayune*, May 5, 1891:

> There is no clew to the $2500 diamond robbery at the Hotel Eastman recently. And the detectives are in darkness as to who stole the $13,000 worth of diamonds and $2,000 in money from Dr. Tumblety, a guest at the Plateau Hotel. The thieves also stole from the doctor a fine gold watch of peculiar mechanism and make, which should be easily traced by a shrewd detective.

Tumblety's gold watch was recovered in 1893 by a woman named Cora Simms. She stated it was hidden in a basement of a deserted house in Hot Springs, Arkansas. According to the *St. Louis Globe-Democrat*, December 29, 1894, Simms turned it over to the chief of police.

In certain cities, such as New Orleans in 1881, Tumblety would stay at least a month before traveling to the next city. Tumblety was quite comfortable with Pittsburgh. He opened an office in Pittsburgh soon after the Civil War in November 1866 and maintained it until August 1867. He then returned occasionally, opening new offices for months on end until May 1872.

JACK THE STRANGLER STRIKES AGAIN – AUGUST 1891

An article in the *Brooklyn Daily Eagle*, August 3, 1891, stated that on Sunday, August 2, 1891, a young woman around the age of twenty was found murdered in a wooded area near Glendale, Long Island. The body was found between bushes and a house lying on its back. The victim was wearing a black skirt, and all of the undergarments were in place, suggesting rape was not the motive. Dr. Vincent Judson performed the autopsy and determined that death had been caused by asphyxiation due to strangulation and that the attack must have been violent. On her fingers were two gold rings set with garnet and rhinestone. A pair of gold sleeve buttons and a black breastpin adorned the victim's clothing. This showed that robbery for financial gain was not the motive.

THE IDENTIFIED GIRL.
From the police photograph.

THE MURDERED GIRL.

THE LONELY ROAD.

According to the *Evening World*, August 6, 1891, Reverend Thomas Martin of Hewletts, Long Island, identified the victim on August 5 as his family's

English servant girl, or domestic, Hannah Robinson. Martin stated to the police that Robinson was missing since Saturday, August 1, so this was likely the date of the murder. They had hired her two months earlier from Hendrickson's employment agency on Fulton Street in Brooklyn. Martin said that the victim left their home and took the 4:29 P.M. train for Long Island City. It, therefore, is possible that the assailant followed Hannah off the train, similar to a number of the cases examined.

Mrs. Martin stated that Hannah planned to continue onto Brooklyn and go shopping. The *Evening World*, August 5, 1891, stated Detective Henry Miller and Constable Earnest Brechter were assigned to the case. They appropriately dug into her life; interviewing family and friends and going through her letters and personal effects. Coroner Homeyer also began his investigation, stating to the press that he would catch the assassin. Half a dozen men were arrested, but all were eventually discharged. The case remains unsolved.

The *Wilkes-Barre News*, August 11, 1891, reported on the detectives being puzzled over a discovery that a fifteen-year-old girl, Mamie Maguire, was attacked and strangled in a vacant lot on Long Island. Maguire, however, survived and stated that the offender was a large, powerful man. The article then states, "The manner in which the fellow seized her has impressed the authorities with the idea that possibly this Long Island 'Jack the Strangler' is a man who is responsible for the English servant girl's death."

As with many of these unsolved murders of women, not only was there no robbery and rape, but there is also a connection to the victim being near or at a train station. The local authorities and press certainly did see a connection to the numerous murders in the same location on Long Island. In the *Evening World*, July 2, 1892, a correspondent reported on yet another unsolved murder and stated,

> Within the past two years *half a dozen women* have been assaulted in the same neighborhood and the assailant never captured. At Glendale, which is only two miles from Maspeth, Hannah Robinson, a young girl, was assaulted and then choked to death last fall, but the guilty one was never brought to justice. [Author emphasis added.]

The use of the word "assaulted" could not have meant raped, since none of them were.

Glendale, Long Island, borders Brooklyn on the east, a city in which Tumblety had an extensive history. Additionally, Hannah Robinson had taken the train, so we see again that the offender of the crime may very well have seen her at the train station. In sworn testimony in 1905, Reverend J. J. Conway, professor of ethics and political economy at St. Louis University and chaplain at St. John's Hospital in St. Louis in 1903, stated he had many conversations with Tumblety just before he passed away. He said Tumblety showed him documents demonstrating that he owned stock in a railroad company in Long Island.

CUT IN TWO – NOVEMBER 1891

As in the case of Amelia Olson, another young woman was brutally murdered in Chicago yet was neither robbed nor raped. According to the *Inter Ocean*, November 6, 1891, the deceased was well-known actress Fannie, or Fanny, Cartwright. At twelve forty-five A.M., Wednesday, November 4, foreman of the switching crew of the Northwestern train yard, Ed Brown, found her body on the tracks. The body was lying diagonally across the north rail, cut in two with the head on the inside of the tracks. Brown also claimed that at eleven forty-five A.M., the body was not at the location. If true, then the body would have been hit by a train when two engines passed over the track at twelve fifteen A.M. In the *Inter Ocean*, November 5, 1891, the reporter described the scene: "Very early yesterday morning unmistakable evidence of a murder, that may have been the work of some Western imitator of Jack the Ripper . . ." Strangely, not a drop of blood was on the ground. The detectives assigned to the case were convinced it was a murder and the murderer placed the body "on the railroad tracks with the expectation that the wheels would remove all evidence that a crime had been committed." The purse was found near the scene and contained jewelry, suggesting robbery was not the motive. Clothing was on the body and was positioned to suggest she was not raped.

The deputy coroner had the inquest the next day on November 5 and concluded it was an accident. This caused an immediate outrage, many complaining that the deputy coroner failed to take into account crucial evidence. For example, how the body was mutilated by the train showed that the victim had her arms out to the side. Also, the blood on the body was dry and congealed, suggesting Cartwright was killed many hours before. There were gashes to the abdomen, and detectives believed that falling in front of a train would not have inflicted wounds like these, but the gashes did resemble a knife attack. The deputy coroner did not even request an autopsy. Police Captain Laughlin stated, "The deputy coroner made a great mistake. Such inquests are worse than useless. The county physician should have been called to make an examination of the body and testify before the jury. I am opposed to rushing matters of so much importance as this."

Ignoring the deputy coroner's conclusions, the police arrested John Beatty. Beatty was the last person seen with Cartwright. They also found out that Beatty was actually arrested seven years earlier for the Amelia Olson murder. While the police released Beatty for the Olson murder, in this case, a Grand Jury was convened to review the evidence. As reported in the *Times Herald*, December 5, 1891, an Associated Press report published the results of the Grand Jury, which returned a "No Bill." The grand jury concluded that there was not enough evidence against Beatty and the case was dropped.

Eyewitnesses stated that Fannie planned on walking from Indiana Street to Roby Street to Austin Street and then going south on Artesian Street. Her body was discovered on the northwestern train tracks at Artesian Street. The path that Fannie walked and the location of where her body was found was near the Oakley Avenue Train Station. Also, Fannie had to cross the Chicago–Milwaukee Street train tracks just half a block north.

THE PITTSBURGH RIPPER STRIKES AGAIN? – FEBRUARY 1892

According to the *Pittsburgh Press*, February 19, 1892, the dead body of a young woman was found at about eleven A.M. near the corner of Bouquet Street and Sylvan Avenue in Pittsburgh, Pennsylvania, in an area known as Oakland. The body was found "about 100 feet below Sylvan avenue, among the rocks." The victim's name was Sarah Joyce, aged twenty-one years. She was about five feet eight inches, weighing about 150 pounds. Her hair was short and black, and she was wearing a "red velvet hat, black beaver coat, plum colored dress, black stockings and a red and black barred flannel skirt." She had a purse containing thirty cents and a handkerchief.

The *Pittsburgh Press*, February 22, 1892, reported that Coroner McDowell began an inquiry. The first witness was Sarah Joyce's brother-in-law, Michael McGinley, who said that Sarah was at his house at five thirty P.M. Thursday evening, which is when he left for work. McGinley identified the body. He also said that Sarah never went out at night and only did so if his wife sent her on an errand. He said Sarah had not been sick. Tony Hasley, a teamster, testified that he found the body and noticed that the ground had been trampled, discovered some blood spots, and saw marks where a man had fallen on the soft earth near what looked to be drag marks coming from the road. He recalled seeing a deep wound under the woman's right eye and seeing her tongue sticking out. James

Hartman and Thomas Sheehan testified to the same facts. In the *Pittsburgh Daily Post*, February 23, 1892, it stated her clothes had been "disarranged" so Hasley, Hartman, and Sheehan first replaced them.

Dr. J. Guy McCandless and Police Surgeon Dr. Moyer held the postmortem and stated that there were marks of violence on the victim's body. There was a scalp wound and a flesh wound on the cheek the size of a lead pencil, which extended into the bone. The bone was slightly fractured. It was Moyer's opinion that the wound was produced by a sharp instrument, such as the tool used to sharpen knives. The fact that Tony Hasley noticed her tongue was sticking out suggests that the assailant strangled the victim. Police Surgeon Moyer stated in the postmortem examination that Joyce died from suffocation. Her blood was dark colored, as is usual in cases of asphyxiation. The *Pittsburgh Dispatch*, February 20, 1892, reported after discussing the postmortem exam, "The physicians found no evidences of injury except the two wounds mentioned. There was positive evidence that no assault had ever been committed." Although there was no physical evidence that Sarah Joyce was sexually assaulted, Dr. Moyer would not definitively swear that rape was not the offender's motive. The only reason he suspected sexual assault was because "her assailant must have had a motive," and since it was not robbery, in his mind, it had to be rape. Clearly, Dr. Moyer had no understanding of serial offender motives.

Nora McGinley, Sarah Joyce's sister, testified as follows: "I am a sister of Sarah Joyce. I last saw her alone at 6:30 Thursday evening at my house. She said she was going to the lady she lived with on Ward street." Nora stated that Sarah would have to go up Sylvan Avenue and saw her go up the road. She stated that Sarah had no marks on her face. Nora stated that she saw a "colored man" on the road a half hour earlier. Nora identified John Pulpus as the man. Pulpus admitted that he was indeed on Sylvan but denied that he was "on that part of the lonely road" where the murder occurred. He claimed that he left the road by a "foot path at a point fully 20 yards further down the hill, and that he went directly from that point to his boarding house down in the ravine."

The jurors concluded that John Pulpus murdered Sarah Joyce in an effort to sexually assault her. Pulpus was arrested. The *Pittsburgh Post-Gazette*, February 29, Pulpus had his supporters stating, "The colored people of the city think Pulpus is innocent and have begun a subscription to retain counsel to defend him. John Scott has been made treasurer of the fund which now amounts to $15; all raised by the waiters in one restaurant."

The police admitted that the evidence against Pulpus was weak, as detailed by the *Pittsburgh Dispatch*, April 11, 1892:

Although they furnished the circumstantial evidence upon which Pulpus was held for the crime, the police admit that the evidence is weak, and acknowledge their belief that Pulpus cannot be convicted on it. The case is expected to come up before the grand jury this week, and it will be no surprise if the bill against Pulpus is ignored. The police declare they have no other evidence of any importance against him than that produced before the Coroner . . . In the meantime no clew has been found leading to any other person as the murderer of Sarah Joyce, and does not seem likely that the guilty man will ever be apprehended.

According to the *Pittsburgh Post-Gazette*, June 22, 1892, a grand jury cleared Pulpus of all charges. The case remains unsolved.

No one saw Sarah Joyce near any man around the time of her murder, so there is no solid eyewitness physical description of a possible suspect, one that indicates Tumblety or excludes him. Even so, this mysterious murder does have some striking similarities to the 1886 Buffalo assaults and the December 1888 Chicago assault by a tall man in an Ulster coat. Recall, these assaults began with the assailant grabbing the women by the throat and attempting to force them to go to a different location. This is exactly what happened to Sarah Joyce. Joyce was walking on Sylvan Avenue, yet her body was found in a secluded place just off the road. Her tongue was out, and she died of asphyxiation, meaning, she was strangled. Further, the murder site was only a block from two separate sets of train tracks and only minutes away from the Laughlin Train Station on the Baltimore & Ohio Railroad, the same railroad near the Kate McGarvey knife attack one year earlier. Also, even though the police surgeon was clearly ignorant of serial offender motives, the Joyce murder certainly does conform to a serial killer with a motive of anger-retaliatory.

THE NEW JERSEY RAILROAD LINE – APRIL 1892

Lizzie Farrell was murdered on April 28, 1892, outside, in Red Bank, New Jersey. This location is just south of Perth Amboy and South Amboy. According to the *Cincinnati Post*, April 29, 1892, Farrell was blonde and about thirty years old. She was found on Bridge Avenue "near the railroad track" with her head crushed in with no signs of rape. She was taken to the hospital but died three days later. The murder remains a mystery. The Red Bank train station, aka, New York & Long Branch Passenger Station, was next to Bridge Avenue, having opened in 1875. It was the next stop after the Perth Amboy and South Amboy stations on the North Jersey Coast Line of the New Jersey Central Railroad system.

In the *Monmouth Democrat*, May 5, 1892, Lizzie Farrell's whereabouts just before her murder were ascertained by interviewing witnesses. The article stated:

> On the night of the assault, Miss Farrell was returning home, after spending the evening in company with Miss [Mary] Leiden, at a friend's on Front street. Near the railroad station she and Miss Leiden parted, each going alone in different directions to their homes. It was only a short time after they had separated that Miss Farrell was found as before described.

If the killer was at or near the train station, he would have seen Lizzie Farrell walk off on her own. This certainly conforms to the pattern of an opportunistic serial killer stepping off a train and finding his next victim, only to quickly leave the area by rail. According to the *Morning Call*, April 30, 1892, the weapon was an "iron bar used on railroad switches." After the attack, the assailant dragged Lizzie "from the sidewalk to the gutter then fled."

Tumblety had been known to stay in this area of New Jersey. Just five miles away along the train route is Long Branch, New Jersey, to the southeast, which is the previous train stop on the New Jersey Central Railroad line. In the *New York Herald*, July 22, 1891, a letter from Francis Tumblety was published because he also provided a check for $323.75 to defray the expenses of an American stowaway. In the letter, Tumblety wrote:

> Returning from Long Branch [New Jersey] this morning I read an account in the brilliant New York Herald . . .

Although dated one year earlier, the published letter does show that Tumblety not only transited through Long Branch and Red Bank by train, but he also stayed in the area for a period of time. This is clear evidence that Tumblety journeyed through Red Bank during his travels. He considered New York City his home, living at 109 East 9th Street in 1891. On May 30, 1892, Tumblety was in Washington DC, the *New York Herald*, May 31, 1892, recording a personal appreciation from him. If Tumblety did travel to Washington DC from New York City in April 1892, then that would have him traveling through Red Bank, New Jersey, in the same month Lizzie Farrell was murdered in that very town.

JACK THE TRIPPER AND JACK THE CHASER, BAD PAIR OF JACKS – MAY 1892

In the *New York Press*, May 12, 1892, an article titled "Bad Pair of Jacks, This" reported upon two cases of a man purposely troubling and threatening women; one with the nickname "Jack the Tripper" and the other "Jack the Chaser." In Washington Square in New York City, a tall, middle-aged, well-dressed man in dark clothing with a dark mustache was tripping women with his gold-plated umbrella as they walked by him. A witness spotted the man hooking a girl's foot with his umbrella, which caused her to stumble and drop all of her books. He apologized but then quickly vanished into the park. The young woman was convinced the man tripped her on purpose. The *New York Herald*, May 12, 1892, reported that moments after he tripped the young schoolgirl, he approached an older woman, a schoolteacher, and tripped her in the same fashion. The man again apologized but then quickly left. The schoolteacher was convinced the acts were malicious, so she went to the local police station. Further description of the man stated that he wore a high silk hat and diamonds:

> He is described as tall, well built, about 40, wearing a high silk hat, black clothing and diamonds on his shirt bosom and fingers. He has the appearance of a retired business man.

The police searched for the man but failed to arrest him. They dubbed him 'Jack the Tripper.'

Jack the Tripper had much in common with Francis Tumblety. Not only was Tumblety in the New York area in May 1892, but he was a tall man with a dark mustache who was known to carry an umbrella. According to the *New York Herald*, December 4, 1888, when Tumblety arrived in New York on December 2 after sneaking out of England, he was carrying an umbrella:

> He wore a long English cloth Ulster, without a cape, a derby hat, and carried an umbrella and two canes tied together. It was the now famous Dr. Tumblety...

L. D. Cain, proprietor of the Waverly Hotel in Hot Springs, Arkansas, stated under oath that he knew Tumblety for at least fifteen years, seeing him annually. He was asked by the attorney about Tumblety's dress and manner. Cain replied:

Well, Tumblety was filthy in his habits, first of all, and peculiar in that, while I don't think Tumblety meant to be a thief, or to pick up things as a thief would do, still he would carry away things in his coat and in his umbrella; 'most always carried an umbrella, in and out of the house.

Tumblety not only traveled with diamond rings, but he also traveled with diamond pins. Under sworn testimony in a 1905 court case, Hot Springs, Arkansas, resident Adolph Marx was asked if he knew Tumblety. Marx owned a cigar and tobacco store and replied that he had lived in Hot Springs for twenty years and knew Tumblety for fifteen years. He also said that he had a personal acquaintance with Tumblety for the last four years. The attorney asked Marx if he knew of Tumblety's financial condition. Marx replied:

> Oh, he says, he said in German to me, "I got plenty of money," and he put his hands in his pockets and took out some diamond rings, and put it on my fingers. Of course I handed them back. He had a scarf pin in his coat pocket, and showed me another pin with a diamond in it.

Tumblety offered that pin to another Hot Springs resident, John Hickey, proprietor of the Milwaukee Hotel. Around the year 1901, Tumblety was sick and asked Hickey to get the doctor. Hickey testified in court under oath, stating, "I went up there he [Tumblety] told me to send for old Dr. Keller. He says, 'I have got a diamond stud here, and I will give it to you.'" Hickey refused. The attorney asked if it was a diamond ring, and Hickey replied, "It was a diamond pin." Just three years earlier, Tumblety was arrested on June 4, 1889, for assault and battery on a young man named George Davis in Manhattan. Tumblety approached Davis and "engaged in conversation," which angered Davis, who called Tumblety "a vile name." This caused Tumblety to strike Davis with his cane. According to the *Pittsburgh Dispatch*, June 6, 1889, at the time of Tumblety's arrest, he was "flashily dressed and sparkling with diamonds."

The actions of Jack the Tripper are clearly misogynistic, and Tumblety was an eccentric misogynist. Also, Tumblety's last known New York City residence ten months earlier was literally 300 yards away from Washington Square Park at 109 E. 9th Street. In 1888, he lived at 79 E. 10th Street, which was also a short walk away from Washington Square Park.

Jack the Tripper may only have been a mean and eccentric man, but this anger-retaliatory type of behavior makes sense if he was a serial killer. He was purposely going out in public, targeting the type of person who brings out his rage—females—then tripping them. Violent offender experts M. R. Sutton and D. Keatley have connected non-homicidal activities with serial killers attempting to suppress homicidal urges. These behaviors are part of what they call "offending-oriented fantasy." Sutton and Keatley suggest that these behaviors would extend the time between homicides, or the cooling-off period. In their research article, "Cooling-off periods and serial homicide: A case study approach to analysing behaviour between murders," in *Forensic Science International: Mind and Law*, 2021, Sutton and Keatley discuss Dennis Rader, the BTK ('Bind, Torture, Kill') Killer, and they identify four cooling-off periods between murders he committed, lasting three years, eight years, five years, and fourteen years, respectively. The offending-oriented behavior they identified with Rader was trophy-taking, engaging in self-bondage, "rigging" potential victims' homes, taunting and sending letters to family members of victims and the police, and reading his name in the newspaper as "the BTK Killer." All of these activities would have suppressed Rader's homicidal urges. Sutton and Keatley also identified offending-oriented behavior in serial killer Lonnie Franklin Jr., the Grim Sleeper. These were trophy-taking and collecting Polaroid photos and videos of his victims. During his cooling-off periods, he would suppress his homicidal urges by reliving the experiences through fantasizing as he viewed these items, images, and videos.

Jack the Tripper's behavior fits well with offending-oriented fantasy, albeit not sado-sexual fulfillment but anger-retaliatory. Imagine the joy he must have felt at his victims' embarrassing, and possibly injurious, expense.

Recall that this was not the first time a serial eccentric misogynist was targeting women in New York City with an offending-oriented fantasy. In the October 1, 1888, issue of the *New York World*, Inspector Byrnes told the reporter:

> We caught a fellow who had a mania for throwing vitriol [sulfuric acid] upon women's dresses red-handed. Immediately after it was reported, his crime was localized. He frequented Fourteenth street. I found victims for him and my men were thickly scattered through the district.

It is difficult not to connect these two cases, meaning, the misogynist was one and the same. They are both cases of a man surprising the victim, committing the act outdoors, then vanishing. Even though one case is tripping a woman and the other is ruining women's dresses with acid, both acts could be considered an offending-oriented fantasy of a misogynist humiliating a woman and having little to no remorse. When Chief Inspector Littlechild stated in his

1913 letter that Tumblety's hatred of women was "remarkable and bitter in the extreme," the kind of unusual, or remarkable, extreme behavior evident in the above attacks comes to mind. It is also not a surprise that the physical description of diamond-wearing Jack the Tripper matches diamond-wearing Tumblety in style and appearance.

Jack the Chaser was across the river in New Jersey, ten miles south of Perth Amboy. Female residents of Red Bank, New Jersey, were being followed and chased by a man at night. This alarmed them greatly because of the recent murder of Lizzie Farrell. According to the *New York Press*, May 12, 1892:

> As Maria Moran and Katie Sherlock, two domestics, were returning home Tuesday night [May 10] they noticed a man standing in the shadow of the old Grace Church building. As the girls passed him he jumped out at them. Both girls ran back to the house where they had just left a companion, followed closely by the man. They rang the doorbell and called loudly for help. The man rushed up the steps and rudely grasped Miss Moran in his arms. As the door was opened the ruffian rudely pushed Miss Moran aside and was soon lost in the darkness.
>
> Moran fainted. The report then stated, "The man is supposed to be a crank, and a great many people have an idea that this is the murderer of Lizzie Farrell."

ANOTHER RAHWAY MYSTERY – JUNE 1892

According to the June 10, 1892, issue of the *New York Sun*, on June 8, in Perth Amboy, New Jersey, a sixteen-year-old servant girl named Mary Anderson had her throat slit. Perth Amboy is situated on the opposite side of the river from New York City, specifically, in the borough of Staten Island. An Associated Press article in the *Democratic Advocate*, June 11, 1892, stated she worked in Rahway: "Mary Anderson, a domestic employed in a hotel at Rahway, New Jersey . . ." An article in the *Daily Times*, June 9, 1892, makes it clear that she was murdered along the train tracks:

MARY ANDERSON.

> The little village of Sewarren is wild today over the finding of the body of Mary Anderson a pretty young Danish girl near the Jersey Central Railroad tracks between Perth Amboy junction and Woodbridge Creek, with her throat cut.

Later, it was discovered that she was first shot with a .32-caliber pistol. Her body was found near the New Jersey Central Railroad tracks between Perth Amboy junction and Woodbridge Creek near a patch of woods. It was very near the Edgar Train Station, which was between Perth Amboy and Rahway. She was lying on her back with no signs of rape. Officials theorized that Anderson was first shot along the tracks, then dragged to the wooded area where she was mutilated with the knife.

Anderson was in the habit of walking the short stretch of train track when traveling to and from work. According to the *Sun*, June 13, 1892, one week later, two boys discovered a ten-inch blade near the location of the crime scene.

Local law enforcement was convinced enough that a local railroad workman, or brakeman, named Harry Schlipf committed the crime that they arrested him and placed him in pre-trial confinement, as published by the *Pike County Dispatch*, June 23, 1892:

> STRONG FEELING AGAINST SCHLIPF
>
> Perth Amboy, N. J., June 17 – Great excitement was caused here when the townspeople learned of the damaging evidence Detective Charles A. Oliver of New Brunswick has against Harry Schlipf, the Lehigh Valley brakeman who is confined in the Middlesex county jail, charged with the murder of pretty 16-year-old Hester Mary Anderson. Mary Anderson's body was found in a patch of woods alongside of the Jersey Central Railroad track, a mile north of here over a week ago, with a bullet wound in her left arm and her throat cut from ear to ear.

Schlipf was working in that area at the time. Another watchman claimed he saw Schlipf running away from the crime scene at five twenty P.M., and the murder had occurred at five ten P.M.

There were also conflicting eyewitness accounts, and other workers claimed that Schlipf could not have been at the crime scene:

> When Harry Schlipf was arrested there were a dozen of his fellow employees who came forward and said that they could swear that he was at work at his post in the Lehigh Valley yards on the Wednesday afternoon of the murder, without leaving it once.

Detective Oliver continued to favor the eyewitness account against Schlipf, who was, thus, held in pre-trial confinement for two months. It took the state

Supreme Court to order his release or take him to court, but they dropped their case against him. According to the *Philadelphia Inquirer*, April 7, 1892,

> The bondsmen of Harry Schlipf, who was accused of the murder of Mary Anderson, near New Brunswick, have been released from the bond by the Supreme Court. Schlipf was arrested on purely circumstantial evidence, and afterward proved an alibi. The guilty party has never been found.

It just does not make sense that Schlipf would have carried a revolver and a knife with him at work, happen upon the victim at a location he was not normally at, shoot her and slit her throat, then casually go back to work. If it was a premeditated murder, it does not make sense that the suspect would kill the person where they worked.

At no time did law enforcement tell reporters that the killer may have been someone unknown to the victim, such as a transient.

Again, Tumblety was reported to possess and even carry a small revolver. Under sworn testimony in 1905, A. R. Smith, proprietor of the Hotel Navarre, Hot Springs, served one term as mayor of Hot Springs in 1882 and recalled Tumblety coming to him requesting permission to carry his gun. Strangely, Tumblety also traveled with railroad bonds, but if he was wandering on the tracks and was approached by law enforcement, claiming to be merely inspecting his investments would have sounded reasonable. Having the jewelry and cash he always carried would have reinforced this because he would have come off as rich. His collection of knives has already been well established.

Shockingly, Tumblety can be placed at the Anderson murder site within a few days of the murder. He sent a personal ad to the *New York Herald* on May 30, 1892, from Washington DC, as reported in their May 31, 1892, issue:

> DR. TUMBLETY'S APPRECIATION. [BY TELEGRAPH TO THE HERALD.] Corner Fifteenth and G Streets, N.W., Washington, May 30, 1893. A man with a breezy air dropped into the Herald Bureau this afternoon and said: — "I see the Herald is at it again, doing good. I would rather give fifty dollars every morning than miss the Herald. It has done more real good than all the newspapers of this country combined. The free Ice project is a practicable idea and it will give great relief and comfort to the poor people and in many cases will save lives. Just send this twenty dollar bill to the New York office. Pardon me for intruding. Good afternoon." The name on the card left by the energetic and mysterious visitor was Dr. Francis Tumblety.

The reason Tumblety was sending money was to get his name into the New York paper so he could publish his philanthropy in his 1893 autobiography. After he published his biography, he never gave to the poor again.

Five days later, the *New York Herald*, June 5, 1892, reported Tumblety telegraphed from Baltimore, Maryland, an intention to donate $40:

> Dr. Francis Tumblety telegraphs the Herald from Baltimore that a donation of $40 from him (his second) is in transit.

In the *New York Herald*, June 6, 1892, Tumblety stated he would bring to the New York office of the *New York Herald* $100 on Monday morning, meaning June 10, 1892. Tumblety had taken the train from Washington DC northeast to Baltimore, Maryland, which is in the direction of Philadelphia, Pennsylvania, then through Red Bank, New Jersey, where Lizzie Farrell was murdered near the train station just a few weeks earlier, through Rahway—the location of the murder mystery in 1887—and finally to his destination of New York City.

This means Tumblety was traveling by train from Washington DC around May 31 to New York City with the intention of arriving by June 11, 1892. Perth Amboy is a train stop in New Jersey just before arriving in New York City. This point cannot be overstated. Mary Anderson was murdered with her throat cut from ear to ear on June 8, 1891, in Perth Amboy, on the train tracks, which means we can place Tumblety—a Jack the Ripper suspect—at the murder site of a woman who had her throat cut between June 4 and June 10! Despite the implications, if we cannot definitively say that Tumblety was the killer, this travel evidence proves that he was at the murder site within just a few days of the murder, and therefore, once again, Tumblety cannot be excluded as the potential murderer in this case.

As noted, the murder of Mary Anderson was only about ten to fifteen miles northwest of where Lizzie Farrell was mysteriously murdered in Red Bank, New Jersey, just over a month earlier. Additionally, the Anderson murder was only four or five miles south of the young woman who was murdered in Rahway five years earlier. None of the three women were robbed or raped and, thus, the motives for their murders were a mystery to contemporary law enforcement. Additionally, all three were located along the same New Jersey train line. This line, the New Jersey Central Railroad, specifically, the Philadelphia–Long Branch Railroad, actually traveled through four other murder sites of women who were neither robbed nor raped, one occurring in 1886, another in 1890, another in 1891, and one four years later in 1896.

A Second Train Mutilation – July 1892

The *Evening World*, July 2, 1892, reported on the discovery of the body of Lizzie Beiler, aged twenty-two: "The body of a young woman, cut diagonally in twain [in two], was found early this morning on the Long Island Railroad at Maspeth, about one hundred yards over the city line in Queens County and near the Bushwick train depot. One-half the body was lying on either side of the track." The engineer stated the victim must have been laid lengthwise face up on the track. At six P.M. on the evening of July 1, Beiler left her parents' home smiling on her way to a dance. The parents insisted that Lizzie would never have committed suicide and was too careful to have been run over.

Ultimately, the coroner and jury concluded Lizzie Beiler was killed by accident, but there are a number of solid reasons why she is on this list of unsolved murders. First are the seemingly weak reasons why the inquest concluded her death was an accident. Because Lizzie's lover, Joseph Easer, had a solid alibi, this meant no clear motive for murder. It is apparent that the coroner and jurors did not take into account serial offender motives. Also, per the *Evening World*, July 8, 1892, an autopsy revealed no evidence of poison. Again, this, in their minds, meant no motive. Lastly, Beiler's right hand was crushed, whereby the coroner concluded that Beiler was holding her hat in a standing position when hit. This contradicts the engineer's conclusion that Beiler was lying on her back when hit.

Second are the connections and similarities to other unsolved murders of women on the list. Beiler was neither robbed nor raped. As reported, at least a half dozen women were assaulted in this particular area in Long Island. Lastly, recall that the body of Fanny Cartwright was also hit by a train and mutilated just one year earlier. In that case, a suspect was charged with the murder, albeit it was dropped. It would make sense that both Cartwright and Beiler were killed by a serial killer with an anger-retaliatory motive. Assaulting and then watching his victims be ripped apart by a moving locomotive would bring a significant level of satisfaction to a suspect with this motive.

Another Mysterious Great Lakes Murder – December 1893

According to the *Evening World*, December 8, 1893, in an Associated Press article titled, "Throat Cut on the Street," Julia Huff, or Hulf, was a young woman employed by the family of M. H. McArthur on Franklin Avenue in Cleveland, Ohio. Cleveland is situated between Chicago, Illinois, and Buffalo, New York, on the coast of Lake Erie. On Thursday evening, December 7, 1893, she was accompanied by a man who walked her up to the McArthur house where he suddenly turned on her and cut her throat from ear to ear. He escaped into the darkness. Suspicion was immediately placed upon her husband, John, who was reported to have left the city Thursday morning. The case was no longer reported in the newspapers, suggesting that the husband was not located, or he was located and cleared.

Notice that the pattern of attack on this woman was very similar to the other attacks mentioned. It was on the street at night, and the victim was neither raped nor robbed. The assailant merely ran off. Also, the Pennsylvania & Ohio Railroad tracks were near Franklin Avenue, so the attack was within walking distance of the railroad. In view of this, and the Ripper-like cut on the victim's throat, this murder deserves discussion as possibly having been committed by Tumblety. Recall, the Hot Springs, Arkansas, resident and friend of Tumblety, George Lower, testified under oath that Tumblety sent at least one letter to him from Cleveland, Ohio, meaning, Cleveland was along the train route Tumblety would take on an annual basis and that he would sometimes stay in Cleveland on occasions in between.

Either way, the case remains unsolved. Tumblety's nephew Michael Fitzsimmons stated under oath in 1905 that Tumblety continued to visit Rochester, New York, generally once a year until 1898. Cleveland was along the train route from Hot Springs, Arkansas, to Rochester, so it would have been a stop along the way.

JACK THE CLIPPER – NOVEMBER 1893

Besides the unsolved murder of Julia Huff, a deep search for mysterious murders of women who were neither raped nor robbed in 1893 and 1894 has come up empty-handed. There may have been murders of this type, but the crimes, for whatever reason, did not make the papers. Coincidentally, this is also the time we see a change of behavior in Francis Tumblety. In 1893, Tumblety changed the city he considered home from New York City to Baltimore, Maryland. While Tumblety never gave a reason for this change, it may very well have been that the New York City Police Department was finally putting pressure upon him. Recall Detective Inspector Byrnes speaking to reporters in October 1888 about finally apprehending and arresting a man who was squirting acid on women as they walked the streets. Then, in May 1892, a tall man wearing diamonds nicknamed by the police as Jack the Tripper was tripping women in

Washington Square and running away. Finally, in November 1893, near the Tenderloin district, a location where Tumblety was known to walk, women and girls were being grabbed, threatened, then abused by getting some of their hair cut off. The man would follow them and even brazenly enter their homes. An article in the *New York Times*, December 1, 1893, titled, "Women and Girls Robbed of Hair," states:

> The police of the west-side stations are searching for a man who has been seizing women and girls in the streets and clipping off their hair . . . The women say he is a tall man, and that he wears an Ulster coat and a soft hat. A few days ago he followed a young schoolgirl into the hallway of her home and caught hold of her long braids. She fainted, and the miscreant cut off the braids with a pair of scissors. He then fled. This was done in broad daylight. The next day Mrs. Annie Smith, a young woman living at 330 West Thirty-eighth Street, when about to enter the hallway of her mother's home at 354 West Thirty-seventh Street, was attacked by a man, who put his hand over her mouth and told her to keep quiet. She felt that her assailant was cutting off her hair, but she could offer no resistance, as she carried her baby in her arms. She screamed, and the fellow threw her severed locks on the steps of the house and fled.

Because the police were involved in all three non-homicidal cases beginning sometime before 1888, if they did indeed know it was Tumblety, then Byrnes, finally being fed up with Tumblety, just may have threatened him to leave New York City or face excessive police harassment. Tumblety would have worn out his welcome.

The year 1893 seems to have been a cooling-off period if there was a serial killer guilty of these murders and assaults in the United States since 1882. This tall man in an Ulster coat was exhibiting aggressive misogynistic behavior and fits perfectly with a serial killer suppressing homicidal urges by acting out an offending-oriented fantasy. A nickname like "Jack the Clipper" would certainly be appropriate.

THE ASSAULT OF MAY BARROWCLIFFE – DECEMBER 1893

According to the *Cincinnati Enquirer*, December 30, 1893, a young music teacher, May Barrowcliffe, was found in a vacant lot in Jersey City with her skull fractured and her body bruised, having been attacked on December 29. She was taken to the hospital unconscious, and the physicians believed she would not recover from her head wound. The article continued:

> Her pocket-book and valuable diamond cluster pin which she wore are missing. Miss Barrowcliffe was an orphan, and was employed at Rockwood's photograph gallery, 1440 Broadway, New York. It is learned that Miss Barrowcliffe left her home yesterday afternoon to give music lessons at Marion, N.J.

The police and press initially assumed that she was sexually assaulted as well as being robbed, however, as reported in the *Evening World*, January 11, 1894, the police became convinced that she was not assaulted. By January 10, May had regained consciousness, but, understandably, her memory was foggy and she did not recall who attacked her. Her cousin, Gertie Dexter, visited her at the hospital when an *Evening World* reporter was also visiting and recorded some of their dialogue. Gertie asked, "How did you get hurt?" May replied, "I don't know. I got lost that night." May told Gertie that she walked down a street alone but did not remember being hit over the head. May had finger marks on her neck, which made it clear that she was also grabbed by the throat. In the *Daily News*, January 24, 1894, she recalled being struck down in a lot a half mile from where she was found. The *World*, March 19, 1894, stated that she was found at Van Wagenen and Sip Avenue, which is just a few blocks from the railroad tracks.

SHE REFUSED TO GIVE HER NAME – APRIL 1894

The *Cincinnati Post*, April 12, 1894, published an article titled, "WHO IS SHE," in which an eighteen-year-old woman was assaulted on the streets at night about three blocks from the downtown Cincinnati railroad terminal. Frustratingly, an eyewitness description of the assailant was not given, other than him being burly, but there are similarities in the crime when compared to nighttime assaults by a tall man in a gray Ulster coat. The story begins:

> The citizens in the neighborhood of Kenyon Avenue and Mound Street are talking about a sensational and mysterious assault that occurred Tuesday evening [April 10, 1894] on Kenyon Avenue, near Mound, about 8 o'clock. At about the time stated, the residents of the neighborhood were startled by piercing shrieks, that grew louder and more terrifying every instant. Men and women rushed into the street, to find a young girl about 18 years old

struggling to free herself from the grasp of a burly ruffian, who had her by the throat and was endeavoring to check her cries. The poor girl shrieked with pain and fright, till Clarence Kruger, who lives on Kenyon Avenue . . . rushed to her rescue.

Kruger wrestled with the "ruffian," but he broke loose, ran away, and escaped. The girl refused to give her name to the police because she feared that her father would scold her if he found out where she was, "calling upon a friend" on Cutter Street. The article then stated:

She says that after she left Cutter Street she noticed that a man was following closely behind her. She quickened her steps, but the man gained steadily upon her. Finally she broke into a run, hoping to meet a policeman. The ruffian, however, increased his speed, and, when she was just in the darkest spot along the block, in the shade of the big college building, with no human being in sight, the man grabbed her.

Yet again, the assailant was unknown to the victim, attacked on the streets at night near the railroad, and quickly grabbed her throat in order to control her.

Tumblety's Baltimore attorney, Robert Simpson, testified under oath about Tumblety's behavior change around the year 1895. This is evidence that his neurosyphilis was in its next stage and was having a significant effect on his mental condition. If Tumblety was rage killing, it is not a surprise that he suspended his murderous agenda and focused on his health. Mysterious, unsolved murders of victims neither raped nor robbed began again in 1895 and continued until 1900.

Around the year 1895 was also the time two interesting events occurred. Recall, this is when Tumblety's Rochester neighbor, Eleanor Elsheimer, saw Tumblety in the city of Rochester at night, suspiciously hiding in a dark alleyway area. It was also around this time that Richard Norris took Tumblety to a brothel for a joke, which showed how much he despised "street walkers."

A series of assaults on women was happening on the streets at night around Pittsburgh, a city Tumblety commonly visited. Also, two mysterious and well-publicized unsolved murders of sex workers did occur in 1895, which bear the hallmarks of anger-retaliatory murders by a serial killer—murders in cities Tumblety was known to visit multiple times a year. Although Tumblety did switch his home of record to Baltimore, he still visited New York City, especially since all of his money was in a New York City bank. Under sworn testimony, Tumblety's banker, Henry Clews, stated that Tumblety would periodically visit the bank.

RASH OF ASSAULTS IN GREATER PITTSBURGH – APRIL 1895

Recall, on March 4, 1891, that Kate McGarvey was attacked on the streets of Pittsburgh near the railroad tracks by someone whom the papers named the Pittsburgh Ripper. Then again near the railroad tracks in Pittsburgh, Sarah Joyce was murdered on February 18, 1892. Both cases remain unsolved. In the *Pittsburgh Press*, April 8, 1895, an article titled, "An Exciting Chase," reported upon an unknown man attacking women and girls along the West Penn railroad tracks in Sharpsburg, Pennsylvania, which is directly on the north side of the river from Pittsburgh, just four miles away from the murder site of Sarah Joyce. The article stated that Officer Pfeiffer gave chase to a man whom he believed was attacking women and girls along the railroad tracks, which border the Allegheny River, the same river that enters the city of Pittsburgh. The article states:

> The officer has been on a close watch for the man, and about 8 o'clock Saturday evening he heard the screams of a girl at the locality mentioned. He ran to her assistance and the man started to run. Officer Pfeiffer followed in close pursuit, but the fugitive managed to make his escape in the darkness. The officer then returned to the spot where he had left the young girl, but she had gone away and her identity is unknown. The assailant is believed to be the man who has of late made a practice of stopping women in the upper portion of the town and attempting to carry them in his arms toward the river bank.

The fact that the offender was attempting to drag the women to the river may very well have been attempted murder. Just two years earlier, in the spring of 1893, in Chicago—the next major city after Pittsburgh along the B & O Railway System—the dismembered body of a woman was found on the beach. According to the *St. Louis Globe-Democrat*, April 8, 1893, "This afternoon the dismembered body of a woman was found buried in the sand in the shore of Lake Michigan, at the foot of Hollinwood [sic] avenue." Only two blocks away was the Edgewater Station, the very same Chicago cable car system that a tall man in a gray Ulster coat had taken just before he attacked young Hulda Johnson in December 1888. Recall, in May 1883, the dismembered body of a woman was found floating in the river off Coney Island. In October 1883, another dismembered female body was found in the Erie Canal. Yet another dismembered body of a woman was found in the river in Boston in July 1885.

The railroad tracks are only feet away from the Allegheny River and parallel the river into Pittsburgh. Although no other reports can be found to give a physical description of the attacker, the rash of attacks there matches the rash of attacks in other cities frequented by Tumblety—and by a tall man in a gray Ulster coat, a description that matches the quack doctor. The other significance of this report reveals that there were other attacks and even rashes of attacks on women on the streets at night that never made the newspapers.

GOTHAM'S JACK THE RIPPER – APRIL 1895

According to the *Wilkes-Barre News*, April 24, 1895, on April 21, 1895, New York City sex worker Alice Walsh had her throat cut in the hallway of the Yorktown Hotel at 143 Thompson Street. She was brought to the Bellevue Hospital, where she died. Alice "had been familiar to them [police] by sight for years, and to many others in that neighborhood she was known as an outcast... The patrons of the Yorktown were chiefly the outcast women who swarm the streets at night in that part of the town, and brought men there of the very lowest and most depraved character. She had been frequently arrested by the police, both in the streets and in raids which had been made on various houses of ill repute in that locality." The *St. Louis Globe-Democrat*, April 22, 1895, titled their article, "Gotham's Jack the Ripper," and stated:

ALICE WALSH WHO RAN AWAY FROM HOME.

> When an autopsy was performed on her body it was discovered that certain mutilations had been made which distinguished the Whitechapel murders, though not of so serious a character... [The coroner] found that the woman was bruised and black and blue on almost every part of the body. He found also that she had been brutally mutilated with a knife or dagger, and the wounds thus resulting had started the hemorrhage which had terminated fatally.

There were no witnesses to the murder, and two suspects Walsh was known to have associated herself with, "Stumpy" Walker and "Big Louis," had solid alibis. No one was arrested for her murder.

Tumblety was known to be in New Orleans in early April, and his pattern of yearly spring travel was to return to New York City immediately after. If Tumblety's annual travels remained the same in the year 1895, then Tumblety would have been in New York City near the time Gotham's Jack the Ripper murdered Walsh.

LONG-LEGGED JACK, HE SCARES WOMEN - JUNE 1895

The *Buffalo Courier*, June 28, 1895, reported a nighttime street attack on a young woman in Buffalo, New York, by a tall man, similar to what the city experienced in December 1886. The article is titled, "He Scares Women," with a subtitle, "Cold Spring Has a Bad Man Who Leaps from Behind Trees." The article suggests that the attack is a continuation of a previous streak of attacks from one month earlier:

> Some strangely constituted individual in the form of a man at Cold Spring is carrying on a campaign similar to that which scared the women of Black Rock half out of their senses a month ago. About 10 o'clock Wednesday night Miss Louise Schramm of No. 37 Holland Place was walking over Northampton Street from Main Street and when a block and a half from Michigan Street she experienced the worst scare of her life. She was in front of a house occupied by a man named Drubar, when a tall, slim figure leaped from behind a tree and attempted to seize her. Miss Schramm screamed with such vigor that she was heard by a woman on Michigan Street. Her cries brought to her assistance several young people who were on a nearby corner, and her assailant fled. Miss Schramm was so overcome by terror that she could give but a poor description of the man.

Even though Louise Schramm gave a poor description, it is clear that the tall, slim man was a stranger to her. It is also clear that he intended to violate her person in some way. His actions were enough to put her in terror. This assailant was at it again the following summer, and this time he was recorded in the *Buffalo News*, December 26, 1896, to have been wearing a dark mackintosh overcoat. The double-breasted version looks just like the Ulster coat. According to the *Buffalo Morning Express*, December 28, 1896:

> A strange feature of the case is that the highwayman resembles closely, both in dress and appearance, the man who has for two years appeared on the West

Side as an annoyer of women, and who had been dubbed by the police Long-legged Jack. Jack always wears a mackintosh and slouch hat; so did the robber who attacked Miss Macduff. Jack is about six feet high and slender.

Recall, a tall man in a gray Ulster threatened and assaulted Buffalo women on the streets at night in December 1886 and, again, young Carrie Bott in April 1890. All three of these locations are near Michigan Street, which is now Michigan Avenue.

ANOTHER BOWERY MURDER – DECEMBER 1895

According to the *Chicago Chronicle*, December 26, 1895, a body was found horribly mangled at 432 East 14th Street on Saturday, December 21, in Manhattan. A Mrs. Jackson visited the morgue and stated she believed the woman was Mrs. Carrie Robinson, an East Side frequenter. According to the *Philadelphia Inquirer*, December 24, 1895, an Inspector Cartwright said that after a thorough investigation, he had concluded that her death was an accidental fall. He stated that the nature of the wounds did not indicate violence. Deputy Coroner Donlin, on the other hand, came to a different conclusion after examining the wounds. According to the *Sun*, December 23, 1895, he concluded that the wounds "could scarcely have been caused by a fall, but had been inflicted by some blunt instrument, a heavy piece of wood or an iron bar." His autopsy revealed

> ...that there were six wounds on the body, and that two of the ribs on the left side were broken. There were two deep incised wounds on each side of the nose extending across the bridge, which had been crushed and broken. There was a third wound on the chin extending almost through the lower jawbone, and the bone over each eye was fractured. There were also two deep abrasions on the top of the head, a large bruise on the upper part of the left arm, and another at the base of the left thumb. The number and position of the wounds could scarcely, it is thought, have been made by a fall either from a window or upon the flagstones.

Since the police department concluded the death was most likely accidental, the investigation effectively ended. Also, the deputy coroner decided not to push the issue. There are a number of reasons why this death should still be considered a murder. First, the autopsy corroborated the deputy coroner's position. Second, bruising indicates an injury while the person is still alive. Bruising in dead tissue is rare. If the fall caused not only the injury but also her death, bruising should not be expected. If it was a murder, it was a brutal one with a motive of neither rape nor robbery.

The location where the woman died—432 East 14th Street—is only yards away from the Bowery and numerous lodging houses where Tumblety was known to rent a room. If Tumblety was in New York City in December 1895, he would have been nearby.

CHAPTER 10

TALL MAN IN A GRAY COAT AND A DERBY HAT

While a tall man in a gray overcoat wearing a derby hat, or cap, attacking women on the streets at night near the railway has become a noticeable pattern, it becomes even more apparent in the mid-1890s. The following St. Louis murder of a sex worker was unusually Ripper-like, the assailant attacking her on the streets at night and ripping her abdomen with a knife, then vanishing. In this case, the attack was witnessed by multiple people.

THAT MAN STABBED ME! – JULY 1895

A woman's abdomen was sliced open by a "tall white man" wearing a gray coat and a derby hat on the streets of St. Louis at night by someone unknown to the victim on July 13, 1895. According to the *Daily Republican*, July 15, 1895:

> A white man, evidently familiar with the Whitechapel manner of murder, took the life of Ella alias "Kid" King, a negress 28 years of age and a dissolute character. The woman, whose abdomen was ripped open by the knife of the assassin in such a manner that the entrails slipped out, died . . .

The *St. Louis Globe-Democrat*, July 14, 1895, began the story with additional detail relating a similar MO to Jack the Ripper:

> An unknown white man, evidently familiar with the Whitechapel code of murder, unsheathed his knife last night and in horrible mutilation let out the life of Ella, alias "Kid," King a negress occupying a room in the alley in the rear

of 811 North Tenth Street. The woman was stabbed shortly before 9 o'clock, and died soon after reaching the hospital. Her assassin had made a sweeping cut, penetrating her vitals and opening the abdomen to such an extent that the entrails dropped out as soon as she was laid on the operating table. The woman was 28 years old and of dissolute character.

The murder occurred between Morgan Street and Franklin Avenue on the east side of 11th Street in St. Louis, Missouri. Authorities arrested Charles Schlick, or Charles Van Slyck, who had lived with King in Kansas City. The *St. Louis Globe-Democrat*, July 16, 1895, reported eyewitnesses who saw the attack and claimed it occurred at eight thirty P.M., and said King then staggered to a brick wall and yelled, "That man stabbed me?" Three eyewitnesses who saw the murder and the murderer also knew both King and Van Slyck and were convinced it was him. Van Slyck was a tall White man, his height at around five feet ten inches.

Van Slyck profusely denied killing King. Supporting his denial was the fact that he owned only one set of clothes, and the killer was wearing something different. Also, if King and Van Slyck were once so close as to have been living with each other, it stands to reason that King would have yelled out his name as opposed to "that man." According to the *St. Louis Post-Dispatch*, February 16, 1896, Van Slyck was acquitted of the murder, having proved his alibi. Also, it was later revealed that King's dying statement was that she did not know who the White man was.

Who, then, was the Ripper-like killer? According to the *St. Louis Globe-Democrat*, July 14, 1995:

> After she was taken away the police began a thorough investigation. Sergt. Hanion and a half dozen detectives entered the alley and interviewed everybody in sight. The negro women, who keep disreputable houses, generally agreed that the murderer was a tall white man, wearing a gray coat and vest, straw hat, with a dark band and dark-colored trousers.

At the coroner's inquest, it was clarified that the assailant wore a derby hat, and Van Slyck wore a straw hat, a significant discrepancy. The eyewitness description of Van Slyck matches Tumblety, and according to numerous eyewitness accounts, when he was staying in a certain city, Tumblety would usually dress down as a homeless person, "slumming it"; however, he would also dress quite well when he went out for the evening. Under sworn testimony,

Tumblety's nephew Thomas Powderly stated that Tumblety would "occasionally dress awfully neat," but "two or three days later he would put on old clothes and go out on the street."

Between 1888 and 1903, Tumblety visited St. Louis annually; indeed, it was the chosen location of his death in May 1903. According to the sworn testimony of St. Louis residents, Tumblety spent upward of three weeks at a time in St. Louis. St. Louis resident and proprietor of the Mona House, Philo W. Smith, stated under oath that he knew Tumblety beginning around 1886 up until his death in 1903. He stated that Tumblety would visit St. Louis and stay at his rooming house once a year, but sometimes twice a year. The Mona House was only about five hundred yards away from the murder site and in a southern direction—the same direction that the suspect ran after murdering King. Smith stated that Tumblety's habits were peculiar, staying in his room all day, then leaving his room in the evening. His nightly habit was to walk the slums in each city he visited and to frequent locations where prostitution was prevalent.

Mysterious assaults and murders by a tall man in a gray overcoat continued into 1896, specifically in New Jersey. A rash of at least a dozen assaults occurred just across the river from New York City in February and March. Just like in Buffalo in 1886 and Chicago in 1888, the specific type of gray overcoat reported was an Ulster coat. A further connection was that the crimes were all committed near, or on, train routes. The most brutal was the murder of Mamie Sullivan.

A TALL MAN IN A DARK SPOT IN A GRAY ULSTER – MARCH 1896

According to *The News* (Paterson, New Jersey), March 5, 1896, on the previous evening of March 4, 1896, a twenty-eight-year-old schoolteacher named Mary, or Mamie, Sullivan was brutally murdered at night in a vacant lot on the corner of 18th Street and Park Avenue in Paterson, New Jersey. The "electric light was not burning," leaving the area dark. Sullivan was beaten in the head repeatedly with a twelve-pound iron railroad coupling pin, which was found five feet from where she lay. The offender had hit her over the head and then dragged her into the dark vacant lot.

MAMIE SULLIVAN.

A reporter for the *New York Sun* stated in the March 7, 1896, issue that the crime was from a different kind of killer:

SCENE OF THE TRAGEDY.
XX where the body was found. X where the coupling pin was found.

The belief is gaining ground that the man who murdered Mamie Sullivan, the young woman who was killed by successive blows on the head with a car coupling pin in one of the main streets of Paterson, and within half a dozen doors of her own home, early last Wednesday evening, was a man of perverted mind who derived pleasure from inflicting torture, one of a class of persons about whom the medical books tell much, a sort of Jekyll-Hyde.

The county physician, W. B. Johnson, relayed this to the reporter, highlighting the excessive rage-related blows to the head. He then stated:

> I believe it is foolish to talk of either robbery or criminal assault as a motive. I have given careful study to this form of perversion in connection to the case. It is a momentary insanity. When the object is attained the fit passes off and the person becomes again apparently sane. It is the kind of insanity that is often shown by an uncontrollable desire to wring a chicken's neck. Acts that are horrible when the frenzy has passed, or before it comes on, are the means of pleasure in the frenzy. If a man is of the character I mention, it is doubtful, I think, whether he will ever be caught.

Dr. Johnson explained what nineteenth-century alienists, or psychologists, referred to as a monomaniac. Otherwise perfectly sane, a monomaniac becomes insane about one particular passion: in this case, murder. Alienists were in general agreement in 1888 that Jack the Ripper was a monomaniac.

According to Chief of Police Grant, Sullivan's rings and diamond pin were not taken, which ruled out robbery as a motive. The police chief also believed the murderer was a tramp. The physician who performed the autopsy examination stated:

> The person who murdered this girl was in a *psychopathic condition*. A regular *Jack the Ripper*. Mind you, I don't mean maniac. The murderer of this girl is sane on every point except on such acts as was committed on Mamie Sullivan. The object of the murder was not robbery, neither was it to ravish the girl. From a careful examination I have come to the conclusion that there was no assault committed. In fact I don't think there was any attempt. The blows which this girl received could be delivered in a minute and a half. The person kept delivering blow and blow and did not stop even after she fell to the ground. I would also say that if revenge or jealousy actuated the assault the assassin would have weakened. The cries of the girl would have struck pity, and the girl would not have been so badly injured. A psychopotic [*sic*] person did the job, and I don't think he will ever be captured as he has left no trace.
> —*The News*, March 5, 1896 [Author emphasis added.]

This certainly fits the modern serial offender behavior of anger-retaliatory. The blows to the head were brutal, personal, and excessive, much like the attacks by the Yorkshire Ripper in the late 1970s.

Another similarity to the Whitechapel murders is that the offender accomplished his task outdoors between the time of two patrolmen, or police constables, walking their beat. The police chief stated that the offender had "no more than three minutes in which to accomplish his work." At the very corner where the murder occurred was a patrol box where the patrolman is required to make a call back to headquarters. Patrolman Bernard Nolan called at 9:10 P.M., and Sergeant John Ricker reported at 9:20. Ricker also stated that after "pulling" the box, he stood at the corner for a few minutes. The man who first happened upon the body was Olaf Petersen, who claimed the attack had to have been no later than 9:25 since he checked his watch. Two young ladies were going eastward on Park Avenue and heard a voice crying in pain in the vacant lot. They screamed and began to run, nearly knocking Olaf Petersen down. Petersen ran into the lot to investigate, finding Sullivan alive but brutally beaten. Sullivan died of her wounds later at the hospital.

OLAF PETERSEN.
[Who discovered the body.]

Reverend Henry Wood, pastor of the Park Avenue Baptist Church, walked near the corner around 9:20 or 9:25 and noticed a woman standing at the corner apparently waiting for a car. As he walked near the "Susquehanna railroad" about 150 yards away, he noticed a man who he believed was Olaf Petersen.

Petersen claimed to have seen a tall man lurking around the Eastside "in a dark spot." According to *The News,* March 5, 1896, "Mr. Petersen also remembered having seen a tall man standing near Jake Rogers' residence. This fellow when he heard the two women scream darted down Madison avenue." According to the *New York Sun,* March 7, 1896, he noticed that the man was also wearing a derby hat. As he passed him, "His hat was down over his eyes and he was standing partly facing down the street; that is looking in the direction of the scene of the crime." Petersen reasoned that he saw the man after the crime had occurred. The *Philadelphia Inquirer,* March 7, 1896, reported it as a tall man in a gray Ulster coat and connected it with an earlier encounter with two other young women, Anna Lynch and another schoolteacher, Miss Graves:

> County Physician Johnson seems to think it is a "Jack the Ripper" crime. The Chief of Police is inclined to the belief that a tramp committed the murder. Detectives Taylor and Lord look wise and think they have a clue. *They are looking for a tall man in a gray Ulster.* They think he is the murderer. The man in the gray Ulster was undoubtedly in the immediate vicinity of the scene of the murder, and within an hour of the commission of the horrible crime he waylaid two young women, Miss Lynch and Miss Graves. Miss Lynch was held up on Sumner street by the tall man, about half an hour before Miss Sullivan's body was found. [Author emphasis added.]

The *New York Sun,* March 7, 1896, gave more detail of the Lynch and Graves assaults:

> Anna Lynch was assaulted in Sumner street. It was about 8 o'clock in the evening and she was going to visit her mother, who worked for Dr. Crooke. A tall man followed her two blocks to the doctor's house and ran up to her and attacked her in a little passage beside the house. He seized her by the throat with both hands so that she could not scream and held her till she was just ready to fall from exhaustion.

Lynch then screamed, which caused the man to run away. The direction the man ran was toward Carroll Street, which is where Miss Graves was assaulted:

This occurred half an hour later, and Miss Graves was the victim. The man seized her and she slipped from his grasp and fell. She succeeded in kicking him in the stomach as well as in screaming, and when he ran away it was in the direction of Eighteenth street. It was in Park avenue, near Eighteenth street, where an hour later Miss Sullivan was murderously assaulted.

Four points match Francis Tumblety to Petersen's recollections. First, the suspect was a tall man; second, the man was wearing a gray Ulster coat; third, the police stated that Tumblety was wearing a derby hat when he returned from London in 1888, as was the assassin here; and fourth, the man was lurking around in a dark spot, which Tumblety was known to do. We have numerous sworn testimonies and eyewitness accounts of Tumblety walking the slums in the darkest areas, or darkest side of the walkway. The assault on Anna Lynch was initially an attack to the throat, which was exactly what occurred in Buffalo in 1886 and Chicago in 1888 by a tall man in a gray Ulster coat.

Years later, in 1915, Olaf Petersen's business partner was murdered. According to the *Courier-Post*, September 9, 1915, police brought Petersen to the county jail as the material witness to the man's murder. The reporters at the jailhouse became aware that this was the same Olaf Petersen who was connected to Mamie Sullivan's murder. A reporter asked if current rumors were true that he was arrested for the Sullivan murder. Paterson stated:

> I never, never was arrested for that crime. That was on a snowy, windy night. I lived at 133 Ward street, Paterson then. I had been calling on Miss Sarah and Jenny Smith, who lived on fifteenth avenue, between Twenty-third and Twenty-fourth streets. When I reached the corner I waited for a car and I found the snow was delaying the cars. I started to walk down Park avenue to keep warm. As I passed the house of Jacob Rogers, a square away, I met a man. He had a big Ulster on and the collar was turned up. I could not see his features. Rev. Harvey Wood, then pastor of Park avenue Baptist Church, Paterson, now secretary of the American Baptist Society, of New York City, was behind me [Petersen] and also saw the man in the Ulster. I walked a square further and suddenly I saw a dark form on the sidewalk. It was not at a vacant lot but in a residential section with plenty of houses on the street. As I neared the form I heard two women scream. They startled me and I nearly stumbled over the body, which I found was that of a woman. The women ran across the street. I ran up the steps of the house in front of which the body was lying. I tried to get the occupants to the door but they did not respond. I ran to the house next

door and they responded. We carried the body into that house. The woman was bleeding badly and she kept moaning, "Oh, don't do that. Oh, don't do that." Policeman Taylor joined us shortly afterward and an ambulance was summoned and the woman was taken to the General Hospital, where she died the next morning. I was never arrested for that murder. I went to my home each night and ate my meals at home. I told my story to Prosecutor Eugene Emley. At the inquest it was found that the woman was murdered but they never arrested the murderer.

Note that Petersen said the tall man's collar was up. This was exactly the case with the tall assailant in a gray Ulster overcoat in Buffalo in 1886 and Chicago in 1888.

In the *Morning Post*, September 10, 1915, the sister of Mamie Sullivan, a Mrs. Copperfield, was interviewed. She told the reporter that "The murderer of Mamie Sullivan has never been found." Mrs. Copperfield stated that on the night of the murder, Mamie left their house to see a sick friend.

There is no direct evidence that Tumblety was in Paterson, New Jersey, on March 4, 1896, since he only transited through the city. Then again, if the killer was a transient merely passing through, it would have been nearly impossible for authorities to prove that anyone of interest was in town. According to two sources under oath, Tumblety's nephew Michael Fitzsimmons and Rochester resident Eleanor Elsheimer, Tumblety would visit Rochester each year or two until his brother's death in 1898. Throughout the 1890s, Tumblety continued to visit New York City as well, primarily because this was where he kept his entire wealth of over three million dollars in today's value. His New York City banker, James Clews, a partner with his father Henry Clews, stated under oath in 1905 that Tumblety made periodic visits to the bank. Clews stated he first met Tumblety at his bank in 1890 and last met him in 1902, one year before Tumblety's death. If and when Tumblety left for Rochester, New York, from New York City, the shortest train route actually made a stop in Paterson, New Jersey. This meant that Tumblety had likely passed through Paterson on numerous occasions in the 1890s. The use of a coupling pin on Sullivan suggests the killer came from the train tracks; the tracks of the New York, Susquehanna, and Western Railroad are near the corner of Park Avenue and 18th Street.

There are numerous details of the Sullivan attack that are nearly identical to the Lizzie Farrell attack in Red Bank, New Jersey, in April 1892. The attack was at night, on the street; it was near the railroad; and the weapon was a metal object used on the railroad. This means that the assailant used an object in the local area as the weapon. Lastly, the assailant dragged the lying victim to a second spot.

The following is an eyewitness account from a young man who gave the name Joseph Murtagh, and, if true, it is a stunning account of him being with the actual killer just before and during the murder of Mamie Sullivan. On page one of the *Boston Globe*, March 26, 1896, an article titled, "Sleuths Busy," begins:

> New York, March 26 – The [New York] Journal this morning prints the following: One witness, Joseph Murtagh, has been kept purposely in the background by the Paterson bureau of prosecution that has been searching into the Mary Sullivan murder mystery. Murtagh's family have for years been well known in Paterson, although the man who avers that he witnessed the murder is at present a resident of this city. He had not visited his parents in over a year, but he returned to Paterson on the night of March 4, in time to witness the killing of Mamie Sullivan. Not only that, but he claims to have accompanied the murderer all the way from Yonkers, New York. The story told by Murtagh is to the effect that on March 3 last he left his home in this city and started for Yonkers. At one time during his career he had been employed in that city, and while there became engaged to a young woman who is at present employed in Smith's carpet works. The day set for the wedding had actually arrived, the banns had been published in the Catholic church, but at the last moment the marriage was declared off for the time being, on account of anonymous letters received by the priest, who decided to investigate. Up to that time Murtagh had been a man of temperate habits. Then, however, his whole nature seemed to change.

It is clear by the details of this article that the reporter was receiving factual information from either Murtagh himself or an official involved in the investigation of the story. The story continues about his excessive drinking habits, him breaking off the marriage, then moving to New York. The ex-fiancée had moved on, stayed in Yonkers, and a few months later was about to marry another man. A distraught Murtagh decided to go to Yonkers and speak with the woman:

> When Murtagh started for Yonkers on the day before Mamie Sullivan was murdered at Paterson, N J, he was considerably under the influence of liquor. He spent all the money he had with him, and on Wednesday morning he waited for the whistle of Smith's carpet works, where he hoped to see the woman with whom he had quarreled. *Up to that time every detail of Murtagh's story has been fully verified.* [Author emphasis added.]

After meeting her in the morning and then again a half hour later, she gave him a dollar to get back to Paterson, New Jersey, to his parents. Clearly upset that he was rejected, he then went directly to a saloon in Yonkers. While there,

> ... he saw a savage-appearing man, clad in a long, gray ulster, who glared at him in a most ferocious manner. When Murtagh started to catch a train the fierce-looking man followed him, and came to New York by the same train. On arriving there he went into a saloon, and invited the man, who had followed him, to have a quick drink with him.

In the *Paterson Evening News*, March 26, 1896, Murtagh clarified that it was not the tall man in the Ulster coat who had the drink with him, but who he thought was an acquaintance of his. Notice that Murtagh said "a quick drink." The train route from Yonkers to Paterson included a transit by ferry across the river. The train traveled through Manhattan and stopped at a terminal at the river's edge. The passengers would then disembark, take a ferry across the river, then embark on a waiting train on the New Jersey line, which traveled straight through Paterson. Even though Murtagh was visiting saloons, he was making his way back to his parents and did not want to miss any connections. It was at this time Murtagh believed the man in the gray Ulster must have put drugs in his drink because he stated he passed out.

He then said he had a dim recollection of buying a ticket to Paterson. Even though he was quite drunk and possibly drugged, Murtagh did recollect some of the trip back to Paterson. In the *Paterson Evening News*, March 26, 1896, he said:

> Once on the journey here I remember waking up and seeing what I believed was the same man who had followed me out of the saloon at Yonkers. I spoke to him, but he would not answer me.

When Murtagh arrived at the train station in Paterson, he stated that he started off toward his father's house but then noticed that the tall man in a gray Ulster coat followed him off the train. He said that the man "laid his hand on" his shoulder, and "told him to come with him." Murtagh stated that he had neither the strength nor the will to resist and was hurried along Park Avenue toward 18th Street. The stranger stopped and leaned Murtagh against a tree and momentarily left him. Murtagh stated that he saw the tall man stop a young woman and drag her into the vacant lot. According to the article, "Murtagh heard a few more words spoken, when suddenly the man took a short, heavy bar of iron from his pocket and struck the woman several blows on the head." Murtagh then stated he ran as fast as he could to his father's house around eleven P.M. but was still in a stupor. In the *Paterson Evening News*, March 26, 1896, Murtagh stated, "I ran away as hard as I could after that. I don't know where, except that sometime after 11 o'clock I arrived at my father's home in a dazed condition."

The *New York Journal* reporter then stated:

> According to his story, the man who claimed to have seen the murder remained at his father's home, in bed most of the time, until the Saturday following, when after reading all the stories published about the murder, he became convinced that he had seen it. Accordingly, he concluded to surrender himself to the police, but decided to first see Rev. Dean McNulty. The latter questioned him closely, then brought him to the office of prosecutor Gourley. The story was repeated there, and soon the work of investigation began. A detective has gone over the ground, step by step, which Murtagh said he covered.

The story went nowhere. According to the *Paterson Evening News*, in its March 26, 1896, issue, Prosecutor Gourley rejected the eyewitness account:

> Shortly after the murder Mr. Gourley admitted to the local newspapermen that he knew a man who claimed to have seen the girl murdered. But, added the Prosecutor, "I think the man was suffering from drink and I take no stock in his story." The man referred to, went first to the Very Rev. Dean McNulty and to him told his story . . .
>
> The above is the fellow's story to the good Dean and to the Prosecutor. The latter had this man's statement investigated and found that the fellow could not have been in this city at the time of the murder, as he did not leave Yonkers until nearly eight o'clock, which would not permit his arrival here in time to witness the affair even if he were in the neighborhood. The Prosecutor denies that the man's name is Murtagh as one New York paper had it, and flatly refused to tell his name for the sake of the young man's family. Mr. Gourley does not take any stock in the man's statements.

There are issues with Gourley's conclusion that Murtagh's story was untrustworthy and, therefore, was all wrong. Gourley admitted to the local Paterson reporter that the primary reason he did not take stock in Murtagh's account of events was because Murtagh was very drunk. It seems Gourley was saying that the young man was in such a state of altered reality that his recollections could not be trusted. This may have been true after Murtagh was in the saloon in downtown Manhattan when he believed he was drugged, but when he was in Yonkers, he was coherent enough to relay a corroborated story. Recall, the reporter stated that the Yonkers part of the story was "fully verified." This means that Murtagh was coherent when he met the tall man in the gray Ulster coat in Yonkers and when he and the acquaintance went to the saloon for a quick drink.

The second reason why the prosecutor discarded the story was because he claimed that Murtagh left Yonkers at nearly eight P.M. and would not have been able to be in Paterson at the time of the murder, which was at or about 9:20 P.M.:

> ... the fellow could not have been in this city at the time of the murder, as he did not leave Yonkers until nearly eight o'clock, which would not permit his arrival here in time to witness the affair even if he were in the neighborhood.

This does not match Murtagh's story, though, as told in the *New York Journal*. Murtagh met the woman in Yonkers in the morning, then had his final meeting with her a half hour later. He then went to the Yonkers saloon, which was less than a mile away. The saloon was near the train station where he was beginning his travels. The prosecutor is apparently claiming that Murtagh spent nearly eight hours at that particular saloon even before he left for downtown Manhattan. Murtagh was given one dollar by his ex-fiancée to make it back to Paterson. Murtagh actually explains how many drinks he had at the Yonkers saloon. In the *Paterson Evening News*, March 26, 1896, Murtagh is quoted, "I think I had three drinks in the saloon, and then hearing the noise of an approaching train, I ran out to catch it. As I did so the fierce-looking man who had been standing apart from the others ran after me, and we both managed to board the same train. We did not speak on the journey." Not only does having three drinks not equate to eight hours in the Yonkers saloon, but Murtagh had a time limit—the very next train arriving at the train station.

There is a possibility that Prosecutor Gourley did not know Murtagh was in the Yonkers saloon so early. He never mentioned this critical fact to the *Paterson Evening News* reporter when he was quoting Murtagh's testimony to him. This part of the story was in the *New York Journal*, and the fact that Gourley refused to tell the reporter Murtagh's real name suggests that the *Journal* reporter spoke to someone else other than Gourley. Regardless, Gourley is incorrect.

Even if we assume the Paterson officials were correct that Murtagh's story between the time he was drugged in downtown Manhattan and the murder in Paterson around 9:20 P.M. cannot be trusted and, therefore, is one hundred percent wrong, note the extremely odd coincidences this conclusion produces. Murtagh met an unknown tall man in a gray Ulster coat; he did, indeed, travel to and arrive in Paterson on the night of the murder; and then a tall man in a gray Ulster coat, likely the killer, was seen near the murder site around 9:20.

Maybe Murtagh lied? Murtagh was so concerned about possibly having information that could help the case that he went to his pastor and discussed it with him. If Murtagh was purposely lying, why would he have done this? He was not getting any money or publicity for telling the police about it. It is even stated that his name was not Murtagh and that the prosecutor kept his true name a secret in order to keep the press away from the family. Also, Murtagh convinced Father McNulty enough that McNulty believed the next step was to go to the prosecutor.

Even before discovering Murtagh's story, the press had related that Mamie Sullivan's murderer was likely the tall man in a gray Ulster coat, which fits the many other assaults and murders where Tumblety cannot be eliminated as having committed the crime. Then, Murtagh relayed a story of a man whose behavior with young men was an exact fit for Tumblety. Time and time again, Tumblety would approach a strange young man and attempt to dominate him. One such case was in 1878. Recall, an elderly Catherine Lyons retained a Manhattan attorney named William Burr in July 1880 when Tumblety had sued her for larceny. In the *New York World*, December 2, 1888, Burr commented upon how Tumblety dominated Catherine's teenage grandson, Joseph Lyons, stating, "Tumblety greeted him [Joseph Lyons] and soon had him under complete control . . . for once he had a young man under his control he seemed to be able to do anything with the victim." Not only did Murtagh's recollection paint a picture of a man very similar to Tumblety in behavior and established residence, but he stated that the man was "savage-appearing." The sworn testimony of numerous eyewitnesses to Tumblety's appearance establishes that his black-waxed mustache made him fierce-looking. The April 18, 1890, issue of the *St. Louis Republic* shows how Tumblety used the cigar as a type of signal for a young man he met:

> Jack The Ripper. The Mysterious Dr. Tumblety Now in St. Louis.
>
> But to his presence in this city. Last night at about 10 o'clock, while Donovan's Exchange, in the Chamber of Commerce building was crowded with billiard players, a large, massively built man strolled into the place. He was six feet

and an inch tall, broad shouldered, dark skinned, with an immense jet black mustache that gave to his face a *fierce, almost fiendish*, expression . . .

[Author emphasis added.]

Rochester neighbor Eleanor R. Elsheimer commented upon an experience she had with Tumblety around 1885. In her deposition on May 8, 1905, Eleanor stated she first met him about 1885, three years before the Ripper murders. She stated that she was frightened when he turned in at their gate, saying he was sunburned and suntanned, then continued:

He was tall with a fierce mustache and odd looking. He had on a fur coat which looked like a spotted dog, this being strange since it was late spring.

Tumblety was darkening his mustache hairs because they were white. Mr. B. McDavid, barber at the Arlington Hotel, Eastman barbershop, Hot Springs, stated under oath:

. . . his [Tumblety's] hair and mustache were perfectly white, but he kept them blackened with a preparation made of lard and charcoal that made *him look very fierce*; blacked his skin and hair with it, and it made him look very peculiar, *fierce*; different from most people. [Author emphasis added.]

OTHER ATTACKS IN NORTHERN NEW JERSEY – FEBRUARY 1896

While Mamie Sullivan's murder was front-page news around the country, less known were similar assaults of women that occurred around the area by a tall man in a gray Ulster coat; two also in the town of Paterson, and two in the nearby town of Montclair, New Jersey. What's more, they all occurred just weeks apart. Murtagh stated that the man wore a gray Ulster coat. An appropriate and perfectly logical conclusion is that the offender in each case was one and the same.

An article in the *New York Sun*, March 7, 1896, stated that earlier in the evening of Mamie Sullivan's murder, Anna Lynch and a Miss Greaves were assaulted in Paterson. The attacks were by a tall man in an Ulster coat and outdoors on the street. The article also commented upon a rash of assaults just across the border in Spring Valley, New York. According to the *Sun*, "Seven or eight girls and women at Spring Valley, twelve miles from Paterson, were assaulted a week to ten days ago," by a man in a long gray coat, or Ulster coat. It seems this man was finally arrested but then let go. A special to the *New York Tribune*, in their March 7, 1896, issue stated,

> David Voght, who lives here, has sent word to the Chief of Police in Paterson to come to this place, as he thinks he can give him a clew to the murderer of Mamie Sullivan. Voght says he knew the man well who was frightening the women and school children in this place last week by springing out from behind buildings and pinching them. Voght says the man told him he was going to Paterson as the officers were making it too hot for him here. The man to whom Voght refers was said to be partially crazy over a woman. When here he wore a long gray ulster.

While the Spring Valley, New York, assaults were by a man in a gray Ulster coat like the man witnessed near the Sullivan murder, David Voght claimed that the man was merely jumping out and pinching women and girls. He also said that it was his opinion he was partially crazy over a woman. Pinching women is a far cry from crushing women's skulls. Plus, if it is true that the assailant was crazy over a woman, this does not sound like opportunistic attacks on unknown women. Additionally, the Paterson chief of police apparently got the name of the Spring Valley pincher, but nothing seems to have come of it.

The Northern New Jersey assaults, though, were much more similar in method and ruthlessness to the Sullivan assault and murder. On February 6, 1896, Lizzie Lamb and May Little in Montclair were assaulted with a wooden club by a tall man in a gray Ulster coat. The reporter stated,

> The assault on Lizzie Lamb and May Little in Montclair might easily have ended as did the assault on Miss Sullivan but in this case the man was armed with a wooden club instead of an iron coupling pin, and the force of his blows could not have been as great.

The reporter noted another similarity to the Sullivan murder in that they "were in the street in Montclair at just about the hour the assault on Miss Sullivan took place." The *Evening Times*, February 7, 1896, goes into further detail about the Montclair assaults:

> ASSAULTED BY AN UNKNOWN
> Mysterious Attack on Two New Jersey Servant Girls
> Montclair, N.J., Feb 7. – Lizzie Lamb and Mary Little, two servants employed here, were on their way Wednesday evening to visit the family of Thomas Lamb, Lizzie's brother. On Harrison avenue they were followed by a tall man wearing dark clothes and a derby hat, and stepped aside to let him pass.

Without warning, the stranger quickly struck both girls on the head with a weapon. Lizzie Lamb fell unconscious. Mary Little screamed "murder," "police," and the man took to his heels. Neighbors came to the girls' assistance. Lizzie's head was badly crushed, and in the interval when the girl was conscious she was unable to give any good description of her assailant. Lizzie Lamb was conscious at intervals yesterday.

The *Montclair Times*, February 8, 1896, stated that the attack was on the corner of Harrison Avenue and Union Street and noted that the assailant selected a dark location to do the attack:

> The deed was committed at a comparatively early hour, but he had laid his plans well, for he had turned off the gas from the two nearest street lights.

This suggests that the offender was purposely selecting a spot to physically attack women—one that gave him the best opportunity to escape after the assault.

Curiously, the Montclair train terminal on the Bloomfield branch of the D. & L. Railroad was just over two blocks south on Union Street. This matches the pattern found with the other assaults made by a tall man in a gray overcoat or Ulster.

Another incident connecting this assailant to the Sullivan murder was relayed by a Dr. Emerson of Paterson. He said he was out at ten P.M. on Wednesday night, just a half hour after the Sullivan murder. A tall man approached him on 17th Avenue and told him he was on his way to Montclair. The man asked Dr. Emerson what time it was. After the doctor told him, the man went on.

After the man attacked and left the servant girls bleeding on the ground, "Like a flash the man was off." The reporter stated that there was no apparent motive, and the girls had no known enemies. This was exactly what the assailant did with Sullivan.

CHAPTER 11

RUTHLESS TO THE BITTER CENTURY'S END

While the New Jersey assaults and murders have been discussed, other locations in the Midwest and Northeast also experienced mysterious murders and assaults, such as New York City in 1895 with Gotham's Jack the Ripper. Even though around 1893 Tumblety began to consider Baltimore, Maryland, his residence, his New York City banker stated under oath in 1905 that not only did Tumblety maintain his wealth in his New York bank, but he also commonly made personal visits to the bank. The reason why it was difficult for the courts to determine which city and state Tumblety considered his home of record—an issue that came up in the 1905 court case contesting his 1903 St. Louis, Missouri, will and testament—was because Tumblety was a transient and only rented out rooms in all of the cities he visited.

Tumblety died in St. Louis, Missouri, in May 1903 at the age of seventy-three, his body finally succumbing to his organs shutting down from complications due to neurosyphilis. If he was releasing his rage against women across the United States after returning from London in late 1888, blaming them for his progressive disease, when would he have stopped? If his overall pattern of behavior—travel, walking in slums, etc.—did not change throughout the nineteenth century, there is no reason to conclude his behavior toward women changed.

While he certainly was a loner and exceedingly private, we actually have a small window into Tumblety's threatening behavior against women in his later years around the end of the nineteenth century. In November 1901, he threatened a woman to the point of her fearing for her life in Baltimore, Maryland. One of Tumblety's Baltimore attorneys, Frank Widner, recalled this event under oath. Widner stated that Tumblety would come to his office, sometimes twice a day, and stay for two or three hours. One day, Tumblety felt dizzy, so Widner allowed him to sit on his couch as he conducted business, and a female client came in:

> Widner: "... If a lady happened to come into my office, he would take a newspaper—he generally had a newspaper in his hands—and hold it in front of his face to shield him from the lady."
>
> Attorney: "Did these incidents actually happen?"
>
> Widner: "Yes, they all happened in my office; not at one time, but at various times. And then another time a lady was talking to me when he came in the office. I remember being called to the telephone. I did not have a C. & P. phone in my office and I went into Tippett's office, across the hall. I left the lady there and went to the telephone and after I finished, I found the lady outside my office. I asked her what was the matter. She said she was not going to stay in there with that fellow. She said she was afraid to stay in there..."

Tumblety clearly wanted to cause fear in the woman. His body language, and possibly what he said, made the woman feel unusually threatened. Tumblety was a man who had a difficult time controlling his rage, and evidenced by Widner's comments made under oath to the attorney...

> [Widner:] "Another time he called and presented me with a cigar... I do not know why, but that cigar laid in my desk for a year or more; I don't know why I should be afraid, but I did not smoke the cigar. Being a doctor, I did not know but that it was loaded..."
>
> Cross-examination—
>
> Widner: "I remember that that incident of the lady being in the office was the first one that really made me seriously doubt the mental competency of the Doctor, and from that time on, I was inclined to watch him more closely than ever."
>
> Attorney: "You have stated, Mr. Widner, that at times Dr. Tumblety appeared to be excited and of a nervous temperament. Do you recall any particular incident in which he indicated this disposition?"
>
> Widner: "I remember one day he came into my office in the period from May 1902 to July 1902, sat himself on the edge of the chair as he usually did, in an attitude that was really threatening. He was talking excitedly... and the attitude he assumed toward me was such that I drew back my chair from my

desk and assumed a position of defense, in case he should spring upon me. I was very much afraid that the man would make some movement, his attitude was so threatening, and he was so nervous; he kept shifting his position and I must say at the time he was quite excited . . ."

Whether Tumblety had the physical capabilities to murder a woman on the streets in 1901 or not was clearly not questioned by Widner's female client and even by Widner himself. Sworn testimony from Tumblety's other Baltimore attorney, Robert Simpson, gives a clue as to which year Tumblety was likely not physically capable of committing crimes against women. Simpson stated under oath that his acquaintance with Tumblety began about the year 1890. Tumblety was visiting Simpson's mother, a former customer back in the mid-1870s in Liverpool, England. Simpson was in law school at the time and only saw him on rare occasions. In 1894, Simpson began his law practice and began to see Tumblety on a regular, yearly basis until late in the year 1902. When asked by the attorney what Tumblety's physical and mental condition was in 1902, Simpson replied:

> Well, there was a vast difference in both his mental and physical condition at the time, between that time and the time I first met him. When I first met him, he was rather stylish, especially in his dress, and very fastidious in his ways. . . . From the time I first met him, until 1894, he was about the same, he always was a little peculiar in his ways, especially in his dress. Along about 1894, he was more so, more peculiar in his dress and eccentric and a little odd. During the year 1898 I was away for very nearly a year, and I did not see him; after that, I was at my office all the time and I used to see a great deal of him. I was his counsel and he seemed to be all right mentally and physically until about the year 1902, along about the fall.

Simpson then explained that in September 1902, Tumblety looked and acted much sicklier. He even recalled a time when Tumblety passed out on the street and collapsed. His speech was disconnected, and he would talk to himself on the streets. Richard Norris, who met up with Tumblety each year between 1881 and 1902, noticed an abrupt deterioration the last time he met him in 1902.

Curiously, Simpson noticed a subtle change in behavior between 1890 and 1894, but not an extreme change. This certainly does follow if Tumblety was afflicted with a progressive disease such as neurosyphilis. His comments suggest that the neurosyphilis was affecting Tumblety's mind but not yet his body.

Philo Smith, the proprietor of the Mona House, the lodging, or rooming, house that Tumblety generally stayed at on his visits to St. Louis, Missouri, stated in court under oath that in the last two years he saw Tumblety, 1902 and 1903, he noticed an abrupt deterioration. Smith stated that he had known Tumblety for the last fifteen or seventeen years, meaning from about 1885 to 1903. Tumblety would rent a room either once or twice a year. Smith stated that he knew Tumblety as a cunning man who never looked you in the eyes. Smith also recalled when Tumblety was arrested in England for the Whitechapel murders.

> ... that he had been arrested as Jack the Ripper, followed to this country from abroad by Scotland street detectives. His habits were exceedingly peculiar, kept to his room most all of the daytime; nighttime he was around.

When the attorney asked if Tumblety was able and competent to handle his own affairs, Smith replied,

> He seemed to be at that time, until the past two years. Failed more rapidly than any person I have ever met. The last time in particular, very feeble and sick all the time he was there. If my memory serves me right, he left my house and went to the hospital.

Tumblety entered St. John's Hospital in St. Louis in May 1903, where he died just a few weeks later. In view of the testimonials of Widner, Simpson, and Smith, we can be confident that Tumblety's physical abilities were not affected in 1901 as they were beginning in 1902, and especially in 1903.

A BRONX BROOK – MAY 1896

According to the *Philadelphia Inquirer*, May 14, 1896, forty-nine-year-old Sarah Schofield's body was found in a brook along Mosholu Parkway, New York City, near the railway connecting to the Bedford Park Boulevard station in the Bronx neighborhood, which is just south of Yonkers where Joseph Murtagh first saw the tall man in a gray Ulster coat just two months earlier. The body had what looked to be a deep knife wound to the brain above her right eye. The coroner's physician, Dr. O'Hanlon, stated that there was no evidence that a sexual assault had been committed. With money found in her purse, the police were sure robbery was not the motive. An Associated Press article in the *Courier*,

May 21, 1896, stated that her husband, William Schofield, was initially arrested on suspicion but was quickly "honorably discharged."

In the meantime, Dr. O'Hanlon performed an autopsy in the morgue, according to the *New York Press*, May 14, 1896, and concluded the victim died due to paralysis of the heart induced by some intense excitement. He claimed the large cut on the right side of the forehead was postmortem and had nothing to do with the death since the skull was not fractured and there was little loss of blood. The other small cuts on the legs and feet were made after death. O'Hanlon convinced the jury at the coroner's inquest held on May 12. According to the *Philadelphia Inquirer*, May 30, 1896, their verdict agreed with O'Hanlon's conclusion.

The case was closed, but the police still had puzzling questions that were left unanswered. There were footprints found near the body that tracked a hundred fifty feet away to a large boulder with blood on it. A clump of bushes near the boulder showed evidence that someone was in it. A man's handkerchief was also found there, with blood on it. O'Hanlon dismissed the tracks and blood, especially since there was no evidence of motive of sexual assault or theft.

Paralysis of the heart induced by some intense excitement? If this confusing cause of death is correct, it begs the question as to what caused Sarah Schofield's intense excitement when she was near the railway. An excellent answer that fits all of the evidence is that she was surprised by someone hiding in the bushes who was intent on causing her harm, she was bludgeoned at the boulder, and she was chased, ending with her unconscious in the brook. The event literally scared her to death. O'Hanlon rejected this idea merely because he saw no motive, but then again, this is exactly the type of mysterious assault and murder committed by serial killers with anger-retaliatory motives—something that was unknown to authorities at the time.

Today, forensics would have tested the blood on the boulder and the handkerchief, and since O'Hanlon's conclusions are so unlikely, Sarah Schofield being murdered by a stranger is still a possibility.

TALL MAN WITH A FLOWING MUSTACHE – JULY 1896

According to the *New York World*, July 13, 1896, seventeen-year-old Jessie Tempary was riding her bike in Flatbush, returning from Coney Island, on Friday, July 10. As she rode through a lonely spot, a tall man of a dark complexion and a flowing mustache walked into the road and blocked her way. He stopped her and said, "I'd like to escort you home, my pretty one." The article then stated:

Surprised and indignant, the young woman looked at him angrily, and, saying not a word, pressed her feet more firmly on the pedals and started away as fast as she could go. But the fellow anticipated that. He sprang at her and threw his arms around her. She screamed at the top of her voice. Cursing her, he dragged her from the wheel, and, despite her struggles, managed to tie a handkerchief over her mouth. Miss Tempary tried to tear away the gag and her assailant knocked her down. She fought with all her might, scratching the man's face, while her own arms and her body were bruised by his violence. She felt her strength going, and with a last effort tore away the handkerchief and shrieked again: "Help! Help!" The brute dealt her a blow that made her unconscious. When she revived Heulet Tempary was kneeling by her, and other men stood around her.

Heulet, her brother, brought Jessie to the 23rd Precinct of Brooklyn where a Detective Bettis worked on her case. Frustratingly, nothing came of it. The assailant vanished.

Recall, in 1883, three women were assaulted in Flatbush on the streets at night. This time, a physical description was given, and it matched "Brooklyn's Beauty," Francis Tumblety.

A Tenderloin Murder – August 1896

New York World, August 5, 1896

According to the *New York Times*, August 5, 1896, a New York City woman was strangled and then had her throat cut. The victim was identified in the press with the note, "All the police learned was that Annie Bock was of a class of women who infest this part of East Twenty-first Street..." This area was the Tenderloin; recall that it was, like the Bowery, known for its prostitution. Bock's common-law husband was Jacob

ANNE BOCK MYSTERIOUSLY MURDERED IN HER FLAT.

Bock, a cigar dealer. Diamond earrings and probably diamond rings were stolen from her. The murder occurred early Tuesday morning on August 4, 1896, in her apartment at 207 East 21st Street. The police stated that there was a sign of a struggle. She was found lying partly on the bed. Half of the upper portion of her back was on the bed, her feet were on the floor, "and the rigid limbs propped the body up in that position." Near the door were spots of blood, and blood was spattered between the center of the room and the bed. "At one side of the room was found a rag with which the weapon had been wiped clean and upon which the murderer had roughly wiped his bloody hands."

Murder site, *New York World*, August 5, 1896

A Jacob Tolker, or Jacob Talt, was first suspected because an eyewitness recalled seeing a man resembling him, tall and dark-haired. Tolker also wore a dark mustache, just as the tall, dark-haired Tumblety did. Multiple arrests were made, but in each case the suspects had solid alibis, including Jacob Tolker, so all were released.

New York World, May 14, 1897

According to the *New York World*, August 6, 1896, the physician who performed the autopsy was a Dr. Weston, who stated to the press that there was enough evidence to furnish a motive for the murder. Weston stated, "It is plain that the work was done by a man, and a man made strong by a fierce hate." There were five cuts on the woman's neck. He continued:

> The first gash began back in the muscle of the neck. The knife had been jammed into the neck until it almost touched the vertebrae. Then it was drawn forward and upward towards the lower jaw with strength enough to put an end to a bullock. But that was not enough to satisfy the murderer. He plunged the knife into the side neck again and drove it in as he dragged it forward and downward parallel with the chin. The cuts indicate a hate that was demoniacal.

Her diamond rings were confirmed to have been stolen, but just as Dr. Weston pointed out, theft was not the motive to ruthlessly murder the woman. Tumblety always had diamonds on his person throughout most of his adult life, so he clearly had an obsession with them. Curiously, another Annie, Jack the Ripper victim Annie Chapman, had her rings stolen from the murderer.

The murder site is located within walking distance of a known common residence Tumblety used at this time, 79 East 10th Street. When Tumblety sneaked out of England in November 1888 and arrived in New York City on December 2, 1888, he rushed to East 10th Street and hid at 79 East 10th Street for three days.

The Bock case was never solved. In the *Leader-Telegram*, October 19, 1900, it states, "Incidentally no one has ever been arrested for the murder of Annie Bock."

JACOB TALT AGAIN – NOVEMBER 1896

According to the *New York Sun*, May 15, 1897, police suspected Jacob Tolker, or Talt, again, this time for murdering Annie Hauff by strangulation on November 26, 1896, in Philadelphia, Pennsylvania, at 725 Noble Street. The Associated Press article that made multiple newspapers wrote the victim's name as Fanny Rauff. The reason why they suspected a New York City suspect is because Tolker again matched the physical description. Of significance is that this physical description also matches Tumblety.

ANNIE HAUFF.

The reporter stated, "It is said that within an hour before she was found dead she had been seen going into her rooms with a dark, tall, heavily built man, who wore a dark mustache." Tolker/Talt was eventually cleared.

Just feet away from the Pennsylvania Railroad tracks and only two blocks away from the train depot, 725 Noble Street is near the corner of Noble and 9th Streets The area was known for prostitution. In the *Philadelphia Times*, May 14, 1897, Annie Hauff was stated to be in the same class of woman as the murdered New York City woman, Annie Bock; this article referred to the deceased as a "Noble street unfortunate." If the offender got off of a train at the train depot, he was then immediately in an area of prostitution—where one would encounter such a woman as Annie Hauff.

Although the Hauff murder was not out on the street, neither was the Whitechapel murder of Mary Kelly. Both were near a train station. The last of the Whitechapel murders, the Mary Kelly murder, was in the western section of the Whitechapel District and was just a few short blocks from the Liverpool Street Station. Incidentally, what is considered by many experts as the first of the Whitechapel murders, the Polly Nichols murder was only feet away from the Whitechapel station across from the London Hospital.

ANOTHER TENDERLOIN MURDER – APRIL 1897

New York World, May 14, 1897

According to the *New York Tribune,* July 14, 1897, New York sex worker and "opium fiend," Diamond Flossie Murphy, out of the Tenderloin, was found in her room strangled at 228 West 24th Street. Fifteen hundred dollars' worth of diamonds were stolen; the victim was known for possessing diamonds.

FLOSSIE MURPHY.

While Murphy was strangled in a unique way, she is still discussed here because of her close proximity to both the Bock murder site and the known rooms Tumblety rented, plus she was a sex worker in the Tenderloin district, which Tumblety frequented. Additionally, Murphy was known to possess diamonds, something in which we know Tumblety had an unusual interest.

"MEANEST MAN ON RECORD" – NOVEMBER 1897 TO JANUARY 1898

On what a *Boston Globe* reporter called the "lonely streets" of Newton, Massachusetts, near Boston, between November 1897 and January 1898, women were being threatened and assaulted at night. According to the *Boston Globe,* January 25, 1898:

> Last week reports reached the police that at least 10 women had been frightened or assaulted on lonely streets, and a number of instances are known in which similar occurrences have been kept quiet by the victims. In most of these instances the women have been merely insulted or frightened, but now this form of persecution has been abandoned for one which is far more serious in its consequences.

The reporter stated that in the past few days, a man has been "squirting sulfuric acid onto the women's dresses with a garden syringe." The reporter stated, "The cases have become so frequent that women are becoming timid about venturing out alone after dark." The police also suspected there might be two separate assailants.

Most of the cases occurred in Newton, mostly along Vernon, Park, and Franklin Streets, but at least one victim was assaulted in Newtonville. The man was never apprehended. One possible significance is that both Vernon and Park Streets are only hundreds of feet away from the Newton Train Station, which was part of the Boston & Albany Railroad line. This pattern of assaults and threats in a particular city and near a railroad or train station is very similar to the numerous other mysterious assaults and even murders.

On multiple occasions, Tumblety transited from Rochester, New York, to Albany, New York, then to Boston, Massachusetts, meaning, he took the Boston & Albany Railway. Of further significance is the physical description of the Newton assailant:

> . . . [a] tall man with long Ulster or overcoat of a gray color and a black derby hat.

Not only was Tumblety considered tall, but he wore a gray Ulster coat, and on occasion, a derby hat. This assailant's behavior was very similar to the behavior of Jack the Tripper in 1892, who was a well-dressed man wearing diamonds and harassing women on the street. Recall, again, what New York's Detective Inspector Byrnes stated about a series of attacks around 1888, *nearly identical* to the series of attacks on Boston women:

> We caught a fellow who had a mania for throwing vitriol [sulfuric acid] upon women's dresses red-handed. Immediately after it was reported, his crime was localized. He frequented Fourteenth street. I found victims for him and my men were thickly scattered through the district. —*San Francisco Examiner*, October 2, 1888

It is difficult not to conclude that these three separate series of attacks were done by the same person, a person with an unusual hatred of women. If so, the man was a traveler, just like Tumblety—who was known to frequent both of the cities in which this particular crime was committed. An act such as this again conforms to a serial killer in their cooling off period, attempting to experience homicidal "offending-oriented fantasy" without actually committing a homicide.

Recall, just two years later in 1900, Tumblety's Baltimore attorney, Frank Widner, stated that a female client of his was forced to be alone with Tumblety in his office as he took a phone call. When he returned, she was waiting outside his office looking frightened. The woman then told him that she would never be in the same room with Tumblety again. It is clear that Tumblety had a hatred for a woman he did not know and made it his intention to intimidate her. He also waited until Widner was out of the room to frighten her.

Curiously, a town that is within walking distance to the north of Newton is Watertown, Massachusetts. This is the location where Etta Carlton was murdered in 1883.

NEAR THE MT. VERNON WEST TRAIN STATION – JUNE 1898

According to the *Evening Times*, July 25, 1898, the decomposed body of a young woman, estimated to be twenty-five years old, was found on July 24 in a clump of bushes near Hartley Park in Mount Vernon, New York. A large pool of blood was found about thirty feet from the body, which suggested that she was murdered outdoors in June 1898. A knife wound was found on the body.

Because the body was badly decomposed, it was impossible to determine if the woman was raped or not, although the body was not in a nude state. Still, a number of facts are strikingly similar to other murders possibly connected to Tumblety. The victim was a woman who was murdered outdoors with a knife thrust into her throat. Mount Vernon, New York, is also near New York City along a train route bound for Boston.

CAYENNE PEPPER AND SHARP METAL SHAVINGS IN THE EYES – JUNE 1899

Danbury, Connecticut, is a train stop on the train routes between Manhattan, New York, and northeast to Boston, Massachusetts. It is also a train stop north to Albany, New York. Just one block north of the Danbury train station on the night of June 20, 1899, nineteen-year-old Ollie Richmond was walking on Main Street when an unknown tall man in dark clothing approached her from behind, placed his hand over her mouth, then splashed a mixture of cayenne pepper and tiny needlepoints into her eyes. According to the *Evening Times*, June 20, 1899,

> She had a brief glance at her assailant, and then she was blinded by a cloud of pepper which was flung into her eyes. Her assailant released her in an instant,

and she heard footsteps as he ran, apparently through an alleyway which leads off from Main Street to that point. Nearly blinded and in great agony, Miss Richmond groped her way to the gate of her home and attracted the attention of her sister, who assisted her into the house. Poultices were applied to her eyes until Dr. Nathaniel Selleck arrived. The physician discovered that mixed with the pepper were many minute pieces of steel, some of which had worked their way beneath the eyelids and were causing excruciating pain... Microscopic inspection showed that the steel points were the sharp ends of many needles... The assailant evidently expected that his victim would rub them into her eyes in trying to wipe away the pepper... Persons in the vicinity saw a tall man, who wore dark clothing and a black hat, drawn over his eyes, loitering about the doors of the vacant store for some time before the attack was made.

While the local police believed the assailant was someone local who had a vendetta against Richmond, nothing came of it. This assault is exactly the type of attack expected from a misogynistic transient hellbent on causing permanent damage to a young woman. It is clear that once the victim rubbed her eyes, the metal needle points had the possibility of inflicting permanent eye damage, possibly even blindness. While this was a non-homicidal attack, the intention was to cause bodily harm that would affect the woman for the rest of her life.

The escape route along Main Street—if the assailant ran southbound—brought him straight to the train station just over a block away, which is exactly what would be expected from a ruthless transient stopping at a location, committing a crime, then getting back on the train. The misogynist Francis Tumblety traveled from Manhattan to Boston almost on a yearly basis, which guarantees he would have been on a train that made a stop at the Danbury Station.

GIRL ASSAULTED IN DAYTON – MARCH 1900

Between Cincinnati, Ohio, and Cleveland, Ohio, by train, is Dayton, Ohio. A tall, elderly man attacked a girl at night on the street, attempting to drag her into an alley. According to the *Dayton Daily News*, March 5, 1900:

> A cowardly attempt to commit a criminal assault was made last night on Jones street, about 9 o'clock, near Brown, almost in the full glare of an electric light.

A tall, elderly man emerged from an alley just as an estimable young lady of Dayton View was passing. In a moment's time he had grabbed her about the neck and was endeavoring to drag his helpless victim into the dark alley way. She fought desperately, and succeeded in part in releasing herself. With an extra effort she finally freed herself from the grasp of the villain, but fell upon the street, striking her head on the curbstone. An ugly gash was inflicted, but this did not deter the intended victim from screaming at the top of her voice. This was the only thing that saved her from the clutches of the demon, who seemed bent upon his purpose. For a second time he grabbed her, and endeavored to drag her into the alley, but she resisted desperately, screaming at every move.

Once help arrived, the man vanished. She told the police that the man was poorly dressed.

There certainly is a pattern in a tall man attacking women at night, first by grabbing their throats, then attempting to drag them into a dark alley, clearly to commit further atrocities. We also know that, by this time, Tumblety was older and dressing shabbily.

ROBBED OF HER HAIR – APRIL 1900

Florence Wright, an eighteen-year-old woman with twenty-one-inch-long hair living on 314 Warren Street, Newark, New Jersey, was assaulted by a tall man with a black mustache on her rear veranda at ten P.M., July 1, 1900. According to the *Passaic Daily News*, July 2, 1900, Wright was sitting on her front porch when a strange tall man with a black mustache passed by several times. Later, on her veranda, she was attacked, the man cutting her hair off with a knife.

> . . . she was going to the refrigerator for a drink of water when she saw the tall man beside her and screamed. He struck her behind the left ear and she knew no more until her parents aroused her. The girl had fine golden hair, and her assailant had evidently hacked it off with a knife. She said that she never saw the man before, and thinks that before he struck her he said, "Where is that watch?"

Recall Jack the Clipper just across the Hudson River in Manhattan in November 1893; he was a tall man in an Ulster coat attacking women and cutting their hair off.

TEXAS TRAIN STATION MURDER – AUGUST 1900

On August 14, 1900, the body of Anna Marone was discovered in the sitting room at the Texas and Pacific train depot in Jefferson, Texas. Her neck was broken and her body mutilated. Jefferson resident Mike Kelly gave testimony that he was approached by a Black man named George Johnson, who told him Anna Marone was at his house drunk and passed out. He assisted Johnson in moving the unconscious Marone to the sitting room at the train depot. They then placed a note on her stating that she be shipped to San Antonio, Texas. Both Kelly and Johnson were arrested for the murder, although they insisted they merely left her at the train station.

Tumblety was reported in the *St. Louis Dispatch*, June 28, 1903, to be in Galveston, Texas, during the Galveston Flood, which occurred on August 27, 1900:

> In the Galveston flood Dr. Tumblety was among the victims. He floated about on a chicken coop until rescued by a tugboat, but his health was permanently impaired.

According to the *Baltimore Sun*, July 7, 1900, Tumblety arrived in Boston on that day. By August 27, he was in Galveston, Texas, and Anna Marone was mutilated at the train station in Jefferson, Texas, on August 14, 1900. The St. Louis train route that connected Hot Springs, Arkansas, and St. Louis, Missouri, with Galveston, Texas, made a stop in Jefferson, Texas. Sworn testimonies from multiple witnesses stated that Tumblety visited both Hot Springs and St. Louis each year, sometimes twice a year.

YOUNG GIRL ATTACKED IN BOSTON – SEPTEMBER 1900

According to the *Boston Globe*, October 1, 1900, fourteen-year-old Alice Whitmarsh was assaulted Saturday, September 28, 1900, between nine and ten P.M.:

> The girl lives at 68 Cornell st, and was on her way home with a number of purchases she had made during the evening. She was accosted by a man about 35 to 40 years of age. He asked her if he could not help her with the bundles. The girl was somewhat frightened and would not let him have any of the bundles. The man continued to walk along with her, all the time talking to her. The girl became more frightened by the trend of the remarks of the man

as they walked along a dark portion of the street. As they came to a short street leading toward the rear of Germania hall the man grabbed her by the throat, forcing her to her knees.

The girl struggled and screamed, and fortunately, someone heard. A man on Beech Street came running to help. The assailant saw the man approaching and fled into the woods. A police officer on an electric car also heard Whitmarsh scream and arrived just after the first man. They then escorted her home. A notice went out to the police substation and a search began.

She described the man the best she could in her fright as quite tall, dark complexion, with a black mustache, dark derby hat, and a mackintosh. A nineteenth-century mackintosh was a double-breasted raincoat, which looked very similar to a double-breasted Ulster coat.

Crossing just one block north across Beech Street is a set of train tracks belonging to the Dedham Branch Railroad, and Central Station is walking distance away. Also, recall that the police officer was on an electric cable car at the end of the street, so mass transit was nearby. Under sworn testimony, Tumblety's Baltimore attorney stated that he helped his client with his will in his Baltimore office in October 1900. This means that, after Tumblety's August/September 1900 visit to Texas, he traveled to the East Coast, so being in Boston in late September 1900 is not out of the question.

ASSAULTS IN THE MIDWEST NEAR THE GREAT LAKES AGAIN – JAN 1901

Recall, in December 1886, there was a series of assaults in Buffalo, New York, by a tall man in a gray Ulster coat, and then in Chicago, Illinois, in December 1888 by a man matching the same description. In both cities, the assailant wore his collar up to hide his face, but the victim in Chicago recalled seeing a dark mustache. And then, in December 1893, young Julia Huff, or Hulf, was murdered with her throat cut along Franklin Street in Cleveland, Ohio, a city on Lake Erie situated by train between Chicago and Buffalo.

According to the *Dayton Herald*, January 31, 1901, the second of two similar assaults on the streets occurred. It was an assault on a young woman at night in Cleveland, Ohio, by a tall man—virtually identical to the assault of a young woman in Chicago by a tall man with a mustache in a gray Ulster coat:

> Miss Minnie Schell, a domestic 20 years of age, living at 99 Glen Park Place, was held up and assaulted in front of the above number shortly after 9 o'clock

on Sunday night. Her assailant knocked her down, and drawing a gun, threatened to shoot her if she made an outcry.

Just before, Minnie Schell had boarded the Wilson Avenue car, and a tall man boarded the car at the same time. He sat opposite her. When she took the next leg on Euclid Avenue, the tall man followed and sat next to her. When she got off at Glen Park Place, so did he:

> The girl hurried along the street, which was exceedingly dark. Just before she reached the house, however, the man came up to her, and knocked her down by a blow from his fist. As she fell, Miss Schell gave vent to a cry of terror, which caused her assailant to draw a revolver, and threatened to kill her.

As he grabbed Schell, she fought back and screamed. Once people came out of a nearby house, he stopped, kicked her repeatedly, then ran off. The police assumed that the assailant was attempting to sexually assault Schell, but that is merely a guess.

Notice how shockingly similar this attack was to the December 1888 Chicago attack by a tall man with a mustache in a gray Ulster coat. The young Swedish girl in the Chicago assault was near the same age as the Cleveland girl and also a domestic, both riding a cable car home from work. In both cases, the assailant sat on the opposite side of the cable car and followed the victim off. Once each girl was in a secluded location, the assailant attacked. Only after the initial attack would the assailant pull out a revolver.

According to the *Dayton Herald*, April 12, 1901, yet another similar nighttime assault of a young woman by a tall man had occurred in Ohio. Again, the assailant attempted to force her into a dark alley. Just like in Cleveland, this was just one of a number of assaults in the area:

> A bold assault that was perpetrated the other night, just came to light today. Miss Stella Haas, of 19 DeKalb street, was the intended victim, but she escaped only through strength and fight . . . She left the Jennings residence shortly after 7 o'clock the evening of the assault, and had proceeded about a square north when a strange man made a lunge at her, at the mouth of the alley just south of the high board fence on the Wilkinson street side of the Cooper Seminary. He did not reach her at the first attempt, but grabbed at her again, and caught her by one of her arms, turning her completely around, and then tried to push her into the mouth of the alley.

Stella Haas fought hard and apparently surprised the assailant with how tough she was. He lost his hold when she elbowed him in the stomach. Haas was then able to run away north on Wilkinson Street. The man chased her all the way to her home, but as she screamed for her brother, her pursuer vanished. Haas was only able to describe her assailant as being a "very tall man." There were other assaults:

> The police were notified, and officers were sent to the Haas residence. They stated that several other young women had been assaulted that same evening, and in each instance the assailant had been a tall man.

Between St. Louis, Missouri, and Cincinnati, Ohio—cities Tumblety visited almost on an annual basis—by train, is Evansville, Indiana, which was the location of an assault of a woman by a tall man with a thick black mustache in November 1901. According to the *Akron Daily Democrat*, November 23, 1901,

> A sensational story was told by the police which may throw some light on the two murder mysteries . . . Mrs. Wm. Springer, living at 1018 West Pennsylvania st., says about dark last night a tall man with a heavy black mustache and wearing a long mackintosh, jumped over her back fence and seized her as she stood in the back yard. The man tried to choke her. Mrs. Springer being a powerful woman, beat her assailant off, but did not report her experience to the police until today.

Curiously, the backyard of 1018 West Pennsylvania Street is next to two sets of railroad tracks and within walking distance of a train station. As stated, a long mackintosh is a double-breasted raincoat that looks surprisingly like a double-breasted Ulster coat, especially in the dark.

CHAPTER 12

A LATE NINETEENTH-CENTURY SERIAL KILLER – THE RAILWAY RIPPER

The majority of murders of women in the United States in the late nineteenth century ended in the conviction of someone local, such as an ex-husband, an old boyfriend, or a farmhand. Most articles about solved and even unsolved murders of women found in contemporary newspapers involved the victim having been raped and/or robbed for financial gain. Some, though, had no obvious motive, causing the papers to call them mysterious murders. Many of these murders occurred at or near a train station or train tracks. Nineteenth-century local detectives and investigators would not have been on the lookout for an out-of-town transient serial killer with the primary motive of murder, dispatching a victim in such a violent, personal manner then disappearing on a train. A serial killer exploiting the US railways would not only have discovered the perfect mode of escape but would also have been able to ply their homicidal trade for years.

That said, American editors and reporters of large newspapers, including the Associated Press, kept up on the network of news cable communications and were primed to discover patterns within unsolved murders across the United States. This was especially the case after 1888, newsmen having lived through the well-publicized Jack the Ripper mystery across the pond. Case in point occurring in the 1890s with some calling the offender of this rash of similar murders "Jack the Strangler," or just the "Strangler." An article in the *Cincinnati Enquirer*, March 21, 1896, titled, "Mysterious. Crimes of a Strangler. Monomaniac Murderer Roams Undetected. From the Atlantic to the Pacific Coast – His Victims Are Always Outcast Women," states,

(New York World) From San Francisco comes the news that the mysterious murderer, everywhere known as the Strangler, is at work again. A few years ago it was Jack the Ripper who was filling the world with horror at his series of long and baffling crimes. Now it is the unknown madman called the Strangler who is perpetrating exactly the same sort of horrors. He is a wanderer, instead of choosing the same city and the same district for the gratification of his perverted desire, his work has not attracted as much attention as did the work of Jack the Ripper. . . . Still, those who have made a study of these matters are of the opinion that the long series of crimes done in various cities of the United States are in all probability the work of the same brain.

The article continued and recalled nine unsolved murders across the United States. What the press saw in common was that most of the murders occurred at the end of the month, most were sex workers, and most were strangled with material wrapped around the neck. All were unsolved cases. It began with Minnie Weldt in New York, May 30, 1894; Josie Bennett in Buffalo, June 30, 1894; Mary Ekhart in Cincinnati, July 25, 1894; Lena Tupper in Denver, September 27, 1894; Marie Contassoit in Denver, October 28, 1894; Kiku Oyama in Denver, November 13, 1894; Jessie Williams in San Francisco, December 22, 1895; Marie McDermot in San Francisco, February 24, 1896; and Bertha Paradis in San Francisco, March 10, 1896. Modern experts may or may not agree with this reporter's conclusion, but what is important is that some in the press were noticing patterns of murders, the fingerprint of a serial killer.

When the reporter stated, "He is a wanderer," he or she was identifying what modern-day experts call a transient serial killer, as opposed to geographically stable serial killers. According to Scott A. Bonn, PhD, geographically stable serial killers have a comfort zone where they commit their murders, possibly close to home, called an anchor point. A classic example was John Wayne Gacy, who enticed young men to his home and eventually buried them under his house. Gacy's anchor point was his home. Bonn, ironically, uses the Jack the Ripper case (exclusively the canonical murders) to show that the killer only killed in and near the Whitechapel district. Bonn states that Ted Bundy did not possess an anchor point since he traveled and killed in multiple locations. Bundy was considered a transient serial killer. Other examples of transient serial killers were Israel Keyes, Aileen Wuornos, and Henry Lee Lucas.

Although there was no federal law enforcement in the late nineteenth century, the *New York World* investigative reporter certainly did take into account alienists', or nineteenth-century psychologists', professional opinions on the murders, stating, "The alienists, however, are rather inclined to believe . . ." The reporter was clearly aware of a class of killers we now call serial killers. Interestingly, the reporter concluded that these murders were not at the hands of Jack the Ripper or another ruthless killer in the United States who killed Mamie, or Mary, Sullivan in Paterson, New Jersey, in 1896:

> While he [the Strangler] belongs to the same class as the Ripper or as the pervert who took pleasure in killing Mary Sullivan down at Paterson as slowly and as painfully as possible, he works in a much [more] stealthy manner. The other two attacked their victims in the open air. This man only operates in the house.

With a modern understanding of violent crimes, these particular US murders similar to the Sullivan murder, covered in detail earlier, actually conform to a unique type of disorganized, opportunistic serial killer, specifically, one having an anger-retaliatory motive focused not on a particular person but a particular time and location. The assaults were vicious and opportunistic; a surprise attack on the streets from a dark area.

If we accept that Mary Kelly was the victim of Jack the Ripper, then this investigative reporter made a slight error. Jack the Ripper generally killed outdoors, but he did indeed murder Mary Kelly indoors. Interestingly, the reporter recognized the similarities in the murders of Jack the Ripper and Mamie Sullivan. If Jack the Ripper was indeed in America murdering other women, then this arguably leads to examining a Jack the Ripper suspect having lived in America: Dr. Francis Tumblety.

When Scotland Yard's First-Class Detective Inspector Walter Andrews told an *Ottawa Daily Citizen* reporter in Montreal on December 20, 1888, that he expected "a similar experience in New York," this can only lead to one conclusion; Inspector Andrews was planning on going to New York. This verifies the newspaper reports that Andrews received new orders from Scotland Yard upon his arrival to Halifax on or about December 9, 1888, to "find the murderer in America," who "left England three weeks ago." It also corroborates Guy Logan's comments in his 1928 book, *Masters of Crime*, about his Scotland Yard source telling him in later years that Andrews "came to America in December 1888, in search of the Whitechapel fiend . . . the nature of which was never disclosed." The suspect both Inspector Andrews and Logan referred to was Francis Tumblety, a Jack the Ripper suspect who sneaked out of England on or about November 23, 1888. To have Andrews head an American investigation on a

Jack the Ripper suspect points to only one conclusion: Scotland Yard took seriously the possibility that Francis Tumblety was Jack the Ripper. Both Andrews and Logan believed the last Jack the Ripper victim was Mary Kelly, who was murdered on November 9, 1888, and as Scotland Yard's Chief Inspector Littlechild emphasized, "... certain it is that from this time [Tumblety having left England] the 'Ripper' murders [in London] came to an end."

Tumblety arrived from England in New York Harbor on December 2, 1888, wearing an Ulster coat and a derby hat and carrying an umbrella. The next day, after two New York newspapers reported in their December 4, 1888, respective issues, on an English detective posting himself outside Tumblety's window to "get the chap" who committed the Whitechapel murders, Tumblety vanished. He sneaked off to his sister's home in Waterloo, New York.

Two related questions come to mind when evaluating the plausibility of Tumblety being Jack the Ripper. First, why would an American doctor hellbent on killing sex workers travel across the Atlantic Ocean to do it? There were plenty of potential victims in the United States. The solution to this answer is that he did kill in the United States, thus, he killed on both sides of the Atlantic. This leads to the second question. Were there any unsolved Ripper-like murders (or assaults) of women in America where Tumblety cannot be eliminated as having committed the crime?

A newly discovered newspaper report suggests that Scotland Yard detectives in the United States were attempting to answer these very questions up to the year 1890. According to the *Oakland Tribune*, December 8, 1890:

> A few days since, the "Jack the Ripper" murders which startled all London about a year ago, and particularly the Whitechapel district, were recalled by the arrest at Scotland Yard of a certain Dr. Tumblety on whom suspicion rests at present... The London police could not learn much of Tumblety's antecedents, and to the present they are trying to identify him with other crimes.

Upon extensive research, the answer to the second question is an overwhelming yes. A few months before the August 31, 1888, Polly Nichols murder, sometime in May or June 1888, Tumblety was reportedly seen in New York City, and then soon left for England. In May 1888, a Bowery sex worker, Minnie Moscowitch, was found murdered in the cellar of her lodging house with *her throat cut from ear to ear*. It is surprising that no researcher ever discussed this Ripper-like murder in connection with the Whitechapel murders. According to criminologist Dr. Brent Turvey, the Whitechapel murders showed anger-retaliatory behavior. The motive behind them was not the usual robbery or rape, and the level of overkill suggests there was an element of hatred and rage. It was concluded that this Bowery sex worker was neither raped nor robbed. Just as the Whitechapel victims were working the streets before being murdered, so was Moscowitch. The Moscowitch murder was clearly Ripper-like. The last person Moscowitch was seen with just after midnight was a tall man with a dark mustache.

Less than one month after the November 9, 1888, Mary Kelly murder, when Tumblety was once more Stateside and hiding out in Waterloo, New York, an unnamed woman was attacked on the street at night in that same town, the man grabbing her by the throat. The Waterloo reporter suspected the offender was Tumblety. Just one week later, a tall man in a gray Ulster coat and a dark mustache attacked a young woman in Chicago, Illinois, first grabbing her by the throat. An Associated Press newspaper reporter stated that Tumblety was thought to be in Chicago at this very time.

Tumblety began his annual trips to Hot Springs, Arkansas, around the year 1880, which is evidence that this was near the time he realized he had contracted syphilis, an incurable progressive disease, and was feeling the negative effects. In the late nineteenth century, Hot Springs was the mecca for syphilis patients. The anger and rage he clearly felt from the knowledge that he had contracted an incurable disease would have been the perfect backdrop to begin exacting his revenge upon a segment of the population he already believed was a curse to mankind. In an extensive search through the digitized newspaper archives in the decade of the 1870s, it was difficult to find any women being murdered in the United States where either rape or robbery was not the motive. Searching through the newspaper archives in the decades of the 1880s and 1890s was a different story, and in each year, there was at least one unsolved murder or assault of a young woman with a clear anger-retaliatory motive. This is the type of pattern expected to develop if a serial killer of this type began assaulting and murdering.

This unusual spree in the United States may have even begun as early as 1880. Recall, in August 1880, an unsolved murder very similar to the murder of Polly Nichols occurred along the railway near Barnstable, Massachusetts. The body of Mary Cassidy, aged fifteen, was found along the side of the road with her *head nearly decapitated* and a butcher knife stuck in the left side of her abdomen. The body of Polly Nichols was found near the Whitechapel train station and had a deep gash along the left side of her abdomen.

Curiously, Tumblety lost a court case in New York City against a woman just days before the murder of Mary Cassidy. Tumblety was so enraged in court that the woman's attorney told the press he thought Tumblety was going to leap from the stand and attack him as he questioned him. This may have been what finally pushed Tumblety over the edge, the trigger that finally caused him to kill—his original bloodlust.

It was in February 1881 that Tumblety began the first of his annual visits to New Orleans, Louisiana, for Mardi Gras, and was witnessed exhibiting astonishing Ripper-like behavior. Recall that Tumblety met up with a young man named Richard Norris in Louisiana each year. Norris testified under oath in 1905 that the first time he went up to Tumblety's room in 1881, Tumblety gave him a drink and showed him the collection of surgical knives he traveled with. Norris stated that Tumblety had a bitter hatred of sex workers and even told him that "all street walkers should be disemboweled." Norris continued meeting up with Tumblety for the next twenty years, enjoying the money he spent on him. After the Whitechapel murders in 1888, Norris held suspicions that Tumblety may have been the killer, and in February 1889, he claimed he confronted Tumblety. Tumblety only admitted to *being* in Whitechapel throughout the entire series of murders—not having any part in them. Norris also testified that Tumblety "had peculiar habits of walking the dark streets at night like a street walker" and staying in the darkest parts of the streets. Damningly, Norris testified that Tumblety's "hobby was that of women should be killed."

In 1881, two assaults in the United States followed a similar pattern of a female victim walking alone on the streets at night and then getting attacked by an unknown person. Luckily, the women survived and gave details of the attacks. Instead of following a sex worker to a more secluded location, as in the case of Polly Nichols, the offender first attacked, then attempted to drag the victim to a more secluded location to complete his heinous task. In the first 1881 assault case, young Minnie Sneideker was assaulted in May 1881 in Brooklyn, New York, on the street at night by a large man who attempted to drag her to a dark, vacant lot. In August 1881, just across the river in Jersey City, a young woman was walking at night then bludgeoned by a man who then attempted to drag her into a dark location. In both cases, the women fought back and screamed, resulting in the assailant running away as people came to the victim's assistance.

Also in August 1881, the dismembered body of Ella Clark was discovered just outside of Brooklyn in Long Island. Her head was decapitated by what was thought to have been a long, sharp knife, such as a butcher's knife. Strangely, her organs were missing, foreshadowing Jack the Ripper collecting abdominal organs from three of his victims. Clark had come from Connecticut to her hometown of Manhattan in May 1881 to get an abortion from a specific quack doctor named Dr. James C. Thomas. According to her Manhattan friend, the morning Clark left her home to see the quack doctor on May 5, 1881, was when she went missing. The quack doctor claimed that he was not in his office and never saw her. His alibi was so solid that investigators quickly eliminated him as a suspect.

Authorities were convinced Clark met up with another quack doctor who botched the abortion, which caused her death. The killer then dismembered the body and discarded it on Long Island across the river in an attempt to hide his tracks. Problem: The only way to identify a murdered victim at the time was facial recognition, yet the head was found with the dismembered body parts. It makes little sense not to discard the head in a separate location if the motive was to stump the authorities.

Who was this other Manhattan quack doctor Clark found? How coincidental that another quack doctor by the name of Dr. Francis Tumblety, who not only would be a future Jack the Ripper suspect but who also had an affinity for collecting anatomical organs, had his office just blocks away. Recall, Dr. J. H. Ziegler, the young physician who spoke with a dying Francis Tumblety nightly for nearly a month in May 1903 stated under oath that, "He [Tumblety] would ask about an amputation; if I had seen any amputations, and I told him I had." If Clark did indeed visit Tumblety and ask for an abortion, she would have told him she wanted to keep the abortion a secret and no one would have known she was visiting him. Talk about a fly volunteering to get caught in the web of a spider! Tumblety stated in his autobiographies that he was in search of an elixir of health that existed in the herbal/botanical world, and Scotland Yard certainly did investigate a claim that Jack the Ripper was searching for an elixir of life by mixing the fluids of the uterus with herbs. With Clark's organs missing—along with the fetus—instead of dying from a botched abortion, she may very well have been the victim of a serial killer with an agenda to find a cure for his syphilis. No contemporary explanations of the missing organs and fetus make greater sense than this.

In common with an unusually large number of the late nineteenth-century murders and assaults along US railway systems was a similar physical description of the assailant or suspected assailant. In nearly every case that reported a physical description, the suspected assailant was a tall, middle-aged man wearing a gray Ulster coat, or gray overcoat, usually with his collar up, blocking his face from view. In May 1882, an eyewitness spotted "a tall man in an Ulster" attacking the murdered woman in Boston. In September 1883, Rose Ambler was murdered along the railroad, and an eyewitness saw a "tall unfamiliar man." In November 1883, Phoebe Paullin had her throat cut, and a tall, well-dressed man in a dark overcoat was seen nearby.

In October 1884, in Brooklyn, New York, near Long Island, on three separate occasions, women were attacked at night on the street, struck in the face, then grabbed by the throat. In December 1884, three women were attacked at different times on the street at night in Plainfield, New Jersey, all near the railroad. In each case, the assailant was a tall man in a gray overcoat wearing a derby hat. In January 1885, a tall man surprised a Mrs. Creaney on the streets of Long Island, struck her head, and grabbed her by the throat. This method of surprise night attack, first striking the victim, is exactly the type of brutal, personal, rage attack serial killer Peter Sutcliffe, the Yorkshire Ripper, used in the late 1970s. Sutcliffe being named as the Ripper was an allusion to Jack the Ripper.

In December 1886, Buffalo, New York, experienced a rash of at least three assaults on women at night by a tall man in a gray Ulster coat with his collar up. One victim stated he first grabbed her by the throat. When she resisted, he pulled out a revolver, but when help arrived, he ran off in the same direction as the train station. On two separate occasions, Tumblety was reported to be in possession of a revolver.

Just two months before Tumblety embarked on the transatlantic steamship *City of Rome* in May 1887 to Liverpool, England, an unknown woman had her throat cut from ear to ear in Rahway, New Jersey. There was no evidence of rape or robbery. An eyewitness at the Rahway Train Station saw a woman who matched the description of the victim leave the station toward the murder site. Less than two months after Tumblety returned to New York City in November 1887, just across the Hudson River in Trenton, New Jersey, a sex worker was strangled to death. Her body was found in a cellar eerily similar to where Bowery sex worker Minnie Moscowitch would be murdered six months later.

Within a month of the Minnie Moscowitch murder in New York City in May 1888, Tumblety left New York Harbor for London for an uncharacteristically long stay of over five months. An eyewitness stated that Tumblety's favorite number was eight, and coincidentally, in the eighth month of the year 1888 (Eighteen-Eighty-Eight) on August 7 (curiously falling upon the eighth new moon of the year), unfortunate Martha Tabram was viciously murdered in Whitechapel. Many experts consider Tabram as Jack the Ripper's first victim. Although Tabram did not have her throat cut, she was an East End unfortunate who was brutally attacked with a knife, having been stabbed thirty-nine times.

Also, the motive was neither rape nor robbery. Lastly, no one in the vicinity heard a thing.

Then, at the end of the eighth month on August 31, 1888, unfortunate Polly Nichols was murdered in Buck's Row near the Whitechapel train station and tracks; first strangled, as she lay on her back, her throat was cut to her spine from ear to ear. The killer had even attacked her abdomen with a long knife, considered by experts to be an amputation knife in a surgical kit. No one in the vicinity heard a thing. Two independent accounts in 1881 had Tumblety carrying with him in his travel chest a surgical kit containing multiple knives.

Eight days after the Nichols murder, on September 8, 1888, Annie Chapman was mutilated in the backyard at 29 Hanbury Street with her throat cut deeply. Other than possibly one witness in the backyard of 27 Hanbury Street, no one in the vicinity heard a thing. Her tongue was protruding, indicating strangulation. Her intestines were lifted out and placed over her right shoulder, and her uterus was missing.

On the night of September 30, 1888, at around one o'clock A.M., Elizabeth Stride was murdered in Dutfield's Yard. Her throat was cut, and it looked as if the killer was interrupted. Less than one hour later, Catherine Eddowes's mutilated body was found walking distance away in Mitre Square in the jurisdiction of the City of London police. Her face was attacked with a knife and her uterus and left kidney were taken. No one in the vicinity heard a thing.

On November 9, 1888, Mary Kelly was found excessively mutilated in her room in Miller's Court. Her body was prone on her bed, thighs stripped of skin, and the abdominal cavity emptied of its organs. Her face was also attacked, and her heart was missing. The killer had hours with the body and treated the corpse as if he were carrying out a complete autopsy. According to the *Daily News*, November 12, 1888, on the morning of Kelly's murder, a man collided with a tall, well-dressed man rushing through Mitre Square with a parcel under his arm and blood splatter on his face, shirt, and cuffs.

After Tumblety sneaked out of England, the murders stopped. Chief Inspector Littlechild recalled in his 1913 letter, "... certain it is that from this time the 'Ripper' murders came to an end."

In New York City in May 1892, a tall, well-dressed man wearing diamonds, nicknamed Jack the Tripper by the police, was walking in Washington Square, tripping women with his umbrella. The wealthy Tumblety lived near Washington Square and was known to walk with an umbrella even if it was not raining. He was also known to wear diamonds, with the *Pittsburgh Dispatch* stating in 1889 that Tumblety was "flashily dressed and sparkling with diamonds."

Additionally, Tumblety was an extreme misogynist. Although it was not reported that the "Tripper" wore a gray Ulster coat, there is a convincing connection to another tall man who wore a gray Ulster coat. Recall that Detective Inspector of the New York City Police Department Thomas Byrnes told a reporter that in 1888 or earlier they finally caught a man who was squirting acid on the dresses of women walking along 14th Street. Even though he was arrested, Byrnes declined to give his name. The 14th Street acid attacks took place only seven city blocks away from the trippings in Washington Square—near lodging houses taken up by Tumblety. Suspicions that Jack the Tripper and the acid-squirting man were the same man, specifically, the extreme misogynist Francis Tumblety, are not unwarranted. It makes sense that Tumblety would have changed his misogynistic behavior since squirting acid on women would have caused Byrnes to throw him in jail and press charges. In Boston, nine years later, a tall man in a gray Ulster coat was squirting acid on women walking the street and was known in the papers as the "meanest man on record." Albeit these assaults were only designed to upset and humiliate women and not kill them, many serial killers do, indeed, stop killing for a period of time. During this cooling-off period, they involve themselves in non-homicidal activities, what experts call "offending-oriented fantasies," in hopes to satisfy their homicidal impulses without killing. Various reasons are given as to why they stop killing, but one reason, as explained by serial killers, is that they stop murdering during times of increased police activity and public awareness.

In November 1893, in New York City, a woman was attacked on the streets by a tall man in an Ulster coat who slashed her hair off. The papers called the assailant Jack the Clipper, which may very well have been another non-homicidal crime during a cooling-off period. It happened again in New York City that same month to Annie Smith, who was attacked by a tall man in an Ulster coat who aggressively cut her hair off with a knife. Then, in April 1894, an unnamed woman was assaulted in Cincinnati, Ohio, again first grabbed by the neck.

Unusually similar assaults of women at night occurred in the Pittsburgh area in April 1895. In this case, the offender attacked the women near railroad tracks and then attempted to drag them to the river. These may have been murder attempts, considering just two years earlier a dismembered body of a woman was found on the beach along the Lake Michigan shoreline in Chicago—Chicago being the next major city after Pittsburgh along the B & O Railway System. Just two blocks away was a cable car station, the very same Chicago cable car system a tall man in a gray Ulster coat traveled on before he attacked young Hulda Johnson in December 1888. Further, a dismembered body of a woman was found floating in the river off of Coney Island in May 1883, another in the Erie Canal in October 1883, and yet another in the river in Boston in July 1885.

In May and June of 1895, Buffalo, New York, again saw a tall man assault two women on the street at night. In every case, the attacker first grabbed his victim by the throat. This certainly does conform to a pattern of a transient offender who periodically traveled through Buffalo. In Tumblety's case, before 1889, he generally traveled to England around June and returned Stateside around September—meaning he was in England during the Whitechapel murders and in the United States for the other aforementioned killings. Beginning in 1889, Tumblety was in the United States all year round. By February of that year, he made his way to New Orleans for the carnival season, only to return to the East Coast around April after a visit to Hot Springs, Arkansas.

One of the most Ripper-like murders of a sex worker in the United States occurred in July 1895 in St. Louis, Missouri. Ella "Kid" King was walking the streets at night and was attacked with a knife by a tall White man. Although the victim did not have her throat cut, the assailant slashed her abdomen so deep it caused some of her entrails to protrude from the wound. Eyewitnesses stated he was wearing a gray coat, albeit the style of coat was not given. They recalled her yelling, "That man stabbed me!" As she fell to the ground, the witnesses noticed a horrible gash to the abdomen. She soon died of the major wound. Even though the papers did not state that the coat was an Ulster, that type of gray overcoat was in style at the time, and Tumblety, to a point, was rather a man of distinguished style.

One slight difference between this assault by a tall man in a gray overcoat and the assault in Chicago by an assailant with the same physical description is that it was not near the train tracks or a train station, although one was still walking distance away. What was even closer was the hotel that Tumblety was known to stay at: the Mona House. In fact, the assailant ran south, in the direction of the Mona House. If Tumblety was the offender, his escape was clearly to his room, as opposed to a train station. In cities where Tumblety stayed for a few weeks or more, such as St. Louis, he would rent out at least one room at a lodging house in or near the slums. This would also explain the events that occurred just after the Jack the Ripper murder of Catherine Eddowes at Mitre Square. Part of Eddowes's apron was found a few blocks away to the northeast on Goulston Street, the killer clearly discarding it as he rushed away from the murder site. For Tumblety not to have rented out a room in the East End would have been out of character, so, if he was Jack the Ripper, he escaped in this instance not to a train station but to a lodging house nearby.

In northern New Jersey in 1896, there was a rash of assaults and murders perpetrated by a tall man in a gray Ulster coat. In February 1896, in Montclair, New Jersey, a tall man in a gray Ulster coat attacked two women on the street with a wooden club. In March 1896, Mamie Sullivan was bludgeoned and murdered in Paterson, New Jersey, on the street, and witnesses saw a tall man nearby in a dark location in a gray Ulster coat. The same man attacked two women in that area just a half hour earlier, and as in the case of the first woman, he grabbed her by the throat. An eyewitness to the attack, Joseph Murtagh, stated that he was in a New York City saloon and a tall man in a gray Ulster coat met him, put a drug in his drink, and aggressively escorted Murtagh back to Paterson. As the drugged Murtagh walked with the man on the street, the man placed Murtagh against a tree, then walked over to the woman and attacked her. Murtagh then ran away.

In July 1896, in Brooklyn, New York, a tall man with a flowing mustache attacked young Jesse Tempary at night along the road, which paralleled the railway. She successfully escaped. In November 1896, in Philadelphia, Pennsylvania, Annie Hauff was strangled. The suspect was a tall man with a dark mustache.

From November 1897 to February 1898, a tall man in an Ulster coat was menacing women at night on the streets of Newton, Massachusetts, a suspect who was reported as the "meanest man" in America. The man was squirting sulfuric acid on the dresses of women, then running off. Similarly, in Danbury, Connecticut, in June 1899, a tall man threw cayenne pepper and metal shavings into the eyes of young Ollie Richmond. The attack was near the railways.

Assaults continued in 1900 and 1901. A "tall, elderly man" grabbed the throat of a young woman on the streets of Dayton, Ohio, at night, in March 1900, and tried to drag her into a darker, more secluded area. The young woman successfully fought the assailant off. In April 1900, a tall man with a black mustache grabbed young Florence Wright in Newark, New Jersey, cut her hair off, then ran. In September 1900, Alice Whitmarsh in Boston, Massachusetts, was grabbed by the throat at night on the streets by a tall man with a mustache, wearing a derby hat. In January 1901, in Cleveland, Ohio, Minnie Schell was followed in a cable car, just like the Chicago woman in December 1888, then knocked down by a tall man with a revolver. In April 1901, Stella Haas was attacked at night near an alley in Dayton, Ohio, by a "very tall man." Lastly, in November 1901, a Mrs. Springer was attacked in Evansville, Indiana, by a tall man with a "heavy black mustache" wearing an Ulster-style overcoat.

In some cases, Tumblety was verified to be in the area at the time of the assaults or murders. Recall, in early December 1888, Tumblety sneaked out of

New York City and made his way to his sister's home in Waterloo, New York. It was at this time that a Waterloo newspaper reported on Tumblety being in town and that a woman was accosted on the street at night, the assailant first grabbing the victim's throat. The reporter made the connection that Tumblety may have been the assailant. Just one week later, a woman was accosted in Chicago, Illinois, by a tall man with a dark mustache and a gray Ulster coat. Reports in the newspaper claimed that Tumblety was likely in Chicago. Two years earlier, when the women in Buffalo, New York, were being accosted at night by a tall man in a gray Ulster coat, a Rochester, New York, Catholic newspaper reported that Tumblety was in town; Rochester is the neighboring city to Buffalo in western New York. In May 1892, in Perth Amboy, New Jersey, Mary Anderson had her throat cut along the railroad tracks. Based upon Tumblety's correspondence to the *New York Herald*, he had to have been near the Anderson crime site within one week of her murder. Lastly, Anna Marone was brutally murdered at a train station waiting room in Jefferson, Texas, in August 1900. Within weeks of the murder, a major hurricane hit Galveston, Texas, which is connected by rail to Jefferson, Texas. Tumblety was reported to have been in the Galveston storm, meaning, Tumblety must have traveled through Jefferson, Texas, and stopped at the train station where the woman was murdered.

All told, there were at least seventy-six murders and assaults of women, who were neither raped nor robbed, discovered in the United States each year between 1880 and 1901. With minor exceptions, they were committed at night, within walking distance of a train depot and/or railroad tracks. The MO of these crimes was almost always a surprise attack out of the darkness upon a woman walking along the street at night in a relatively secluded area. The motive in each case was neither rape nor robbery for financial gain but what appeared to have been anger-retaliatory; specifically, a misogynist exacting rage upon innocent women.

After plotting the seventy-six unsolved murders and assaults on a map, then superimposing the determined train routes Tumblety took each year between 1880 and 1901, a stunning match is revealed. When leaving Grand Central Station in Manhattan, Tumblety traveled northeast through Connecticut to Boston, Massachusetts; west through Albany and Saratoga Springs, New York, to Buffalo; south through Cleveland, Ohio, or Pittsburgh, Pennsylvania, to Cincinnati, Ohio, or Chicago, Illinois; then to Hot Springs, Arkansas, and eventually to New Orleans, Louisiana, for carnival season. Sometimes, Tumblety traveled to Texas from Hot Springs and to Mexico from New Orleans. At times, Tumblety traveled east from Cincinnati to Philadelphia, along the coast

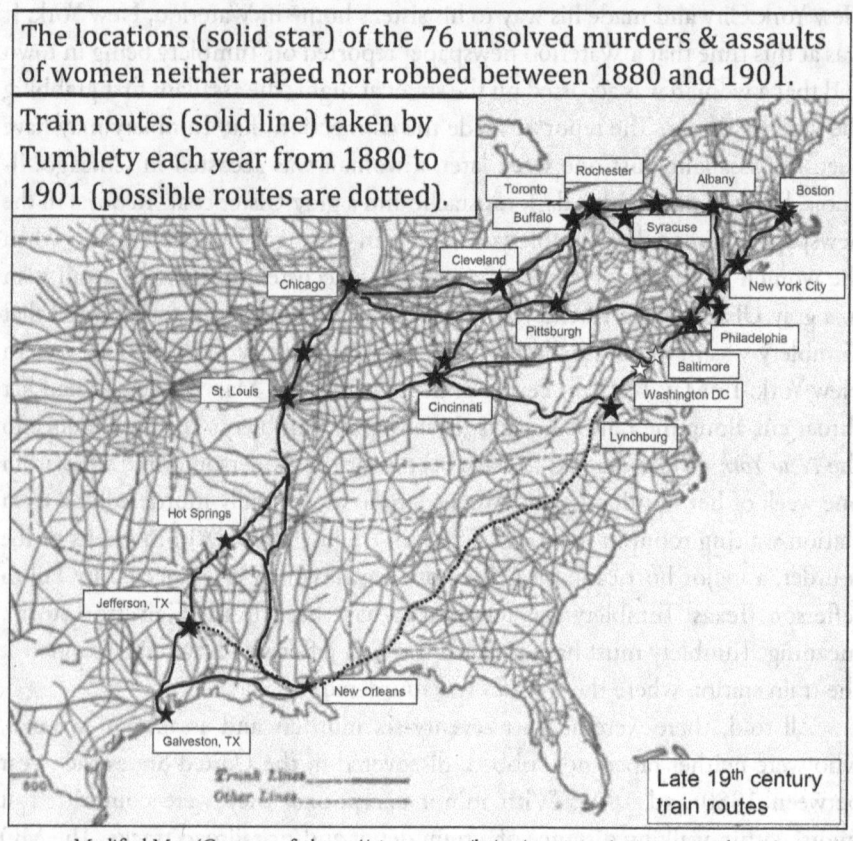

Modified Map (Courtesy of <https://vizettes.com/kt/rta/retrainingAmerica-part1.htm>.)

of New Jersey, then to Jersey City, taking a ferry into Manhattan or traveling to Brooklyn, taking the Brooklyn Bridge into Manhattan. The locations of each and every mysterious assault and murder fit into these annual travel routes.

These murders happened in the late nineteenth century, at a time when investigators had no idea there was a type of remorseless killer we now know as a serial killer. It makes sense that contemporary nineteenth-century detectives rarely detected a transient serial killer disembarking a train, committing murder, then vanishing from the area by train. This is especially true since there was no federal law enforcement monitoring multi-jurisdictional murders in the United States at this time; the FBI did not form until 1908. A serial killer in the habit of constantly traveling by train would quickly have recognized the overwhelming advantage he had.

The pattern is nearly identical to the modern-day long-haul trucker serial killer, which took modern investigators decades to recognize. It should not be a surprise that there was a nineteenth-century version of the truck-driving serial killer taking advantage of the only interstate transport system at the time—the railways—which the modern world is largely oblivious to. Further, there was no FBI searching for serial killer patterns in the nineteenth century. To make reality more complicated, patterns in MO change with a particular offender. Recall, it is a misconception that the MO of serial killers never changes; they can evolve due to changing times and environment. As noted, the Sunday Morning Slasher, Carl Eugene Watts, almost always killed young White women, but his methods of killing varied, using strangulation, stabbing, bludgeoning, and drowning. He sometimes sexually assaulted his victims, but on other occasions, he did not. British serial killer Peter Tobin who murdered into his sixties, would sometimes strangle his victims, sometimes stab them, bludgeon them, and/or even decapitate them. The New York Ripper, Richard Cottingham, would generally strangle his victims, but he also murdered by stabbing, bludgeoning, drowning, and even decapitating.

All seventy-six murders and assaults may not have been caused by one serial killer. There certainly are slight variations in the assaults and murders, but even these variations come in patterns. While it can't be stated factually that there were seventy-six independent attacks, identifying patterns makes a case for one offender making some—or all—of these attacks. It is clear that serial killers were active in the United States in the late nineteenth century.

All of these crimes have significant facts in common, leading to the realistic possibility of just one offender. None of these women were raped or robbed, and the assailant in all of these cases seemed to conform to anger-retaliatory behavioral patterns. Almost all victims were women on the street at night and near railroad tracks or a train station, suggesting a type of railway anchor point. Remember, it was only after identifying the Golden State Killer through familial DNA that we found out he was also the Visalia Ransacker, the East Area Rapist, the East Side Rapist, the East Bay Rapist, the Creek Bed Killer, the Diamond Knot Killer, and the Night Stalker. Prior to that kind of concrete evidence, those different monikers were thought to belong to completely different suspects; without DNA evidence, we may never know if London's Jack the Ripper and the offender(s) of these seventy-six attacks are the same. However, the details and the commonalities to these crimes do indeed suggest one Railway Ripper stalking the United States in the late nineteenth century. This was also the case in the 1970s with the Yorkshire Ripper; the brutal and personal attacks also occurred to women on the streets at night. It is quite appropriate to have used the Ripper moniker as an allusion to Jack the Ripper, and so it is in the case with the nineteenth-century Railway Ripper.

Was Jack the Ripper responsible for some, if not all, of the mysterious unsolved murders and assaults in the United States from 1880 to 1901? In other words, are the Railway Ripper and Jack the Ripper one and the same? Assuming the canonical five Whitechapel victims, Polly Nichols, Annie Chapman, Elizabeth Stride, Catherine Eddowes, and Mary Kelly, were all truly Jack the Ripper victims, with regards to MO, the similarities are very striking. Most of the Whitechapel victims were murdered outdoors, which is the same with the US murders. This means that all of the women murdered had, at some point, walked the streets at night, regardless of if they were sex workers or not. At least two of the Whitechapel victims were first strangled and then had their throats cut. Most of the US murders involved cut throats but also involved strangulation. Victims on both sides of the Atlantic show evidence of a killer with a bitter hatred of women who released his rage upon their bodies.

While the October 1884 Brooklyn, New York attacks; the December 1884 Plainfield, New Jersey, attacks; the December 1886 Buffalo, New York, attacks; the November 1893 Manhattan, New York attacks; and the February 1896 northern New Jersey attacks conform to the pattern of a woman being assaulted on the street at night in a surprise attack by a tall man in a gray overcoat, they do not conform to the attacks having been quite close to a railroad or train station. At the same time, though, a second pattern is revealed. These particular attacks are always in cities, there are multiple attacks, each on separate days, and they then suddenly stop in a short period of time. If they have the same offender, it means the transient offender stayed in the area for a relatively short time, as opposed to leaving town immediately after one attack. It also means that the offender then abruptly leaves the area, effectively ending that particular violent spree.

Each of these patterns—the unsolved murders and assaults of a woman at night near the railways, and the multiple assaults, each on a different night, occurring in one city—actually matches the Jack the Ripper murders. The pattern of unsolved murders and assaults of women in the United States near a railroad or train station is surprisingly similar to what was arguably the very first Jack the Ripper murder, that of Polly Nichols. Recall, Nichols was on the street at night when she encountered the killer. Once at a more secluded location, the offender attacked, first strangling her, then cutting her throat. Nichols was neither raped nor robbed. The Whitechapel train station was less than a block from her murder site. Jack the Ripper may very well have arrived by train at the Whitechapel station, walked down Whitechapel Road just a few hundred yards, met up with Polly Nichols, and followed her to Buck's Row.

The Jack the Ripper murders taken as a whole have the appearance of having been committed by a stationary serial killer with an anchor point, but, especially given the limited duration of the killing spree, they could just as easily have been committed by a transient serial killer who temporarily took up residence in or near Whitechapel. This closely conforms to the second pattern of multiple attacks in cities in the United States, each on separate nights, but then abruptly ending. This occurred in Brooklyn, New York, in October 1884; Plainfield, New Jersey, in December 1884; Buffalo, New York, in December 1886; Long Island, New York, in August 1891; Manhattan, New York, in May 1892; Pittsburgh, Pennsylvania, in April 1895; Buffalo again in May 1895; and Newton, Massachusetts, between November 1897 and January 1898. The Jack the Ripper murders began abruptly in August 1888, then abruptly ended in November 1888. The answer to why the Whitechapel murders suddenly ended just like they began is that the transient serial killer left the area.

The most significant connection between the mysterious United States murders from 1880 to 1901 and the 1888 Whitechapel murders is Francis Tumblety. He was taken seriously by Scotland Yard as possibly being Jack the Ripper. He also cannot be eliminated from having committed most, if not all, of the above-mentioned United States murders and attacks, as they all happened along his usual travel routes. Tumblety's intersex condition guaranteed he could not rape (nor would he have ever wanted to, disgusted as he was by women), and his motive would not have been robbery, as he was wealthy. Also, Tumblety fits the physical descriptions in being tall, having a mustache, owning an Ulster coat, carrying a revolver at times, and having a habit of walking the dark streets each night in every city he visited. How curious that the annual travel pattern of a Jack the Ripper suspect, Dr. Francis Tumblety, exactly matches the double pattern of the United States murders and assaults. Tumblety was always on the move from one city to the next, traveling through and temporarily stopping at countless train stations, but he also stayed at selected cities for a few weeks to a few months.

Also of significance is what Francis Tumblety traveled with. Recall when Tumblety was arrested in the slums for being a "suspicious person" that he was constantly reported as having in his pockets expensive jewelry, such as diamonds, and a large roll of cash. It showed he was wealthy and was only slumming for some personal reason. Tumblety knew law enforcement treated persons of higher status differently. He used his signs of wealth as a tool, or a get-out-of-jail-free card, in order to live outside of social norms and prowl for young men. Tumblety also traveled with railroad bonds. When his room in Hot Springs was broken into in 1891, what he reported stolen were his diamonds and railroad bonds. Tumblety also owned railroad bonds in the early 1880s, as evidenced by the court case involving a young man named Joseph Lyons. Tumblety claimed Joseph Lyons and his mother cashed out Tumblety's railroad bonds.

Researcher Joe Chetcuti introduced the possibility that Tumblety was also using the railroad bonds as an excuse to be around train stations and tracks. If he was indeed prowling along the train tracks for nefarious reasons, he could tell a police officer who approached him that he was on the tracks because he was either considering buying more railroad bonds or checking on his current investments. This, along with being a man of high status, would have been quite effective. After a murder in the area, being on the tracks without a credible excuse would have guaranteed an arrest and deep suspicions from the authorities and the press.

With regards to offender signature, specifically anger-retaliatory, Tumblety's specific hatred and rage against women was similar to Aileen Wuornos and her hatred of middle-aged men. Wuornos had a girlfriend but would prostitute herself for extra money. At times, she ended up shooting the john for no real reason other than releasing her rage. Additionally, she did not begin killing until later on in life, even though she prostituted herself years earlier. Another example could be Dellmus Colvin. He did, indeed, seek out sex worker victims, but he admitted that, before strangling her, he did not always have sex with her. He claimed his motive was misogyny and stated that, if he were not imprisoned, he would do it again.

Our narcissist, Dr. Francis Tumblety, had a lifelong belief that women were the "curse of the land," where it was not Adam who committed the Original Sin but Eve, by deceiving Adam. Included with this misogynistic interpretation, all disease that has affected mankind came from Original Sin; thus, by extension, women are the cause of disease. And then, sometime between 1878 and 1880, Tumblety discovered he was afflicted with the incurable, progressive disease of syphilis. He did not blame his syphilis on himself and his voracious sexual appetite for young male sex workers, rather, he blamed women, especially those confounding streetwalkers. Oh, the anger and intense rage he must have felt knowing that the gender he despised so much ruined him. Not being able to cure himself was like an itch he could not scratch, further enraging him. Throughout the 1880s, Tumblety began to tell acquaintances of his kidney and heart problems. By around 1886, we see corroborating evidence that Tumblety knew his syphilis had entered a tertiary stage called paresis, or paralysis of the insane—what is now known as neurosyphilis. Neurosyphilis occasionally causes cardiovascular issues and also lesions on the kidneys. In January 1888, Tumblety told a Toronto reporter that he was constantly in dread of sudden death because of kidney and heart disease. This "cure-all" quack doctor had publicly announced he could not cure himself. It was as if Tumblety's despair had reached a crescendo, compounded by the fact that neurosyphilis had affected his thoughts.

He then made his way to London, at a time when he was convinced his kidney and heart disease would be the death of him. Tumblety, a man who was known to acquire anatomical organs *and* had a special affinity for the uterus, was connected to the very organs Jack the Ripper collected: the uterus, the kidney, and the heart. If Francis Tumblety was going mutilate sex workers and collect these organs, either as a last-ditch attempt to concoct a potion, or elixir, to cure himself—a motive Scotland Yard did, indeed, investigate—or just for collecting trophies, it would have been at this time. In his autobiographies, Tumblety claimed there was an undiscovered elixir of health. In his 1893 autobiography, though, he finally admitted that "there is no panacea that can give us everlasting youth"; thus, it seems his motive to collect organs vanished while his rage against women on the street continued.

A counterargument might be: "But there's just no public record of Tumblety ever violently attacking women, which is so distant from the actions of a prolific serial killer. This can't possibly be right." Nor was there with transient serial killer Israel Keyes, who murdered between 1996 and 2012, and even placed "murder kits" in selected locations around the United States. Nor was there with "normal, polite, and well-mannered" church leader, Cub Scout leader, and family man Dennis Rader, aka, the BTK Killer. Nor was there with the charismatic and well-educated Ted Bundy, who murdered between 1973 and 1978. Nor was there with husband and father of three, Andrei Chikatilo, aka, the Rostov Ripper, who killed at least fifty-two women and children in Russia between 1978 and 1990. Nor was there with police officer Joseph DeAngelo, aka, the Visalia Ransacker, the East Area Rapist, the Original Night Stalker, and the Golden State Killer. If it was not for familial DNA testing, DeAngelo would have carried his homicidal secrets to his grave. His wife and adult children were shocked he was able to hide this heinous side of himself all their lives. Nor was there with the New York Ripper, Richard Cottington. His wife and kids were completely blindsided. The list goes on. While these modern-day serial killers eventually got caught, few would argue that many serial killers who maintained normal, mostly law-abiding public lives—especially in the nineteenth century—were never caught.

While the answer to the original question of Francis Tumblety not being able to be eliminated as having involvement in over seventy-six unsolved murders and assaults in the United States between 1880 and 1901 is to the affirmative, the evidence is quite compelling that we can make one additional assertion. Francis Tumblety may very well have been the actual offender of most, if not all, of these crimes. Of significance is the underlying reason for asking the original question, specifically, Francis Tumblety having been suspected of the Whitechapel murders. Expressing it in the reverse reveals how damning the connection really is. This tall, misogynistic narcissist who walked the dark alleys and streets each night, and who cannot be eliminated as having been a decades-long transient serial killer in the United States, was also taken so seriously as possibly being Jack the Ripper that Scotland Yard followed him to America in hopes of collecting further incriminatory information. Lost to history is what Chief Inspector Littlechild read in Tumblety's dossier that made him state unequivocally that Tumblety's "feelings toward women were remarkable and bitter in the extreme." Maybe Scotland Yard was onto something in late 1888. Even if Tumblety was responsible for just one of these unsolved US murders, this Jack the Ripper Suspect was a killer of women.

CHRONOLOGY OF THE UNSOLVED MURDERS & ASSAULTS FROM 1880 TO 1901

Victims were women neither raped nor robbed.

Each of these attacks occurred along the annual train travel pattern of Francis Tumblety. Most attacks were outdoors at night near a train route.

Note: (H) homicide, (A) assault

#	Name	Date	City	Suspect, Additional details
1.	Mary Cassidy (H)	Aug 1880	Barnstable, MA	Nearly decapitated, mutilated
2.	Minnie Sneideker (A)	May 1881	Brooklyn, NY	Attempted to drag victim to dark area
3.	Ella Clark (H)	May 1881	New York City	Quack doctor, dismembered, near railroad tracks
4.	Unnamed Girl (A)	Aug 1881	Jersey City, NJ	Bludgeoned, attempted to drag victim to dark area
5.	Boston Woman (H)	Mar 1882	Boston, MA	Throat cut, tall, thick mustache, Ulster coat
6.	Anne Moorman (H)	Mar 1882	Lynchburg, VA	Throat cut/gun, along train route
7.	Alice Faulkner (H)	Mar 1882	Syracuse, NY	Body in ditch, along train route
8.	Etta Carlton (H)	Mar 1883	Boston, MA	Crushed skull, suspect slouch hat, near railroad
9.	Unknown Woman (H)	May 1883	Coney Isl, NY	Throat cut, in river
10.	Rose Ambler (H)	Sept 1883	Stratford, CT	Strangulation, along road, rail, tall unfamiliar man
11.	Zora Burns (H)	Oct 1883	Lincoln, IL	Throat cut, outside, along train route
12.	Unk Woman (H)	Oct 1883	Rochester, NY	Dismembered, Erie Canal Lock 65
13.	Phoebe Paullin (H)	Nov 1883	Orange, NJ	Throat cut on road, tall, well-dressed, dark overcoat
14.	Amelia Olson (H)	Jan 1884	Chicago, IL	Strangled outside, near train station, cable car
15.	Mary Hatton (A)	Oct 1884	Brooklyn, NY	Flatbush, grabbed by throat, strike to face
16.	Unk Woman (A)	Oct 1884B	rooklyn, NY	Flatbush, similar to Hatton
17.	Unk Woman (A)	Oct 1884	Brooklyn, NY	Flatbush, similar to Hatton
18.	Annie Madison (H)	Oct 1884	Covington, KY	Ax/Throat cut, near Cincinnati, OH, older man
19.	Mrs. Stevens (A)	Dec 1884	Plainfield, NJ	On street, tall man in gray overcoat, near railroad
20.	Nellie Overbaugh (A)	Dec 1884	Plainfield, NJ	On street, tall man, overcoat, derby hat
21.	Annie Buist (A)	Dec 1884	Plainfield, NJ	On street, tall man, overcoat, derby hat
22.	Mrs. Creaney (A)	Jan 1885	Long Island, NY	Street, tall man, grabbed throat, strike to head
23.	Ellen Mitchell (?) (H)	Jul 1885	Boston, MA	Dismembered, river, strangled, cut
24.	Carrie Whitney (H)	Dec 1885	Boston Area	Neck broken, left train station, sex worker
25.	Annie Doran (A)	Jan 1886	Jersey City, NJ	Railroad cut, 50-foot drop attempt
26.	Annie Dugan (H)	April 1886	Camden, NJ	Strangled, found in woods along train route
27.	Mamie Holweger (H)	Jul 1886	Franklin, OH	Clubbed and mutilated, near train station/route
28.	Buffalo Assault (A)	Dec 1886	Buffalo, NY	Tall man, gray Ulster, grabbed throat, had gun
29.	Buffalo Assault (A)	Dec 1886	Buffalo, NY	Tall man, gray Ulster, grabbed throat
30.	Buffalo Assault (A)	Dec 1886	Buffalo, NY	Tall man, gray Ulster, grabbed throat
31.	Rahway Mystery (H)	Mar 1887	Rahway, NJ	Throat cut, road, near train route

#	Name	Date	Location	Description
32.	Ellen Quinn (H)	Nov 1887	Trenton, NJ	Sex worker, strangled in a cellar, near train route
33.	Minnie Moscowitch (H)	May 1888	Bowery, NY	CThroat cut, cellar, tall man, mustache, sex worker

— **Whitechapel Murders, August to November 1888** —

#	Name	Date	Location	Description
34.	Unnamed Woman (A)	Dec 1888	Waterloo, NY	Grabbed throat, reporter suspected Tumblety
35.	Hulda Johnson (A)	Dec 1888	Chicago, IL	Tall man, mustache, gray Ulster coat, throat
36.	Annie Laconey (H)	Sept 1889	Camden, NJ	Throat cut, kitchen, along NJ train route
37.	Annie Miller (H)	Sept 1890	Camden, NJ	Throat cut, road, along NJ train route
38.	Kate McGarvey (A)	Mar 1891	Pittsburgh, PA	Slashed with knife, near railroad, Pittsburgh Ripper
39.	Hannah Robinson (H)	Aug 1891	Long Island, NY	Jack the Strangler, Road, railroad station
40.	Mamie Maguire (A)	Aug 1891	Long Island, NY	Aged 15, strangled, survived, large, powerful man
41.	Fanny Cartwright (H)	Nov 1891	Chicago, IL	Mutilated by train, cut in two
42.	Sarah Joyce (H)	Feb 1892	Pittsburgh, PA	Strangled, knife wound, near train station/tracks
43.	Lizzie Farrell (H)	Apr 1892	Red Bank, NJ	Head crushed, outdoors near NJ railroad track
44.	Jack the Tripper (A)	May 1892	Manhattan, NY	Tall middle-aged, mustache, wearing diamonds
45.	Jack the Tripper (A)	May 1892	Manhattan, NY	Victim 2, young girl, other victims, using umbrella
46.	Mary Anderson (H)	Jun 1892	Perth Amboy, NJ	Near Rahway, throat cut, railroad tracks
47.	Lizzie Beiler (H)	Jul 1892	Long Island, NY	Mutilated by train, near Hannah Robinson murder
48.	Jack the Clipper (A)	Nov 1893	New York City	Unnamed woman, cut hair off, tall, Ulster coat
49.	Annie Smith (A)	Nov 1893	New York City	2nd Jack the Clipper victim, tall man, Ulster coat
50.	Julia Huff/Hulf (H)	Dec 1893	Cleveland, OH	Throat cut, on street, along train route
51.	May Barrowcliffe (A)	Dec 1893	Jersey City, NJ	Skull fracture, dark vacant lot
52.	Unnamed Woman (A)	Apr 1894	Cincinnati, OH	Outdoors, grabbed throat, burly ruffian
53.	Pittsburgh Assault (A)	Apr 1895	Sharpsburg, PA	Near railroad tracks, dragging to river
54.	Pittsburgh Assault (A)	Apr 1895	Sharpsburg, PA	Second assault, dragging to river, more victims
55.	Alice Walsh (H)	Apr 1895	New York City	Gotham's Jack the Ripper, throat cut, sex worker
56.	Black Rock women (A)	May 1895	Buffalo, NY	Women assaulted on street at night by a tall man
57.	Louise Schram (A)	Jun 1895	Buffalo, NY	Assaulted at night on street, tall, slim, man
58.	Ella "Kid" King (H)	Jul 1895	St. Louis, MO	Abdomen cut, sex worker, tall man, gray coat
59.	Carrie Robinson (H)	Dec 1895	Bowery, NYC	Mangled on street, along train route
60.	Liz Lamb/May Little (A)	Feb 1896	Montclair, NJ	Iron coupling pin hit on head, tall, gray Ulster coat
61.	Mamie Sullivan (H)	Mar 1896	Paterson, NJ	Iron coupling pin hit on head, tall, gray Ulster coat
62.	Sarah Scofield (H)	May 1896	Bronx, NYC	Wound on head, blood on boulder 150 ft away
63.	Jessie Tempary (A)	Jul 1896	Brooklyn, NY	Flatbush, night, road, tall man, flowing mustache
64.	Annie Bock (H)	Aug 1896	Tenderloin, NYC	Throat cut, strangled, sex worker, in room, tall
65.	Annie Hauff (H)	Nov 1896	Philadelphia, PA	Strangulation, street, tall man with mustache
66.	Flossie Murphy (H)	Apr 1897	Tenderloin, NYC	Strangulation in room, NYC sex worker
67.	Meanest man (A)	Nov 1897	Newton, MA	Squirting sulfuric acid on dress, tall, Ulster coat
68.	Meanest man (A)	Jan 1898	Newton, MA	Nine more menaced by threats, tall, Ulster coat
69.	Unk Woman (H)	Jun 1898	Mt Vernon, NY	Knife thrust to throat, along train route
70.	Ollie Richmond (A)	Jun 1899	Danbury, CT	Cayenne Pepper and metal shavings in eyes, tall man
71.	Unnamed Girl (A)	Mar 1900	Dayton, OH	Tall elderly, grabbed throat, drag into dark alley
72.	Florence Wright (A)	Apr 1900	Newark, NJ	Cut hair with knife, tall man with black mustache
73.	Anna Marone (H)	Aug 1900	Jefferson, TX	Broken neck, mutilated, train station waiting room
74.	Alice Whitmarsh (A)	Sept 1900	Boston, MA	Grabbed by the throat, tall, mustache, derby hat
75.	Minnie Schell (A)	Jan 1901	Cleveland, OH	Followed on cable car, knocked down, gun, tall man
76.	Stella Haas (A)	Apr 1901	Dayton, OH	Attacked at night near alley, "very tall man"
77.	Mrs. Springer (A)	Nov 1901	Evansville, IN	Tall, heavy black mustache, Ulster-looking coat

BIBLIOGRAPHY

Arkowitz, H. & Lilienfeld, S.O., "Do the "Eyes" Have It?", *Scientific American Mind*, 20, 7, 68-69, Jan 2010, doi:10.1038/scientificamericanmind0110-68.

Appignanesi, L., *Trials of Passion: Crimes Committed in the Name of Love and Madness*, Virago Press, 1969.

Barrat, D., The Prosecution of Francis Tumblety, *Ripperologist 163*, Jan 2019.

Begg, P., Fido, M., & Skinner, K., *The Jack the Ripper A – Z*, Headline Book Publishing PLC, 1996.

Benis, Anthony, M. M.D., *NPA Theory of Personality* (2017).

Benis, Anthony, *Toward Self & Sanity* (1985, 2nd edition 2008).

Birbaumer N., Veit R., Lotze M., Erb M., Hermann C., Grodd W., et al., Deficient fear conditioning in psychopathy: a functional magnetic resonance imaging study, *Archives of General Psychiatry*, V. 62, pp. 799–805, 2005.

Blondheim, M. *News Over the Wires*, Harvard College, 1994.

Bondeson, J., *The True History of Jack the Ripper by Guy Logan (1905)*, Amberley Publishing, 2013.

Casebook: Jack the Ripper, available at www.casebook.org, Stephen P. Ryder & Johnno, 1996-2013, Thomas Schachner.

Central Criminal Court Calendars, London, England, November and December 1888.

Chronicling America Historic American Newspapers, Library of Congress and the National Endowment for the Humanities, 2023, <https://chroniclingamerica.loc.gov/>.

Circuit Court Archives, City of St. Louis, State of Missouri, Case Number 31430, Series A., 1904 – 1908.

Conway, J., *Big Policeman: The Rise and Fall of Thomas Byrnes*, Lyons Press, 2010.

Crawford T.C., *English Life*, Frank F. Lovell & Company (Princeton University), 1889.

Cumming, C., *Devil's Game: The Civil War Intrigues of Charles A. Dunham*. Univ. of Illinois, 2004.

Decety, J., Chenyi, C., Harenski, C., and Kiehl, K., An fMRI Study of Affective Perspective Taking in Individuals with Psychopathy: Imagining Another in Pain Does Not Evoke Empathy, *Frontiers in Human Neuroscience*, September 24, 2013.

DoveMed, Champaign, IL, 2018. <https://www.dovemed.com/diseases-conditions/cardiovascular-syphilis/>.

Edwards, R. 1896: Journals & Newspapers in the Campaign. Vassar College, 2000. projects.vassar.edu/1896/journals.html.

Evans, S. and Rumblelow, D., *Jack the Ripper, Scotland Yard Investigates*, Sutton Publishing, 2006.

Federal Bureau of Investigation, U.S. Department of Justice, *Serial Murder Multi-Disciplinary Perspectives for Investigators,* Behavioral Analysis Unit National Center for the Analysis of Violent Crime, 2005.

Gitlin, M, Pfaff, D.: *Joseph Pulitzer: Historic Newspaper Publisher,* Abdo Publishing Co., 2010.

Hamilton, J M. *Journalism's Roving Eye: A History of American Foreign Reporting,* LSU Press, 2009.

Hardy, A., The World's Foremost Authority on Mardi Gras, <http://www.mardigrasguide.com/index.php?number=5&start_from=5>.

Hawley, M., Charles A. Dunham: for the Better Good, *The New Independent Review* (Issue 2), pp. 10-17, January 2012.

Hawley, M., Charles A. Dunham Part II: Tumblety's Anatomical Collection Reconsidered, *The New Independent Review,* Issue 3, April 2012.

Hitchcock T., Shoemaker R., Emsley C., Howard S., and McLaughlin L., et al. *The Old Bailey Proceedings Online, 1674-1913* (www.oldbaileyonline.org, version 7.0, 24 March 2012).

IPUMS-USA, University of Minnesota, <https://usa.ipums.org/usa/volii/80sick.shtml>.

JTRForums, Howard & Nina Brown, 2000 – 2005, www.jtrforums.com. Kulbarsh, P., The Malignant Narcissist, April 21, 2008, *Officer.com,* <https://www.officer.com/investigations/article/10248968/the-malignant-narcissist.>. Kuntz, J., Francis A. Stevenson's "Black and Tan", *gangsannotated.blog,* <https://gangsannotated.blog/2020/04/28/francis-a-stevensons-black-and-tan/>.

Littlechild Letter, dtd September 23, 1913. Sent privately to George R. Sims.

Logan, Guy, *Masters of Crime,* S. Paul, 1928.

Macilwain, G., *Memoirs of John Abernethy, F.R.S.,* Harper & Bros Publishers, New York, 1853.

Masarik, E.G., DigPodcast.Org: *Selling Sex: 19th Century New York City Prostitution and Brothels,* September 3, 2017,< https://digpodcast.org/2017/09/03/19th-century-new-york-city-brothels/>.

Matters, L., *The Mystery of Jack the Ripper,* Hutchinson & Company, 1929.

MedlinePlus, U.S. National Library of Medicine, Bethesda, MD, 2019, <https://medlineplus.gov/ency/article/000748.htm>.

NYS Historic Newspapers, Northern New York Library Network and Empire State Library Network, 2023, <https://nyshistoricnewspapers.org/>.

New York Times. *The Reminiscences of a Colleague,* October 23, 1898.

Newspapers.com, Ancestry, 2023, <https://www.newspapers.com/>.

Old Fulton NY Post Card Website, 2013, https://www.fultonhistory.com/Fulton.html/.

Palmer, R., Inspector Andrews Revisited, *The Casebook Examiner,* Issues 1, 2, & 4, April, June, & October 2010.

Pemment, J., MA, MS, What Would We Find Wong in the Brain of a Serial Killer?, *Psychology Today,* April 5, 2013, https://www.psychologytoday.com/blog/blame-the-amygdala/201304/what-would-we-find-wrong-in-the-brain-serial-killer.

Pokel, C., *A Critical Analysis of Research Related to the Criminal Mind of Serial Killers*, Graduate Research Thesis (Advisor Biggerstaff, E.), University of Wisconsin-Stout, August 2000.

Riis, J., *How the Other Half Lives*, CreateSpace Independent Publishing Platform, October 2, 2009.

Rumbelow, Donald, *The Complete Jack the Ripper*, Virgin Books Limited, 1988.

Samuel, D.B., & Widiger, T.A., Clinicians' judgments of clinical utility: A comparison of the DSM-IV and five factor models. *Journal of Abnormal Psychology*, 115, 298-308, 2006.

Sereno, M., *Types of Crimes: The Relationship Between Narcissistic and Antisocial Personalities*, Department of Psychology, Published by Lavin, M., Ph.D., St. Bonaventure University. <http://web.sbu.edu/psychology/lavin/abbey.htm>.

Shepherd, H., *History of Baltimore*, Maryland, S. B. Nelson, 1898.

Skodo, A., Gunderson, J., McGlashan, T., Dyck, I., Stout, R., Bender, D., Grilo, C., Shea, M., Zanarini, M., Morey, L., Sanislow, C., and Oldham, J., Functional Impairment in Patients with Schizotypal, Borderline, Avoidant, or Obsessive-Compulsive Personality Disorder, *American Journal of Psychiatry*, Volume 159 (2): 276-83, February 2002.

Slijper, F. M., Drop, S. L., Moleaar, J. C., Muinck, Keizer-Schrama, S. M.: Long-term psychological evaluation of intersex children. *Arch Sex Beh*.1998; 28: 103-5. <https://www.ncbi.nlm.nih.gov/labs/articles/9562897/>.

Smith, P., and Brain, P., Bullying in Schools: Lessons from Two Decades of Research, *Aggressive Behavior*, Volume 26, pp. 109, 2000.

Storey, N., *The Dracula Secrets: Jack the Ripper and the Darkest Sources of Bram Stoker*, The History Press, 2012.

Strand, Ginger, *Killer on the Road: Violence and the American Interstate*, University of Texas Press, 2012.

Thompson, L.O., *Syphilis*, Lea & Febiger, 1920.

Tumblety, F., *A Few Passages in the Life of Dr. Francis Tumblety, The Indian Herb Doctor, 1866*, (Originally self-published in Cincinnati). Casebook: Jack the Ripper, <www.casebook.org>.

Tumblety, F., *A Narrative of Dr. Tumblety: how he was Kidnapped during the American War, His Incarceration and Discharge, A Veritable Reign of Terror*, 1872, (Originally published at Russells' American Steam Printing House, New York, NY.), Casebook: Jack the Ripper, <www.casebook.org>.

Tumblety, Francis, *A Sketch of the Life of the Gifted, Eccentric and World-Famed Physician, Presenting an Outline of His Wonderful Career*, 1889. (Originally published in Brooklyn, Eagle Book and Job Printing Department). Casebook: Jack the Ripper, <www.casebook.org>.

Tumblety, F., *A Sketch of the Life of Dr. Francis Tumblety, Presenting an Outline of His Wonderful Career as a Physician*, 1893, (Originally published in New York, NY), Harvard College Library, 1918.

Turvey, B., *Criminal Profiling: An Introduction to Behavioral Evidence Analysis*, Academic Press, 2012.

Turvey, B. *Forensic Victimology*, Academic Press, 2009.
U.S. Dept. of the Interior, *Annual Report of the Department of the Interior*, Volume 2, 1885.
Vaknin, S., *Malignant Self-Love: Narcissism Revisited*, 2015 (10th Revision).
Vronsky, P., *Serial Killers: The Method and Madness of Monsters*, Penguin Random House, 2020 (2nd ed.).
WTSRS, The Maiden Tribute of Modern Babylon I: The Report of our Secret Commission, W. T. Stead (*The Pall Mall Gazette*, July 6, 1885), W.T. Stead Resource Site (WTSRS). <https://www.attackingthedevil.co.uk/pmg/tribute/mt1.php>.
Ward, P., Simon Baruch: Rebel in the Ranks of Medicine, 1840-1921, Univ of Alabama Press, 1994.
Warren, J., Burnette, M., South, S., Chauham, P., Bale, R., and Friend, R., Personality Disorders and Violence Among Female Prison Inmates, *Journal of the American Academy of Psychology and Law*, Volume 30, Number 4, 2002.
Water-cure Journal, Volume 56, *The Herald of Health*, July 1873.
Welles, C.A., *The Doctor*, Volumes 2-3, 1888.
Wijngaards, J., Wijngaards Institute for Catholic Research, *Women Can Be Priests*, 2014, <www.womenpriests.org>.

INDEX

Abberline, Inspector Frederick, 63
Ambler, Rose, 127–29, 217, 231
Anatomical (Florentine) Venus, 33
Anderson, Mary, 164–67, 223
Anderson, Sir Robert, IX, XI, 2, 4–6, 19, 29, 37–39, 51, 232
Andrews, Inspector Walter, 14–25, 27–29, 37, 49–50, 90, 213–14
Antisocial Personality Disorder (APD), 91–92

Barnet, Roland Gideon Israel, 14–16, 18, 20, 25
Barrowcliffe, May, 170–71, 232
Bartley, George F. (New Orleans attorney), 40
Baxter, Coroner Wynne E., 30–31, 35–37
Beiler, Lizzie, 168, 232
Benis, Anthony, 91
Blackburn, Luke, 81
Bloom, C.A., 8
Bock, Annie, 199, 201–202, 232
Bond, Thomas (police surgeon), 37
Bowery, 33, 54–55, 57–59, 61, 65, 78–79, 176–77, 214–15, 218
Brisbane, Arthur, 30
Brooks, John, B. (Hot Springs physician), 70, 87–89
Brown, Frederick Gordon (surgeon), 37
Bulger (boy from Toronto), 66–67
Buck's Row, 58, 129, 219, 226
Buist, Annie, 138
Burns, Zora, 130–31, 134, 231
Burr, William P., 105–106, 112, 190
Byrnes, Thomas F., 2, 13, 23, 59–61, 67, 163, 169–70, 203, 220

Caine, Thomas Henry Hall, VII–VIII, 34, 46
Calusio, Maria, 57–59
Campbell, Patrick, 2, 38
Carlton, Etta, 124–25, 204, 231
Cartwright, Fanny, 156–57, 168, 232
Cassidy, Mary, 105–106, 114, 215, 231
Central Criminal Court, 2–3, 8–10, 12, 23, 26
Chapman, Annie (aka, Dark Annie), 36–37, 53, 63, 74, 95, 127, 133, 144, 201, 219, 226
Clark, Ella, 108–14, 140, 216–17, 231
Clews, Henry, 82–83, 173, 185
Clews, James B., 185
Coles, Frances, 28
Colvin, Dellmus (Interstate Strangler), 79, 123, 228

Conway, J.J., Father, 156
Conway, William A., 56–57
Cottingham, Richard (New York Ripper, Time Square Killer, Torso Killer), 63–64, 225
Cox, David A., 75
Crawford, T.C., 1
Creaney, Mrs., 218, 231
Crowley, Patrick (Chief of Police), 2, 38–39, 52

DeAngelo, Joseph (Golden State Killer), 52, 229
De Puy, W.H. (Reverend), 83–84
De Tatham, Hamilton, 10
Di Cantio, Vincenzo, 57–59
Diagnostic and Standard Manual of Mental, 91
Director of Public Prosecution (DPP), 6
Disorders, fourth edition (DSM-IV), 91
Doran, Annie, 141, 231
Double Event murders, 59, 147
Dr. Jekyll and Mr. Hyde, 3, 34–35, 181
Druitt, Montague John, 5–6
Dugan, Annie, 142, 150, 231
Dunham, Charles A., 32

Eddowes, Catherine, 8, 33, 37, 39, 53, 63, 219, 221, 226
Elsheimer, Eleanor R., 131–32, 134, 172, 185, 191
Evonitz, Richard (serial killer), 62
Farrell, Lizzie, 159–60, 164, 167, 185, 232
Faulkner, Alice, 119, 231
Fisher, Albert, 3, 8
Fitzsimmons (Fitzsimons), Mary (niece), 77
Fitzsimmons, Maurice, 12–13
Fitzsimmons (Fitzsimons), Michael H., 13, 77, 119, 130–31, 169, 185
From Hell Letter, 39

Galveston flood, 207
Geary, John, 100–101
Govan, Henry, 43–44, 113, 153
Greaves, E. (Edwin) Tracy, 1–3, 12, 26, 30, 34, 42, 60

Haas, Stella, 209–10, 222, 232
Hall Caine, Sir Thomas Henry, VII–VIII, 34, 46
Hammond, Graeme M., 83, 85–88, 104
Hammond, William A., 85–87, 89–90
Hannay, James L., 8–10
Hare Psychopathy Checklist, 92

Hatton, Mary, 135, 231
Hauff, Annie, 201, 222, 232
Hernandez, Gabriel (Judge), 29, 64
Holloway Prison, 3, 9–11
Holt, Alfred H., 124
Holweger, Mamie, 142–43, 231
Hotchkiss' Seven Deadly Sins of Narcissism, 93
Huff/Hulf, Julia, 168–69, 208, 232

Jack the Clipper, 169–70, 206, 220, 232
Jack the Strangler, 63, 154–55, 211, 232
Jack the Tripper, 161–64, 169, 203, 219–20, 232
Johnson, Hulda, 68–69, 173, 220, 232
Jones, John B. (Hot Springs judge), 70, 93
Joyce, Sarah, 157–59, 232

Kelly, Mary Jane, 9, 30, 33, 37, 42, 49, 53, 60, 63–64, 95, 201, 213–15, 219, 226
King, Ella "Kid", 178–80, 221, 232
Kruger, Clarence, 172

Laconey, Annie, 144, 147, 232
Lamb, Liz, 192–93, 232
Little, May, 192, 232
Littlechild, John George, Chief Inspector, VII, 4–6, 8, 11, 12, 25–27, 29–30, 45, 163, 214, 219, 230
Logan, Guy, 24–25, 27–29, 31, 49, 90, 213–214
London Hospital (Royal), 40, 202
Lusk, George, 39–40
Lyceum Theatre, 3, 34
Lyons, Joseph, 105–106, 190, 228

Macnaghten, Sir Melville, 5–6, 25
Madison, Annie, 136, 231
Maguire, Mamie, 155, 232
Maiden Tribute of Modern Babylon (Criminal Law Amendment Act of 1885), 3, 6, 31
Malignant Narcissism, 92
Mansfield, Richard, 3, 34
Marlborough Street Police Court, 5, 10, 42
Marone, Anna, 207, 223, 232
Marsh, Emily, 39–40
Marx, Adolf, 162
Matthews, Henry (Home Secretary), 19
McClellan, Major General George B., 32
McDavid, B. (barber), 191
McGarry, Martin, 89, 101–102, 113, 118, 120, 129, 146
McGarvey, Kate, 151, 153, 159, 173, 232
Meanest man, 202, 220, 222, 232
Metropolitan Police Force, 5
Miller, Annie, 147–50, 232
Mitchell, Ellen, 139, 231
Mitre Square, Aldgate, 11, 42, 219, 221

Monomaniac, 181, 211
Moore, Julia (Judith), 12–13
Moorman, Anne, 115–16, 231
Moscowitch, Minnie, 57–59, 61, 76–77, 79, 214–15, 218, 232
Murphy, Flossie, 202, 232
Murtagh, Joseph, 186–91, 197, 222

Narcissistic Personality Disorder (NPD), 91–92
National Vigilance Association (NVA), 6
Neill, Thomas, 28
Nichols, Mary Ann (aka, Polly), 37, 53, 58, 63, 74, 95, 127, 129, 202, 214–16, 219, 226
Norris, Richard S., 29–30, 36, 43–44, 47–48, 64, 78, 88–89, 96–97, 116, 153, 172, 196, 214, 216

O'Donovan, Daniel, 126
O'Malley, Dominick C., 43–45, 48
Olson, Amelia, 133–4, 156–57, 231
Overbaugh, Nellie, 138

Paullin, Phoebe, 132–33, 218, 231
Phillips, George Bagster (surgeon), 37
Pinkerton, William, 85, 86, 90, 134
Powderly, Elizabeth (sister), 13, 66
Powderly, Thomas (nephew), 66–67, 97–98, 101, 106, 180

Quinn, Ellen, 76–77, 232

Rahway Mystery, 74–76, 141, 164, 231
Richmond, Ollie, 204–205, 222, 232
Robinson, Carrie, 176, 232
Robinson, Hannah, 155

Schell, Minnie, 208–209, 222, 232
Schram, Louise, 175, 232
Scofield, Sarah, 197–98, 232
Simpson, Robert H. (Baltimore attorney), 38, 50, 94, 172, 196–97
Sims, George R., VII, 4, 6, 25–27, 29, 31, 36, 45
Smalley, George W., 30–31
Smith, A.R., 71, 166
Smith, Annie, 152, 170, 220, 232
Smith, Bridget, 145
Smith, Charles, 111–12
Smith, D.J., 103–104
Smith, Jenny, 184
Smith, Louis, 126
Smith, Philo, 180, 197
Smith, Raynor, 108
Smith, Sidney, 111
Smith, Tillie, 57
Smith, William, 145–46
Sneideker, Minnie, 107, 216, 231

INDEX

Springer, Mrs., 210, 222, 232
Steamships
   City of Rome, 3, 75–76, 83–84, 218
   La Bretagne, 11, 13, 31, 64–65, 70
   Oregon, 16–18
   Sarnia, 16–17
Stevens, Mrs., 137, 231
Stoker, Bram, VII, 34
Stride, Elizabeth (Long Liz), 8, 63, 219, 226
Sullivan, Mamie, 180–86, 190–93, 213, 222, 232
Sutcliffe, Peter (Yorkshire Ripper), 62, 122, 218
Swanson, Donald Sutherland, Chief Inspector, 28

Tabram (Turner), Martha, 3, 114, 218
Tempary, Jessie, 198–99, 222, 232
Thomson, Sir Basil, 25

Tobin, Peter, 225
Turvey, Brent, 95, 214

Urdiales, Andrew, 114

Walsh, Alice, 174–75, 232
Watts, Carl Eugene (Sunday Morning Slasher), 63, 225
Way, Catherine, 12
Whitmarsh, Alice, 207–208, 222, 232
Whitney, Carrie, 140, 231
Widner, Jr., Frank M. (Baltimore attorney), 94, 194–97, 204
Wright, Florence, 206, 222, 232

Ziegler, J.H., 114, 217

ABOUT THE AUTHOR

MICHAEL HAWLEY is the author of both True Crime nonfiction, specifically, the 1888 Jack the Ripper murders mystery, and Mystery/Crime fiction. He has appeared on true crime TV documentaries as an expert on the History Channel in the *History's Greatest Mysteries* series and on the Travel Channel in the *Legend Hunter* series. He has recently been asked to be on Netflix's *Unsolved Mysteries* as an expert for their upcoming Jack the Ripper episode. Michael has lectured on Jack the Ripper suspect Dr. Francis Tumblety in Liverpool, England, as well as multiple cities across the eastern United States. He is a cohost on NBC Radio's House of Mystery and has been a guest on both national and local radio. He has also participated in over a twenty national and international podcasts. Michael holds a Master's degree in science (invertebrate paleontology) and secondary science education at State University of New York, College of Buffalo, and a Bachelor's degree in geology and geophysics at Michigan State University. He is a commander and naval aviator in the U.S. Navy (retired), and is currently enjoying a career in secondary science education. He resides with his wife and six children in Greater Buffalo, New York.

www.ingramcontent.com/pod-product-compliance
Lightning Source LLC
Chambersburg PA
CBHW011956150426
43200CB00016B/2915